PROTECTING THE REPUBLIC

The Education and Training of American Police Officers

JAMES O'KEEFE, Ph. D.

Director of Undergraduate Criminal Justice Studies
Associate Professor of Criminal Justice
St. John's University

Director of Training (Ret.)
New York City Police Department

D0024195

PEARSON

Prentice Hall

Upper Saddle River, New Jersey 07458

Library of Congress Cataloging-in-Publication Data

O'Keefe, James.
  Protecting the republic: the education and training of American police officers / James O'Keefe.
    p. cm.
  Includes bibliographical references and index.
  ISBN 0-13-097778-0
  1. Police training—United States. 2. Police—Education—United States. I. Title.

HV8143.O44 2004
363.2'071'073—dc21   2003043377

Editor-in-Chief: Stephen Helba
Executive Editor: Frank Mortimer, Jr.
Assistant Editor: Sarah Holle
Marketing Manager: Tim Peyton
Editorial Assistant: Barbara Rosenberg
Managing Editor: Mary Carnis
Production Liaison: Brian Hyland
Production Editor: Janet Bolton
**Director of Manufacturing
  and Production:** Bruce Johnson
Manufacturing Manager: Ilene Sanford

Manufacturing Buyer: Cathleen Petersen
Creative Director: Cheryl Asherman
Cover Design Coordinator: Miguel Ortiz
Cover Design: Joseph Sengotta
Cover Art: Gen Umekita, Getty Images, Inc.
Interior Design: Janet Bolton
Composition Electronic Art Creation: Laserwords
  Private Limited, Chennai, India
Printing and Binding: Phoenix Book Tech
Copy Editor/Proofreader: Maine Proofreading
  Services

10 9 8 7 6 5 4 3 2 1
ISBN 0-13-097778-0

CONTENTS

3

EDUCATING AND TRAINING NEW POLICE OFFICERS   27

Building the Form and Function

4

EDUCATING AND TRAINING NEW POLICE OFFICERS   56

Teaching Police Science

5

EDUCATING AND TRAINING NEW POLICE OFFICERS 86

Teaching the Law

6

EDUCATING AND TRAINING NEW POLICE OFFICERS 113

Teaching the Behavioral Sciences

7

EDUCATING AND TRAINING NEW POLICE OFFICERS 136
Teaching Physical Education

8

EDUCATING AND TRAINING NEW POLICE OFFICERS   155
Teaching the Use of Force and Firearms

9

A FIELD TRAINING MODEL FOR NEW POLICE OFFICERS   177

10

EDUCATING AND TRAINING IN-SERVICE POLICE OFFICERS   190
Building an In-Service Model

11

TRAINING POLICE SUPERVISORS AND MANAGERS   213

12

A MODEL FOR EXECUTIVE DEVELOPMENT IN LAW ENFORCEMENT **238**

13

BUILDING A LAW ENFORCEMENT ORGANIZATION TO SUSTAIN THE AMERICAN REPUBLIC **247**

PREFACE

In 1994, I was fortunate enough to be appointed by the police commissioner of the City of New York, William J. Bratton, to one of the most challenging and important jobs in the world: I became the director of training for the New York City Police Department. In that capacity, I was responsible for training about 3,000 newly hired police officers per year. Due to the enormity of the agency, the New York City Police Department hires and trains more police officers in one year than most agencies do in decades. During my eight-year tenure, approximately 13,000 newly hired police officers were screened and trained by the New York City Police Academy. It was my personal responsibility to ensure that every single recruit officer was provided with the necessary knowledge and skills to go home safely at the end of their shift. During the process, I learned a lot about exactly what it takes to educate and train a civilian to be a police officer.

Additionally, with an annual budget of $26.7 million and a staff of approximately 600 sworn and 128 civilian instructors, the New York Police Academy provided regular in-service training for an additional 41,000 uniformed members of the service and 13,000 civilians every year.

This massive professional responsibility included designing and delivering annual in-service training for all the various ranks; promotional training for newly promoted sergeants, lieutenants, and captains; an endless array of specialized and advanced training courses covering every imaginable subject; and a comprehensive executive development program.

As I assumed this awesome responsibility, I considered myself to be as prepared as anyone could possibly be for such a compelling task. After serving for ten years as a uniformed and plainclothes police officer in Houston, I was confident that I understood the actual day-to-day responsibilities and challenges of being a big-city cop. I understood what police officers needed in terms of knowledge and survival tactics, and I fully appreciated how much they hated breaking their daily routine to attend in-service training sessions, especially when their time was wasted.

Since I had earned a Ph.D. along the way, I was equally as confident that I had the appropriate academic background, requisite knowledge, and professional credibility to build a world-class police educational and training facility. All things considered, I was prepared to establish a genuine institute of higher education with all the necessary intellectual and practical support functions required to educate and train adults for an intensely difficult, if not impossible, mandate. Indeed, the men and women of the New York City Police Department deserved nothing less.

As the director of training, every single day there were extremely important and fairly complex problems to be solved. I expected that, and I was surrounded by some of the most talented individuals in the world to help solve them.

After all, the New York City Police Department was the largest police department in the country and was responsible for policing "the city that never sleeps." But as I talked to my colleagues, people who were involved in law enforcement training around the world, I realized that they were struggling with many of the exact same issues that we were in New York. I did not expect that.

During my tenure, I had the wonderful opportunity to meet law enforcement people involved in training from every state in the United States. I also had occasion to meet with training directors from around the world. Representatives from England, Ireland, the People's Republic of China, Indonesia, Sweden, Israel, Japan, and many other places all visited the New York City Police Academy to exchange ideas and concerns. At times, I had fascinating conversations with representatives from emerging democracies around the globe and discussed how the police have to be trained to respect individual rights before freedom can flourish.

Even on the federal level, there is significant interest in law enforcement training. Many of the tactics and strategies are of interest not only for federal law enforcement officers but also for the U.S. military. As it turns out, there are some similarities between urban policing and global warfare.

Finally, even outside of law enforcement, I noticed an astonishing interest in law enforcement education and training. John Q. Citizen, community groups, university professors, politicians, and many others sincerely want to better understand why police officers do the things they do.

So this book was published for a very wide audience. Throughout the world wherever freedom is important, the police always seem to be the subject of great public debate. Since that is the case, as many people as possible should know exactly how extensively police officers are prepared for their role. Maybe that way, they can light a candle instead of simply cursing the darkness.

On all fronts, it is my experience that the more people know about the way police officers are educated and trained, the more respect they have for the profession. Hopefully, the following pages will provide a framework for some positive public discussion.

I would like to thank the following professors for reviewing this manuscript: Steve Egger, University of Springfield, Springfield, IL; Mike Grabowski, Prairie View A&M University, Waller, TX; David Graff, Kent State University–Tuscarawas, New Philadelphia, OH; Brian Joyner, Western Wisconsin Technical College, Sparta, WI; David Kotajarvi, Lakeshore Technical College, Oostburg, WI; and Earl Sweeny, New Hampshire Police Academy, Belmont, NH.

ACKNOWLEDGMENTS

Normally, writing the acknowledgments section of a book is the one part an author looks forward to the most. Of course, you think about thanking your wife, your children, and other family members because we all know how critical their support is in everything one accomplishes in life. You think about acknowledging your partner or friends from work because it was so much fun learning how police work is *really* done with them by your side to keep you safe along the way. You might consider thanking a former police commissioner you worked for a long time ago who served as a role model for you as a young police officer, even if it was from a distance . . . a very large distance. You even consider acknowledging a former university professor who may have had a particularly profound impact on your intellectual development early on in your life by teaching you to look into complex issues a little more deeply.

Naturally, you consider thanking your parents because you love and respect them so much, and because they made all things possible for you in life, from your very birth through the luxury of a college education. I must admit that all of these people crossed my mind, and of course, I wholeheartedly thank them all.

But on September 11, 2001, the world as I knew it changed forever. On that date, without any notice or provocation, international terrorists hijacked four commercial airliners and flew two of them directly into the towers of the World Trade Center in New York City. Moments later, a third plane crashed into the Pentagon in Washington, D.C., and the fourth crashed on an open field in Pennsylvania, en route to who knows where.

In the World Trade Center in New York City, the top portions of the buildings collapsed first and the entire structures came down in approximately 12 seconds! In comparison, one of the original architects of the towers remarked, "A stone dropped from the top of the towers would have taken 9.2 seconds to fall to the ground." The subsequent explosions and fireballs, crumbling buildings, confusion, chaos, and devastation defied human comprehension. In the end, the death/missing toll stood somewhere in the thousands, and the actual total number of victims may *never* be known. The number of lives and families completely destroyed by the incident was astonishing. As a New Yorker, everyone I knew from my work, church, and neighborhood lost someone they loved! The largest and most deadly terrorist attack in history had just taken place on the American Republic.

On that date, hundreds of my personal friends and colleagues in the New York City Police Department responded to the scene. My cousin and lifelong friend, Captain Billy O'Keefe (F.D.N.Y., Division 15, Brooklyn), and hundreds of other firefighters, Port Authority police officers, and other emergency workers just like him responded as well. When they arrived on the scene, regardless of the patch on their shoulder, they all did the same exact thing—*exactly what their agency trained them to do.* Caution went out the window and instinct kicked in, instinct thoroughly developed by years of practice, experience, astonishing personal courage, and, of course, education and training.

They all rushed to the scene and into the buildings and immediately focused on saving lives and helping innocent civilians escape the devastation. Because of the way they were trained, they never stopped to consider their own personal safety. They instinctively rushed into the buildings and up the stairs when everyone else was running out. *This dreadful scenario captures the very essence of why the education and training of emergency service personnel are so very critical in the real world.* In an emergency situation, these brave men and women do *exactly* what they are trained to do. Sometimes there is no time to stop and consider the options; you just do what you are trained to do, *so it better be right!* Lives literally depend on it.

The American Republic cannot exist without the core principles of freedom and justice, and even more importantly, it cannot exist without the individual heroes who dedicate their lives to protecting these principles. This book is dedicated to Captain Billy O'Keefe, F.D.N.Y., and all the heroic souls—police officers, firefighters, rescue workers, and civilians alike—who lost their lives in the World Trade Center, the Pentagon, and the Pennsylvania tragedies. Their heroism, sacrifice, courage, and commitment to a greater purpose are beyond words.

GOD BLESS AMERICA AND MAY THEY ALL REST IN PEACE!

James O'Keefe

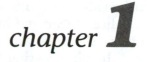

THE MODERN-DAY REPUBLIC AND AMERICAN POLICING

"Government is not reason. It is not eloquence. It is force!
Like fire, it is a dangerous servant and a fearful master."

—George Washington

INTRODUCTION

Every day in America, average citizens read the newspapers and watch the television news. It seems in every city or town across the country, the news is dominated by lead stories about violence, crime, criminals, social disorder, and, ultimately, the police. Moreover, as if the morning newspapers and the nightly television news are not enough, even primetime network television shows that are designed for entertainment purposes are full of reality-based police dramas. As a rule, these television police shows are not very accurate and do not necessarily portray the police in a very positive light.

But they do serve to raise the public interest in law enforcement. Collectively, the constant media exposure to police in action has created somewhat of a public fascination with the police.

It has also served to create public interest in exactly who becomes a police officer and how they are trained and prepared to do such an exciting yet dangerous job.

It is interesting to think about these issues and to explore and attempt to answer these questions. Perhaps the public fascination with the police is also fundamentally connected to the deeply rooted philosophical principles involved in American **democracy**, principles which are played out and resolved every day by the police in American neighborhoods.

After watching the television news each night, most citizens simply wake up the next morning and go about their daily lives, working and taking care of their families. From an individual perspective, they are constantly striving to make their personal world a better place in which to live, a place that is safe and happy for their loved ones.

But at the same time, from a more collective perspective, citizens of a free society essentially rely on local, state, and federal governments and elected officials to make society-at-large a better place. As individuals strive to provide love, money, shelter, and food for their families, they simultaneously expect the federal government to protect them from foreign aggression, and state and local law enforcement to protect them from domestic crime and violence.

This great American **social contract** continues to exist as a conceptual framework to provide a balance in which essentially good yet self-serving people can peacefully coexist in a good and just society.

THE SOCIAL CONTRACT

With the publication of *The Social Contract* in 1761, Jean-Jacques Rousseau established the concept of the "social contract." Essentially it provides an agreement, or a theoretical contract, between a democratic government and citizens of a free society.

It calls for the citizens to allow the government to infringe upon some of their individual freedoms; in exchange for this infringement upon their freedoms, the government provides protection for them against anyone who tries to advance their interests at the expense of others. The social contract is grounded in an understanding of human nature, which is basically good but which can be corrupted by conflicting interests within a society. This is the concept of the social contract.

A modern-day example of the social contract in action can be seen in the area of public safety and international terrorism. Citizens of a free society agree to suspend some of their individual freedoms and allow governmental agents to search them and their vehicles at airports, bridges and tunnels, and other public locations in exchange for an expectation that these measures will facilitate the government's actions to protect them and their loved ones from random acts of terrorism.

Most reasonably intelligent and curious people strive to understand the larger principles and ideas beneath the surface of the events witnessed in society—events that constantly seem to involve random and senseless violence, school shootings, and cruelty against and by children, an endless array of stories about **physical**, **psychological**, and **sexual abuse**. This condition, or at least the perception of such a condition, seems to threaten the desire to create an **ideal state** for the children and all the citizens of a free and just society.

For example, every citizen in a free society is concerned about their right to be free from crime, perhaps the most important civil right of all. Everyone wants to live in a society where the most fundamental virtues of justice, equality, **individual autonomy**, compassion, moderation, courage, and freedom are secure. Indeed, we fight wars to secure these rights; we serve as jurors, elect legislatures, appoint judges, and vote in politicians to see that these lofty principles are realized in our everyday lives. But are they? The struggle is ongoing and constant, yet the very existence of the U.S. **Republic** is contingent on the belief that such an ideal state is possible.

In the meantime, as the great American social contract continues, public cries of "**No justice—no peace!**" can be heard on the streets of America by angry citizens. Conversely, cries of "**No justice—no police!**" can be heard equally as loud from police who serve on the front lines. Social conflict exists in New York City; Los Angeles and Inglewood, California; Oklahoma City; and many other cities as communities protest in the streets against the police and the perceived lack of justice.

The critical importance, however, in both of these perspectives is that they are visible symbols of the struggle that goes on just below the surface of society to maintain a social balance. *They must not be ignored because a society with no justice, or even the perception of no justice, is a society in serious trouble and susceptible to collapsing.* Justice, perhaps the most critical virtue of all, is especially consequential to a free society.

But before such profound ideals as justice and individual autonomy can even begin to be realized, some very fundamental questions must first be considered. For example:

- What is justice?
- Is justice relative to an individual perspective, or is it an objective reality that can actually be achieved?
- Is justice defined as attaining a position of balance in society and fundamental fairness for the overall good of everyone, or is justice simply an individual getting his or her own way by winning a private dispute?
- If not first and foremost to provide justice, why should a government even exist?
- What is the nature and the purpose of government?
- Who should govern?
- Why should free citizens allow a government to infringe upon their individual rights and obey its laws?
- Perhaps most importantly, who should enforce such laws, and how will those persons be selected, trained, and held accountable?

Finally, even if it is agreed by the majority that the best way to build an ideal state is to have a social structure that provides government and laws, and the need for someone to enforce the law is agreed upon, it is still of great public interest to know specifically how these enforcers are to be selected and trained so they can be trusted to act in the best overall interest of the republic at large.

THE PHILOSOPHY OF POLICING

These are compelling questions and are probably considered by everyone at one point or another, for instance, shortly after receiving the first traffic summons requiring them to pay a significant fine. Such questions are answered in the philosophy of policing. Philosophy stands at the foundation of all things, even police work...*especially police work*. In order to more effectively deal with the concrete problems of the world, the more abstract philosophical foundations involved must first be understood.

The good news is that these very same philosophical foundations have already been considered and explored by some of the finest minds of all time, and they have some splendid thoughts on the matter. *The Republic*, by Plato, is generally acknowledged as the cornerstone of all such works. Clearly recognized as one of the world's great books, *The Republic* is rich with classic dialogue about the various questions surrounding the creation of the kind of world that good and just citizens want to live in. Important public policy questions are raised and discussed, all for the purpose of examining exactly what kind of world free and thoughtful citizens should design to sustain their most important freedoms.

In the dialogues of Plato, fundamental virtues, questions about the way to create an ideal state, and many other timeless issues are examined. For example, in *The Republic*, the relationship between power and knowledge is examined. The question of "Does might make right?" is considered and rejected as a foundation for a republic. In fact, it is argued that the reason for the mere existence of a republic is to provide structure and form to control **man's nature** to dominate. Today, one could argue that this same dynamic is still played out between governmental authority and individual freedoms. Usually, the police officer represents the authority figure, and the actions of the citizens represent their desire for freedom. Both, paradoxically, depend on a government of some sort to support their respective positions and protect their interests.

The bad news is that no matter how balanced the underlying **political philosophy** or social structure of a society is, such philosophical answers are only as good as the individual who, on behalf of society, applies them in the day-to-day encounters with free citizens. Notice: only as good as the *individual*, not the great book, **political theory**, written text, law, principle, **constitutional amendment**, or Supreme Court opinion. Even though building an ideal republic is very much a collective or global effort, in the end, actually realizing and sustaining one is very much an individual or local effort.

In the various classic dialogues of political philosophy, original democratic ideals emerged and were discussed, the very same democratic ideals that loom beneath the surface of almost every police–citizen encounter today. Whether it is realized or not, in today's society, a uniformed police officer is both the philosophical and the actual manifestation of these ideals as well as of the republic that exists to advance them.

While the critical principles of justice, equality, individual autonomy, and freedom are all well established in the political philosophy and protected in the written laws, they must actually be experienced and applied to life to become reality. More often than not, such a reality takes place through such events as an encounter with a twenty-three-year-old white male police officer in the middle of the night on some street corner in a calamitous circumstance. In the real world, the quality and outcome of such an encounter directly contribute to an individual's belief in the existence of justice, equality, autonomy, and freedom.

While Plato and **Socrates** may have had the luxury of standing on a street corner philosophizing about the virtues of a great republic, a modern-day police officer has to put on a bullet-resistant vest and a semiautomatic pistol every day to actually bring such virtues to life. Given this realization, the process in which police officers are selected, hired, educated, trained, and held accountable for their actions becomes more than just an exercise in philosophy, and more of a **moral imperative** to sustain freedom.

CONCLUSION

All this talk about the nature of man and political philosophy is important because it is the foundation of American society as we know it, or as we hope it to be. As the nation stands today, the **criminal justice system** in general, and the police in particular, is responsible for protecting all free citizens in terms of controlling human behavior and advancing the virtues America proposes to represent.

Understanding how complex this mandate is in theory provides a better understanding of why it is so difficult to accomplish it in practice. The actual link between the theory of justice and the practical application of justice lies in the hands of the criminal justice system. For this to work even close to what the Founding Fathers envisioned requires a special type of police officer with a special type of selection, education, training, integrity, and account-ability. To advance this purpose, this text is designed to examine many of the issues that should be considered in the education and training of U.S. police officers.

KEY TERMS

Constitutional Amendment

Criminal Justice System

Democracy

Ideal State

Individual Autonomy

Man's Nature

Moral Imperative

No Justice—No Peace!

No Justice—No Police!

Physical Abuse

Political Philosophy

Political Theory

Psychological Abuse

Republic

Sexual Abuse

Social Contract

Socrates

QUESTIONS FOR DISCUSSION

1. Why is there so much crime and violence in society?
2. Compare the number of stories in the local news dealing with crime and violence to other subjects covered in the news. What percentage of time is dedicated solely to crime and violence?
3. What examples can be found in the criminal justice system to illustrate the balance sought in the social contract?
4. How serious is it when a large group of citizens gather together in the community and chant "No justice—no peace!"? What is at stake?
5. All citizens of a free society want justice, but is justice an objective reality that can be achieved, or is it relative to the individual?
6. What systems of government exist to provide justice in soci-ety? How do the different systems and/or agencies differ in their jurisdiction?
7. What is the *most important* purpose of government in a free society?
8. Why should an individual studying to become a police officer read *The Republic*?

9. What common denominators, if any, can be found between philosophy and American policing?

10. How important is an individual police officer to the realization of justice and freedom?

SUGGESTED READINGS

Albert, Ethel, Theodore C. Denise, and Sheldon P. Peterfrund. (1984). *Great traditions in ethics*. Belmont, CA: Wadsworth Publishing.

Barry, B. (1973). *The liberal theory of justice*. Oxford: Clarendon Press.

Bentham, Jeremy. (1988) (originally published in 1781). *The principles of morals and legislation*. Buffalo, NY: Prometheus Books.

Black, Donald (editor). (1984). *Toward a general theory of social control*, Volume 1 and Volume 2. New York: Academic Press.

Blok, Anton. (1974). *The mafia of a Sicilian village, 1860–1960: A study of violent peasant entrepreneurs*. New York: Harper & Row.

Bolton, Ralph. (1970). Rates and ramifications of violence: Noted on Qolla homicide. Paper presented at the International Congress of Americanists, Lima, Peru.

Brown, Paula. (1964). Enemies and affines. *Ethnology* 3: 335–356.

Buckley, William F. (1984). *Up from liberalism*. New York: Stein and Day Publications.

Cranston, Maurice and Richard S. Peters (editors). (1972). *Hobbes and Rousseau: A collection of critical essays*. New York: Doubleday and Company.

Teilhard de Chardin, Pierre. (1965). *The phenomenon of man*. New York: Harper Torch.

Ebenstein, William. (1965). *Great political thinkers: Plato to the present*. New York: Rinehart and Winston.

Felstiner, William. (1984). The logic of mediation. In *Toward a general theory of social control*, Volume One. New York: Academic Press.

Gluckman, Max. (1965). *Politics, law and rituals in tribal society*. New York: Mentor.

Grabosky, Peter N. (1984). The variability of punishment. In *Toward a general theory of social control*, Volume One. New York: Academic Press.

Griffin, Edward. (1964). *The fearful master: A second look at the United Nations*. Boston: Western Island Publishers.

Griffiths, John. (1984). The division of labor in social control. In *Toward a general theory of social control*, Volume One. New York: Academic Press.

Hamilton, Alexander. (1788). The Federalist. No. LI. *New York Packet*, February 8.

Hardie, William. (1980). *Aristotle's ethical theory*. New York: Oxford University Press.

Hobbes, Thomas. (1988) (originally published in 1651). *The leviathan*. Buffalo, NY: Prometheus Books.

Jaeger, W.W. (1934). *Aristotle.* New York: Methuen Publishing.

Joachim, H.H. (1954). *Aristotle: The Nicomachean ethics*. London: Oxford University Press.

Kant, Immanuel. (1987) (originally published in 1785; translated by Thomas K. Abbott). *Fundamental principles of the metaphysic of morals*. Buffalo, NY: Prometheus Books.

Koch, Klaus-Friedrich. (1984). Liability and social structure. In *Toward a general theory of social control*, Volume One. New York: Academic Press.

———. (1974). *War and peace in the Jalemo: The management of conflict in Highland, New Guinea*. Cambridge, MA: Harvard University Press.

MacCormick, Geoffrey. (1976). Procedures for the settlement of disputes in simple societies. *The Irish Jurist* 11 (N.S.): 175–188.

Madison, James K. (1787). *The Federalist*, no. X. *New York Packet*, November 23.

McLean, George. (1978). *Man and nature.* London: Oxford University Press.

Merry, Sally E. (1984). Rethinking gossip and scandal. In *Toward a general theory of social control*, Volume One. New York: Academic Press.

Middleton, John and David Tait (editors). (1958). *Tribes without rulers: Studies in African segmentary systems*. New York: Humanities Press.

Nell, O. (1975). *Acting on principles: An essay on Kantian ethics.* New York: University Press.

Paine, Thomas. (1987) (originally published in 1774). *Rights of man being an answer to Mr. Burke's attack on The French Revolution.* Buffalo, NY: Prometheus Books.

Plato. (1986) (originally published in 387 B.C.; translated by Benjamin Jowett). *The Republic.* Buffalo, NY: Prometheus Books.

Popkin, Richard and Avrum Stroll. (1956). *Philosophy made simple.* New York: Doubleday and Company.

Quinney, Richard. (1982). *Social existence: Metaphysics, Marxism, and the social sciences.* Beverly Hills, CA: Sage Library of Social Research.

Rawls, John. (1958). Justice as fairness. *Philosophical Review* 67: 164–194.

———. (1971). *A theory of justice.* Cambridge, MA: Harvard University Press.

Rieder, Jonathan. (1984). The social organization of vengeance. In *Toward a general theory of social control*, Volume One. New York: Academic Press.

Roberts, Simon. (1979). *Order and dispute: An introduction to legal anthropology.* New York: Penguin Press.

Rohrl, Vivian, J. (1984). Compensation in cross-cultural perspectives. In *Toward a general theory of social control*, Volume One. New York: Academic Press.

Rousseau, Jean-Jacques. (1988) (originally published in 1761). *The social contract.* Buffalo, NY: Prometheus Books.

Wilson, James Q. and Richard Herrnstein. (1985). *Crime and human nature.* New York: Simon & Schuster.

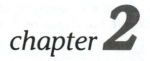

chapter **2**

WHO SHOULD PROTECT THE REPUBLIC?

"It is a matter of real importance whether our early education confirms in us one set of habits or another. It would be nearer to the truth to say that it makes a very great difference indeed, in fact, all the difference in the world."

—Aristotle

INTRODUCTION

If, in fact, the premise of this text is that the police officer is the guardian of the American Republic, it stands to reason that the recruitment, selection, and training of the proper person would be of the utmost importance. Clearly, such individuals would have to believe in and embody the very same virtues of the society they are sworn to protect. Virtues such as integrity, respect, character, compassion, and genuine respect for justice and individual freedoms would all be necessities.

Normally, selecting the proper person for a job is a fairly routine task, one that is essentially guided by logic and common

11

sense. For example, if a job description calls for physical labor, the most appropriate candidate would possess a good work history, a record of coming to work every day and working hard, and a good deal of physical strength. These are all characteristics that are relatively easy to recruit and verify before appointment.

Conversely, if a job description calls for a well-educated, articulate, cerebral individual who enjoys working unaccompanied, is good with technology, and enjoys paperwork and details, a somewhat different recruitment and selection process would be appropriate, and probably a very different type of applicant would apply. If a third type of employment opportunity was available for an individual who was simply not inclined to work in an office and do paperwork but was more drawn to getting excitement, helping people, having adventures, and doing something different every day, that would require yet another recruitment and selection approach, a recruitment and selection approach that the U.S. Armed Forces have apparently practiced with accomplishment for many years.

As a matter of practice, it would appear that selecting the right person for the right job is a relatively straightforward and commonsense process, once given a clear job description and accompanying personality traits that one would need in order to be successful. But what if the job description is not so clear and the personality traits for success are not so obvious? What if the job calls for a great deal of physical size and strength with a real sense of adventure sometimes, but extraordinary communication skills and compassion, without any regard to physical size, at other times? What if the job description is incredibly complex, depending on the time of day one works, the nature of an assignment, or the actions of a third party? What if the job description varies according to who the mayor and/or police commissioner is at any given time, and the priorities of their political affiliation? What if the day-to-day job description changes in a very fundamental fashion according to the latest trend in American policing and a different style of enforcement is forced on an agency by elected officials who may not really understand what police officers do anyway? These are some of the challenges facing American policing today!

For these reasons, simply selecting the right type of person to do police work sometimes can become more complex than it may appear on the surface. In a free society, police officers are asked to be many different things to many different people. Historically, the police mandate seems to be "to be all things to all people."

In some basic underlying ways, the job of a police officer is different from most other civilian jobs in America. Applicants must be carefully recruited and screened before they can be afforded an opportunity to earn the public trust that goes with such a job. Police departments must be extraordinarily selective about who they will empower to have a direct impact on the safety and freedom of the community.

Most citizens would expect that a police officer candidate should be selected for an ability to fight crime and disorder in their community, a quite reasonable expectation. Yet it is clear, based on the complexity of what it means to "fight crime," that it takes more than simply recruiting the high school football team to successfully meet this mandate.

In addition to fighting crime in the community, police officers spend a significant amount of time standing by waiting for something to happen, handling vehicle accidents, and resolving verbal disputes. Police officers also direct traffic; work special events involving the gathering of large crowds; write reports, memos, and book entries; prepare other administrative documentation; respond to property damage calls; guard prisoners in the hospital; and basically handle an endless variation of problems that arise in the community.

Such responsibilities are important and necessary to maintain public order, especially in a nation that has produced an underclass with poverty, unemployment, broken homes, broken dreams, poor educational opportunities, and many other elements of social disorganization. Like it or not, this social disorganization becomes the job of the American police. As complex as such social problems are, by default police officers are expected to handle the resulting disorder. The perfect society has never existed, and it never will as long as it is comprised of human beings. Because of all this, the professionalism and effectiveness of any police organization depend, to a great extent, on the effective recruitment, selection, and training of the right people to be police officers. Accordingly, any society is only as inclusive, just, respectful, responsive, and compassionate as the police officers it employs.

RECRUITMENT

Right from the start, it is important to realize that the recruitment, screening, selection, and hiring process of police officers, by itself, will never produce a perfect officer. It is an oversimplification to attack the hiring process every time a police officer violates the oath of office and gets into some type of trouble.

Although the hiring process should constantly be reviewed, many other factors can potentially be involved in problem officers. Not until a perfect society is found to recruit from will policing be able to select perfect officers. In the meantime, one must believe that a comprehensive recruitment campaign and a thorough personnel selection process, in conjunction with capable education and training, effective supervision, and strict accountability, can produce a professional police officer capable of deserving the public trust.

Police agencies must be as comprehensive and inclusive in their recruitment campaign as possible. Because of the varied nature of the job, as well as the increasingly diverse nature of society, many different types of people are drawn to police work and many different types of people are needed to make it successful.

To attract as many qualified applicants as possible, police departments should be very proactive in their efforts by utilizing many different approaches. Individuals should be assigned to the recruitment function on a continuous basis. These individuals should be extraordinarily knowledgeable about the requirements of the agency, the realities of the profession, the career opportunities available within an agency, the salary structures of the various ranks, and any other relevant questions about the career.

Successful police recruiters should focus their efforts on as many different venues as possible to ensure diversity. The Internet has emerged as a valuable recruitment tool for policing, and it promises to be more and more valuable in the future. Neighborhood fairs, local job fairs, local high schools, military bases, and local colleges and universities all provide access to potential candidates.

At local college and university recruitment efforts, students of *all* majors should be offered the opportunity to explore the option of policing as a career. The diverse and often complex nature of the job allows for individuals of all academic interests to apply. It would be hard to think of any legitimate academic major that would NOT qualify an individual for policing. Police agencies of all sizes, both large and small, can normally think of many career opportunities for students of the behavioral sciences, physical sciences, or essentially any other field of study. Character, integrity, and a desire for public service are not defined or bound by the artificial boundaries of academic disciplines, and the police recruiter should not be either. Due to retirements, organizational growth, and many other factors, most police departments can sustain a constant recruitment process.

In recruitment efforts, it is important to consider a couple of factors. First, recruitment units should be careful how they define success. A "successful recruitment drive" may not necessarily be defined as filling the next academy class with a predetermined number of police recruits. For various reasons (for example, in response to the pressures of political mandates or funding deadlines), police agencies may consider appointing marginal applicants who would not have been hired in a different situation. History has taught that this is clearly a recipe for disaster. *This practice must change. If the anticipated number of quality applicants are not available, quality cannot be compromised for quantity.* Police administrators must not lose sight of the big picture and settle for individuals with questionable backgrounds who may later embarrass the agency.

The definition of a "successful recruitment drive" is the identification of a number of special qualified individuals who are prepared to enter the next academy class, whatever that number may be. With the integrity of an organization at stake, it is always better to pay a smaller number of police officers overtime and do the job right than to hire marginal applicants who may go on to tarnish the shields and the reputation of an entire agency. A bad police officer can almost single-handedly destroy years of social capital built in a community. If there is any question about an individual applicant, the benefit of the doubt should be given to the community and the law enforcement agency, and the individual should not be hired.

Ongoing personnel recruitment in policing must always be a priority, and character and integrity will always be crucial factors in hiring, but they will probably never be available en masse.

SELECTION

While recruitment efforts should be as expansive and inclusive as possible, the actual selection process is where the field should be narrowed with an eye toward elimination. In big cities and small police agencies throughout the country, becoming a police officer is much more difficult than most people realize, as it should be. While most jobs are simply based on a resume, an interview, and a few professional references, the selection process for a police officer is long, time-consuming, and competitive.

Each sequential step in the hiring process must be successfully completed before an applicant will be allowed to move on to the next step. Many of the requirements require a significant commitment of departmental resources in terms of time, money, and manpower, and the investigative process cannot be rushed or abbreviated simply to meet upcoming police academy class schedules. Actual requirements to become a police officer vary from one jurisdiction to another. However, the selection process usually requires some or all of the following:

- A written test to measure the applicant's general knowledge
- A medical examination to determine if an applicant has any medical conditions that might prevent him or her from the physical demands of police work
- A psychological exam to measure emotional stability and general psychological well-being
- A physical test to measure basic levels of physical fitness and agility
- A background investigation to check an applicant's criminal history, credit history, traffic tickets, military record, educational background, and other public records
- A character investigation to interview friends, teachers, neighbors, and other long-term associates of an applicant to assess character

Additionally, during the selection process, or at least by the time of appointment to the police academy, most police agencies require applicants to have the following qualifications:

- Be a U.S. citizen
- Be at least eighteen years of age (although most law enforcement agencies require age twenty-one)
- Possess a certain level of educational achievement (some departments require high school diplomas, some require sixty college credits with a certain G.P.A., and a few require bachelor's degrees)
- Possess a valid driver's license

- Have no felony convictions or convictions for domestic violence offenses
- Be a resident of a certain city, county, or region

While the exact requirements vary from one agency to another, the basic requirements are almost all consistent in any municipal law enforcement agency. As one goes up the ladder from municipal to state to federal law enforcement positions, the overall requirements do generally increase.

At all levels, collectively they serve to identify individuals with the necessary and proper characteristics to be a good police officer. They also constitute the most common selection standards historically used by police departments to identify and select police officer candidates, and they have been in place for a long time. It is significant to realize, however, that all of these standards are predictors of good people only most of the time at best.

For example, since most police officer positions are civil service jobs with municipal governments, the selection criteria must be applied equally across the board. The **egalitarian principles** on which civil service laws are based are essentially a double-edged sword. On one hand, egalitarian principles are designed to keep the system fair, even, and free of any systematic and/or individual discrimination. On the other hand, the focus on fundamental fairness forces a police agency to stick to measures that can be graded en masse, statistically counted, evenly measured, and fairly ranked. In most cases, this system severely limits the use of any subjective criteria such as personal interviews, written essays, and (often difficult to document but noticeable) personality traits.

In general, there are no disagreements about which personal characteristics are needed to become a successful police officer in a free society. Character, integrity, compassion, intelligence, maturity, psychological wellness, physical and moral courage, and effective communication skills, to name a few, are all principal traits. The challenge lies in exactly how to identify, measure, document, and test for such traits.

Education

For example, in the search for individuals with the appropriate reading, writing, and thinking skills, some police agencies have instituted an educational requirement varying from forty-five hours of college credits to a bachelor's degree. Intuitively, this approach seems to be a valid measure of intelligence. But does it mean that an individual candidate with no college hours is not intelligent enough to be a police officer? Moreover, does it mean that a candidate with sixty college hours is smarter than a candidate with no college hours? Finally, is there any guarantee that smart individuals are also people of character and integrity?

Even in the face of such uncertainty, it is interesting to point out that the call for education for police officer candidates is nothing new. As early as 1922, **August Vollmer** stated that the university was an indispensable tool to prepare young adults for the police service (Vollmer, 1922). Shortly after that, in 1931, the **Wickersham Commission** recognized the same need for police officers to be educated. Accordingly, it was publicly agreed that the most effective means of improving the quality of the individual police officer was through the imposition of higher educational standards. Ever since August Vollmer first suggested the utilization of higher education for the police as a key ingredient to professionalize them, many important issues have been discussed and debated about education as a requirement of becoming a police officer.

August Vollmer and many others believed that if the various municipal police agencies could recruit "truly exceptional men and women to serve" as police officers, individuals who were of "superior intellectual endowment, physically sound, and free from any mental and nervous disorders," that such officers could command the respect of the community and their associates (Vollmer, 1922).

Yet it was not until the extensive and highly visible social unrest erupted in the 1960s that public concern about the quality of policing once again appeared on the public agenda. As a result of some of the police actions taken in response to the social unrest and the urgent pleas to regain an orderly society, August Vollmer's position again gained popular acceptance. This time, however, public sentiment was behind the movement.

The public interest was based, at least in part, on the live television coverage of the frequently violent police response to public disorder. For the first time, average middle-class American citizens could actually sit in the safety of their living rooms, turn on the television set, and witness the sometimes violent encounters between the police and the community. Clearly, the publicity associated with such a vivid demonstration of prevailing police tactics and strategies caused many citizens to sit back and consider the role of the police in America as well as the qualifications that should be required for police service.

To this very day, the qualifications to be utilized in hiring police officers consistently vary in accordance with current events and the resulting political climate. In response to especially violent police actions sometimes captured on videotape and covered extensively by the media, the community in general, elected officials, and well-organized special-interest groups of all affiliations frequently call into question the qualifications for police officers and collectively call for improvements. This dynamic was apparent in Los Angeles following the **Rodney King** case and in New York City in the wake of the **Abner Louima** case.

It is usually in light of such high-profile situations that it is once again realized that effective law enforcement and order maintenance are relatively easy to obtain. However, effective law enforcement and order maintenance in a free, democratic, pluralistic society within the confines of the U.S. Constitution and **Bill of Rights** are not quite so simple!

Throughout history, in the wake of public controversy regarding a police action, public hearings are held, committees are formed, debates are entertained, especially vocal members of the community are consulted, commissions are convened, and reports are published. In 1967, the **President's Commission on Law Enforcement and the Administration of Justice** stated:

> The failure to establish high professional standards in the police service has been a costly one, both for the police and for society. Existing selection requirements and procedures for the majority of the departments do not screen out the unfit. The quality of the police service will not improve until higher education requirements are established for its personnel.

Interestingly enough, this same committee later recommended the eventual establishment of a bachelor's degree requirement for all police personnel. The **National Advisory Commission on Criminal Justice Standards and Goals** took this recommendation one step further and suggested a specific timetable for the complete implementation of this requirement (*Report on the Police*, 1973). These same calls requiring higher educational standards for the police were echoed by practically every governmental commission in existence since.

For example, the **Governor's Mutual Assistance Program for Criminal Justice** stated that "improvement for police personnel is the most important facet for improving the police function" (*Where We Stand in the Fight Against Crime*, 1973). The **Police Foundation** stated that one of the primary justifications for its existence should be to "stimulate massive, imaginative, and systematic recruitment of college graduates for police departments" (Police Foundation, 1972).

Even the **American Bar Association** (1972) became involved and offered this recommendation:

> College graduates should be encouraged to apply for employment with police agencies. Individuals aspiring to careers in police agencies and those currently employed as police officers should be encouraged to advance their education at the college level. Communities should support further educational achievement on the part of police personnel by adopting such devices as educational incentive pay plans, and by gradually instituting requirements for the completion of specific periods of college work as a prerequisite for initial appointment and for promotion.

The principal point to be made is that the community, police experts, and elected officials alike all agreed that the quality of the police had to be upgraded. Rapid changes in the complex nature of policing a free society further created a need for increased numbers of well-educated police officers, and access to higher education appeared to all to be the most logical method to accomplish this task. Since that time, a number of academic studies have been published that have attempted to measure actual police performance as it relates specifically to higher education (Bozza, 1973; Cohen and Chaiken, 1972; Finckenauer, 1975; Levy, 1967; McGreevy, 1964; Ostrom, 1976; Smith, 1976; Smith and Ostrom, 1974; Spencer and Nichols, 1971; Van Maanen, 1974; Ostrom, 1978).

Three of these studies found that more educated officers did better on such measures of performance as arrests and fewer civilian complaints. Yet another found that more educated officers were more likely to resign or be dismissed. A fifth study found that more educated officers received higher departmental performance evaluations, utilized less sick time, and were better communicators and better decision makers (Spencer and Nichols, 1971). The remaining studies generally report findings of no relationship between educational levels and the particular measurements of performance they focused on during the research (Sherman, 1978). As mentioned earlier, many of the personal characteristics assumed to be associated with higher education are difficult to isolate and even more difficult to measure, not to mention that some of the more specific questions with regard to this matter are even more difficult to resolve. For example, what is the best major or curriculum for a police officer to study?

In terms of identifying who should police a republic, it is difficult to identify specific characteristics that a college education would furnish an individual that would make him or her a better all-around police officer. Again, because of the complex and changing nature of the job description, a college-educated police officer may not necessarily be a better police officer in every possible circumstance.

Like most controversial public issues, the courts have been asked to review the issue of the college requirement. Around the country, the courts have addressed the question of educational requirements for employment as a police officer, and they have uniformly recognized the unusual nature of the job. Because of that, they have held that college requirements are appropriate, job-related, and valid (*Davis* v. *City of Dallas*, 1979). Even though the courts have also "consistently condemned as discriminatory the requirement of a high school diploma" for some public government positions, and by implication any college requirement, educational requirements for police officers have been consistently sustained.

While many professional-type positions require and utilize skills and abilities that are extremely formidable to define with significant precision and even harder to test for or measure, this is especially true for police officers. Again, how can it be determined exactly which skills are desirable for an individual police officer when the actual job and the public expectations surrounding it continue to change?

In the end, how could one argue that a republic, any republic, would not be better off with a police officer who possesses a liberal understanding of human behavior built around the social and behavioral sciences? Within the confines of such human insights, a police officer would almost certainly be in a better position to preserve the constitutional guarantees and best utilize the broad range of discretion that they are allowed. Certainly in the American Republic, any government official would have to be intelligent enough to understand that differences exist between cultures, mature enough to control emotions, and knowledgeable about social and political conditions.

Such an intuitive belief, if not an empirical one, that a college experience will provide such characteristics simply cannot be denied. Finally, it seems eminently clear that policing is a responsibility that one not only trains for but educates for.

Maturity

Maturity is yet another criterion in which police departments simply have to do the best they can in identifying an elusive character trait. Many departments have instituted a minimum age for their candidates. Requiring an applicant to be at least eighteen years old in some jurisdictions, twenty-one years of age in most, appears to be a relatively reliable criterion for maturity. The problem lies in the fact that age and maturity don't always correlate. Since some people are mature at eighteen and others remain immature well into their thirties, this remains a difficult criterion to effectively measure.

Acknowledging all the difficulties inherent in selecting the right person to protect a republic does not diminish the importance of it or change the reality that it simply must be done. The reality of the police officer selection process is that most police departments do a reasonably effective job. Through the utilization of written exams, educational requirements, thorough background checks, psychological tests, physical exams, credit checks, and other methods, a sensible profile of an applicant can be established.

However, yet another reality of the police selection process is that regardless of how thorough and comprehensive it is, the process will almost certainly be challenged by individuals and groups of individuals represented by special-interest groups who have been eliminated by the selection process. Individuals and/or groups of individuals who have been disproportionately eliminated by a certain selection criterion will challenge that criterion in court. An apparently endless array of individual and collective allegations of systematic bias and discrimination continue to face most civil service commissions and probably always will. No one likes to be told they are not qualified for a career they desire.

Every so often, throughout the nation, police misconduct cases continue to arise and almost always invite public questioning as to how corrupt individuals managed to elude such an exhaustive pre-hiring selection process. Over the years, major cities such as Miami, Houston, New York, and Washington, D.C., have all faced major police misconduct, brutality, and/or police corruption cases that directly led to a review of the selection process utilized to hire police officers. The small communities and law enforcement agencies that constitute the majority of police departments in America share the exact same challenges.

Regardless of how large or small a police department is, history has proven that relaxing the time-consuming process of selecting the right person for the job can lead to disastrous results and can cause more damage to the republic than good. Certain responsibilities of public administration are just too important to be rushed because of time constraints or ignored for financial reasons, and conducting background checks for police officers is one of them!

CONCLUSION

To realize significant improvements in American policing, proactive measures must be taken up front to control the quality of police applicants actually hired. Although it may be difficult and time-consuming to thoroughly investigate and screen each and every applicant, the integrity of the selection process must not be compromised to save time. An excellent education and training program can do a great deal to provide the necessary structure and guidance in the transformation from civilian to police officer. Organizational controls, supervisory oversight, and a progressive disciplinary process are also important ingredients in sustaining a department's integrity. But ultimately police officers operate with an enormous amount of personal discretion, and individuals who are determined to abuse their power and authority will inflict an enormous amount of damage on their victims, a community in general, an entire police department, and, in due course, the overall confidence in government. Nothing can be worth such a price.

KEY TERMS

Abner Louima

American Bar Association

August Vollmer

Bill of Rights

Davis v. *City of Dallas*

Egalitarian Principles

Governor's Mutual Assistance
Program for Criminal Justice

National Advisory Commission
on Criminal Justice Standards
and Goals

Police Foundation

President's Commission on
Law Enforcement and the
Administration of Justice

Rodney King

Wickersham Commission

QUESTIONS FOR DISCUSSION

1. Explain why it is so difficult for law enforcement to eliminate all potential problem police officers up front in the recruitment and selection process.

2. Write a list of personality traits that are desirable in a police officer.

3. What is the police mandate in a free society?

4. Should all potential police officer candidates be required to be criminal justice majors?

5. List and discuss the various reasons that a law enforcement recruitment drive should be as inclusive as possible.

6. List the various steps in the police officer selection process. Why is each criterion important?

7. Should municipal police departments consider utilizing more subjective selective criteria such as interviews or essay questions to select police officer candidates?

8. List and discuss the various reasons it is believed that college-educated individuals would make better police officers.

9. What is the American Bar Association? What is its organizational standing in relation to its concern about the quality of police officers?

10. Discuss and explain the distinction between training for a job and educating for a job. How is this distinction relevant to American policing?

SUGGESTED READINGS

American Bar Association. (1972). *American Bar Association project on standards for criminal justice. The urban police function.* New York: American Bar Association.

Aristotle. (1958) (translated by J.A.K. Thomson). *The ethics of Aristotle: The Nicomachean ethics.* Hammondsworth, Middlesex, England: Penguin Books, Ltd.

Bozza, C.M. (1973). Motivations guiding patrolmen in the arrest process. *Journal of Police Science and Administration* 1: 468–476.

Cohen, B. and J.M. Chaiken. (1972). *Police background characteristics and performance: A summary report.* Washington, DC: Law Enforcement Assistance Administration.

Davis v. *City of Dallas.* (1979). 483 F. Supp. 54,56 (N.D. Tex.).

Finckenauer, J.O. (1975). Higher education and police discretion. *Journal of Police Science and Administration* 3(4): 450–457.

Foster, J.D. (1973). Criminal justice faculty. A survey of employment practices in higher education criminal justice programs. Youngston State University. Mimeo.

Levy, R.J. (1967). Predicting police failures. *Journal of Criminal Law, Criminology, and Police Science* 58: 266–267.

McGreevy, T.J. (1964). A field of study of the relationships between the formal educational levels of 556 police officers in St. Louis and their patrol duty performance records. Master's thesis, School of Public Administration and Public Safety, Michigan State University.

National Advisory Commission on Criminal Justice Standards and Goals. (1973). *Report on the police.* Washington, DC: Government Printing Office.

Ostrom, E. (1978). *Police departmental policies toward education.* Washington, DC: Police Foundation.

Police Foundation. (1972). Education and training task force report. Unpublished report of the Police Foundation.

President's Commission on Law Enforcement and the Administration of Justice. *Task force report: The police*. Washington, DC: Government Printing Office.

Sherman, L.W. (1973). *Team policing: Seven case studies*. Washington, DC: Police Foundation.

————. (1978). *The quality of police education: A critical review with recommendations for improving programs in higher education*. Washington, DC: Police Foundation.

Smith, David. (1978). Police professionalism and performance: An analysis of public policy from the perspective of police as producers and citizens as consumers of police services. Unpublished doctoral dissertation, Indiana University at Bloomington.

Smith, D.C. and E. Ostrom. (1974). *The effects of training and education and police performance*. Washington, DC: Police Foundation.

Spencer, G. and R. Nichols. (1971). A study of Chicago police recruits. *The Police Chief* 38(6): 50–55.

Van Maanen, J. (1974). Working the streets: A developmental view of police behavior. In H. Jacob (editor), *The potential for reform in criminal justice*. Beverly Hills, CA: Sage.

Vollmer, August. (1966). *Professionalism*. Englewood Cliffs, NJ: Prentice Hall.

————. (1922). Aims and ideals of the police. *Journal of the American Institute of Criminal Law and Criminology* 13: 251–257.

Wilson, James Q. (1969). What makes a better policeman. *Atlantic Monthly*, March 1969.

chapter 3

Educating and Training New Police Officers

Building the Form and Function

"Order or disorder depends on organization."

—Sun Tzu

Introduction

Establishing a successful police academy of any size and complexity, whether it is a small agency academy, a medium-size regional academy, a training facility affiliated with a local community college, or even a large independent big-city academy, is difficult under the best of circumstances. Moreover, in public administration, the best of circumstances are extraordinarily rare and, if they appear at all, appear just for a fleeting moment. Exactly like police chiefs or police commissioners, training directors are asked to effectively accomplish their job responsibilities within the ever-changing, politically turbulent realm of public administration. Public administration is, by definition, characterized by political uncertainty, unrelenting media coverage of police actions, competing special-interest groups, scarce resources, economic swings, hiring schedules driven by budget mandates and inappropriate educational standards, and constant politically commissioned studies, committees, commissions, and investigative reports. Collectively, these factors make it very difficult to establish and maintain a steady course in the administration of a training facility.

None of these factors, however, can impact the administration and operations of a police academy like the two that seem to invariably emerge in American policing every so often: a change in administration and/or a police scandal.

A change in administration of either a mayor or a police chief can, and should, have a profound impact on the operations of a police academy. A new top public official will almost always appear on the scene with a fresh vision for the future and immediately begin rearranging priorities to move in the new direction. In a society built on the principles of a democracy, this fresh vision will be based on the priorities articulated during the election process. Therefore, if an individual is elected to public office, one can only assume that his or her vision and priorities are, in fact, the will of the people.

In this day and age, political platforms and agendas are almost always built around some type of law and order or public safety agenda. Public concerns about crime, disorder, overall quality of life, and, most recently, terrorism are perennial political considerations. The major public concern soon becomes a major training issue because newly conceived law and order agendas always have, and always will, begin with the training function.

Indeed, the best way to actually align individual police officer behavior with a broader, more philosophical political vision is through effective education and training of that vision. Elected officials either know this when they assume command or learn it very quickly. Many are elected with a full appreciation for the value of **organizational development** and education and training for the implementation of a vision. Others simply reach out to the training managers in the wake of an unfortunate incident and in response to relentless public questions about exactly how police officers are trained.

Either way, it seems clear that pure public opinion, political will, and even traditional command and control techniques alone simply do not produce a desired behavior change in police officers.

In most all city police departments, police officers are protected with civil service status and, as a general rule, are not easily intimidated or influenced. Ultimately, these are the character traits that make them good street cops! Instead, the police academy should take the lead in aligning police officer behaviors with official expectations, and that is best accomplished through the education and training agenda.

In addition to a change in administration, police scandals of various sorts can have an enormous effect on a police training agenda. The history is clear in that in response to police scandals, investigative, legislative, political, and/or judicial inquiries into such an issue will inevitably lead right to the front door of the police academy and a careful review of the way police officers are selected, hired, and trained. The standard issues—police scandals alleging abuse of force, corruption, brutality, and even just police arrogance—always seem to begin with the assumption that police officers were never provided with the necessary skills to do things correctly. Most police behavior is instinctive, and instinct comes from repetition, and repetition comes from training, so sooner or later, the criminal or civil liability trail leads directly back to the police academy. This is a crucial legal battleground for police administrators. If a police officer is involved in some type of official misconduct, plaintiff attorneys are not interested in suing an individual officer.

Instead, attorneys will typically claim that the individual officer's behavior was not a case of individual failure but instead was a case of systematic wrongdoing actually taught, sanctioned, and indeed institutionalized by an agency through its training practices. Using this legal strategy, the significantly deeper pockets of a municipal government are exposed to a judgment instead of the somewhat limited pockets of an individual police officer.

In the best-case scenario, a preliminary review by the attorneys will reveal a police curriculum that is sound, current, inclusive, academically appropriate, and comprehensive in scope. The pedagogy is at the appropriate conceptual level and consistent with that of area colleges or universities. The **instructional methodology** utilized to deliver the materials was innovative and reflective of the latest instructional technology available. The lesson plans and resource materials, handouts, and textbooks were recently updated, mainstream in content, and without any type of controversial historical, intellectual, or factual references.

The police academy instructors were not only content experts but also state-certified law enforcement instructors. Written exams were utilized in all critical subjects and are available to document that certain materials were not only taught but also learned. Finally, all the training records for an officer's entire career are available in a training archive and are accurate, properly documented, and defendable in a court of law.

If all of these administrative considerations are met, a legal position can then be sustained that any misconduct of an individual officer is the responsibility of the individual and the result of an isolated human shortcoming, not the result of the way all officers are trained, in short, an individual failure and not a systemic problem.

If, conversely, the professional structure of the training function can be successfully attacked on any of the above-mentioned levels, a legal argument can and will be made that the behavior in question is systematic and a clear result of the way officers are trained by an organization to perform. If the organizational integrity of a police department's training function can be successfully called into question, the house of cards can rapidly begin to fall and an organization's ability to defend itself, and its members, from civil liability, criminal liability, and even career liability can be effectively diminished.

For all of these reasons, the best way to establish and administer a police academy that will be capable of sustaining such inevitable attacks and examinations is to firmly establish in the form and function of the institution the three essential building blocks of a professional police training facility: a training philosophy, an organizational structure, and an operational structure (see Figure 3-1).

TRAINING PHILOSOPHY

The first pillar of proper form and function of a professional police training facility is a **training philosophy**. As mentioned earlier in this text, philosophy stands at the foundation of all things, even police work . . . *especially police work!* A written training philosophy establishes a police department's fundamental beliefs and the overall value or importance of training. A training philosophy must be established first because all other operational and administrative decisions should effectively flow from the philosophy and

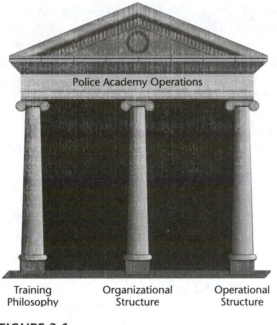

Training Philosophy   Organizational Structure   Operational Structure

FIGURE 3-1
Building the form and function

be consistent with it. In order to correctly deal with the day-to-day policy and operational decisions facing a training administrator, the underlying philosophical issues must be resolved up front and signed off on by the senior command staff. Once this philosophical foundation is accomplished and implemented, the surrounding sea of uncertainty seems to take on a new calm. Without it, knee-jerk reactions, political considerations, special-interest group pressures, or even the short-term "crisis of the day" challenges can distract or disrupt an ongoing well-thought-out training agenda. For example, the following philosophical proclamations can perhaps be considered as guidelines for academy operations:

- Provide a continuing process of **individual development** and organizational development, both designed to align individual behavior with organizational priorities, as a core function.
- Have the commanding officer of the police academy be an active member of the department's executive staffing in order to effectively accomplish its core mission.
- Always directly link instruction at the police academy to the most current priorities of the department.

- Staff and structure the police academy to provide education on the **conceptual level** and training on the **perceptual level**.
- Provide members of the service with training opportunities when they enter the organization, assume new responsibilities, get promoted to a new level of responsibility, or demonstrate a desire to enhance their job performance, as well as when operational changes dictate new skills.
- Provide continuous in-service training opportunities to all sworn and civilian members at all ranks that are designed to prepare them for current job responsibilities as well as prepare them for future professional aspirations.
- Have the police academy always solicit recommendations from members of the community, educational institutions, and other interested parties so that it remains open and responsive to community concerns.
- Utilize current and emerging adult learning theories to be sure instructional methods are consistent with the way adults learn best.
- Expect and demand high performance standards from instructors and class participants so that they aim higher and achieve more.
- Create an environment of free thinking, questioning, and problem solving to enable police personnel to provide law enforcement services in a more innovative and proactive way.
- Implement "discipline with a purpose" in recruit training, designed to instill confidence and purposefulness, not mindless conformity, in members of the service. Military precision and critical thinking skills are not mutually exclusive.
- Teach and always expect physical and **moral courage** in all personal demeanor. The physical courage to face a perpetrator and the moral courage to face a tough decision can *never* be compromised in the police service.
- Instill personal and professional integrity in all actions.
- Enhance public and officer safety by integrating proven verbal and physical tactics into all aspects of academy training. **Voluntary compliance** is the best compliance in a free republic. The purpose of a police confrontation is *to end it, not to win it*.
- Teach and demonstrate courtesy, professionalism, and mutual respect to all members in order to enable them to do the same for the public.

- Build a police academy that is operationally and organizationally prepared to address educational and training challenges, not disciplinary challenges. Officers who don't know how to perform their role will be prepared, but those who choose not to will be disciplined.

These are just a few examples of the types of philosophical proclamations that can offer direction and guidance for policy decisions as they arise. They can provide consistent and direct answers to some classic questions typically asked by interested citizens, involved elected officials, and others:

- Can a professor from the local college sit in on a class?
- Why don't you run the police academy more like a boot camp?
- Don't you teach police officers how to properly speak to people?
- Why are police officers so arrogant when all I did was ask a simple question and I got my head bit off?
- Does the **blue wall of silence** actually start at the police academy?
- How do you teach police officers to use force?

These types of questions, and more that emerge along the way, are simply answered by the training philosophy of an institution. Either things are philosophically consistent with the operation or they are not. The training philosophy offers not only answers to single questions but also operational consistency to the issues that constantly arise. It serves as a public and private proclamation as to the beliefs and values of the training institution.

A police academy without a training philosophy is like a building without a solid foundation. At any time, a storm can come along and bring the entire structure down with it. A police academy that doesn't stand for something will fall for anything.

ORGANIZATIONAL STRUCTURE

The second pillar of form and function is an effective **organizational structure**. Indeed, the age-old saying "Order or disorder depends on organization" applies to public administration and the administration of a police academy. In this case, the organizational structure is the form, and the actual delivery of educational and training services is the function. The way a training academy is structured and organized is critical to the effective administration and operation of the command. A sound organizational structure will provide for the smooth flow of command and control practices, verbal and written communications, power, authority, and overall operational effectiveness. It will also help to ensure that the many support and administrative functions required in a professional training academy are present and accounted for. Finally, it can serve as a protective mechanism and provide consistency for a police agency against the apparently invariable turnover of mayors, police commissioners, training directors, and patrol and investigative commanders as well as the kaleidoscope of changing organizational priorities.

In policing, there is no organizational model that is best for every agency. Indeed, across the country, there are as many variables in size and structure of police academies as there are agencies. The variance in this regard is wide, starting with the numerous small police agencies that may assign one officer to administrative duties, which can include some part-time training responsibilities. Other middle-size agencies may belong to a regional police academy with other law enforcement agencies in their region and send their members there on an as-needed basis. At the other extreme is the New York City Police Academy, with an annual operating budget of $26.8 million and a full-time training staff of approximately 750 people. Both sides of this extreme, as well as the majority of structures in between the two, should dedicate considerable thought to building the best organizational structure possible to support their respective missions.

It is the premise of this text that the education and training function is imperative to a police agency's overall performance. But for this to actually come together, the training director should be an active participant in essentially all policy-making decisions from the very beginning. While training directors, especially civilian training directors, may not necessarily be content experts on all policy conversations, ultimately creating the desired behavior required to implement any new policy will rest with the training function. Before operational orders can be written and distributed, resources moved around and positioned, or other agencies notified about an expected increase in activity, the training function should be activated to provide the members of the service with the necessary operational expertise to successfully and safely accomplish the mission. Practically every conceivable law enforcement mandate implemented carries with it officer safety and survival considerations that *must* be addressed in training before an operation commences.

THE RING OF GYGES

In *The Republic*, Plato tells a story of the **ring of Gyges**, which is a ring that can make whoever wears it invisible. The dialogue considers how people would behave if they could make themselves invisible and presumably be free of individual accountability. What makes people change their wrong behavior, the fear of detection or their own integrity? Plato concludes that only persons who are good enough to care about behaving correctly for their own integrity, and not just so they don't get caught, can become better.

Perhaps the same is true of police administration. Policy directives, rank, direct orders, press conferences, and other traditional command and control practices all serve a purpose. But exactly what organizational strategy will guide an officer's behavior at 3 A.M. when no one else is around to witness it? Probably an effective education and training strategy that took the time to explain to an officer what was expected, why it was expected, and exactly how to accomplish it behaviorally. Only operational directives that are accompanied by the requisite training instructions and understood in the proper context will be observed when the bosses and independent witnesses are invisible, and that is when most police work takes place.

Training at the police academy before a major operational initiative not only can provide the necessary and proper skills expected to make an operation tactically safe and operationally sound but also can put the initiative in the proper context to win the hearts and minds of the police officers.

Operations orders that are not explained and simply forced on the officers at roll call more often than not assume a negative connotation before they ever reach the desired rank. To a veteran police officer, "Every silver lining has a cloud," and a failure to effectively communicate the intent and the context of a new operations order will only serve to promote such a negative mind-set.

However, for a training director to enjoy such inclusion in the traditional paramilitary world of American policing, he or she must have the appropriate rank in the department's organizational hierarchy. While the rank is important to the individual who happens to occupy the position at any given time, it is more notably symbolically important to the training function as a recognition of its role in the organization.

Flexibility in Structure

For any organizational structure to survive in the public sector, it must be firm on the outside yet adaptive and able to be responsive to the changing operational priorities on the inside. Since policing operational priorities constantly change in response to newly emerging crime patterns, threat levels, crime trends, and operational strategies quickly designed and implemented to combat them, this can be a real challenge. If properly designed, a police academy can respond to such changing priorities with equal success.

Finally, the type of officer an agency expects to produce at the end ultimately dictates the organizational structure of any police academy. For example, a police academy built to produce the prototypical state trooper would conceivably be organized differently than a police academy built to produce the typical big-city municipal police officer. To allow for such distinctions, paradoxically, the "pillar" of organization must not be overly rigid and carved in stone. In the end, however, a police academy's organizational structure must provide clear and unequivocal guidance for the following types of questions:

- Is it clear that all the service delivery units actually involved in the delivery of training are in the same reporting structure?
- Are the various educational support units in the same reporting structure?
- Are all of the various functions and subfunctions clearly identified and not repetitive?
- Do all the necessary educational support functions, such as library access, training archives, research and development, training assessment, and instructional technology, exist?
- Do the officers involved in training assessment report to a different chain of command than the officers involved in delivering training? Do they have the necessary autonomy to provide a true and accurate assessment?
- Are the sworn members of the command utilized in an appropriate fashion and involved in teaching police topics?

- Are the chain of command and span of control considerations clearly spelled out for everyone?
- Are the civilian members of the command deployed in an appropriate fashion and involved in teaching civilian topics?
- Do the personnel function, the budget function, and the integrity control function report directly to the commanding officer or director of training?

The establishment of an effective police academy organizational structure to support the often-complex operations of American policing is a seriously meaningful factor in the overall success of any police agency. In the sometimes turbulent and frequently controversial world of public administration, mayors, police commissioners, commanding officers, and training directors will come and go. The existence of a solid training structure can add stability to such a situation and ensure the continuance of a department's best practices.

Service Delivery Model

There are many different types of examples of organizational structures that work. One is the **service delivery model** (Figure 3-2). In a service delivery model, all of the operational units that are directly involved in the delivery of service (in this case, law enforcement instruction) are established and illustrated in the organizational chart. At a glance, individuals can understand the structure that is superimposed over the proper flow of verbal and written communication, chain of command, reporting structures, and other important organizational considerations.

The following service delivery model is just an example of the type of organizational chart that can be utilized to manage both small and large organizational needs.

Educational Support Model

Yet another option would be to provide an additional organizational chart illustrating the various units involved in the educational support of the service delivery units (Figure 3-3). Critical functions of running a successful police academy, such as instructional technology, research and development, training archives, the library, and instructor development, can be designed on an organizational chart demonstrating their reporting relationships. This can be organizationally helpful because many of the support functions normally associated with law enforcement training are highly specialized.

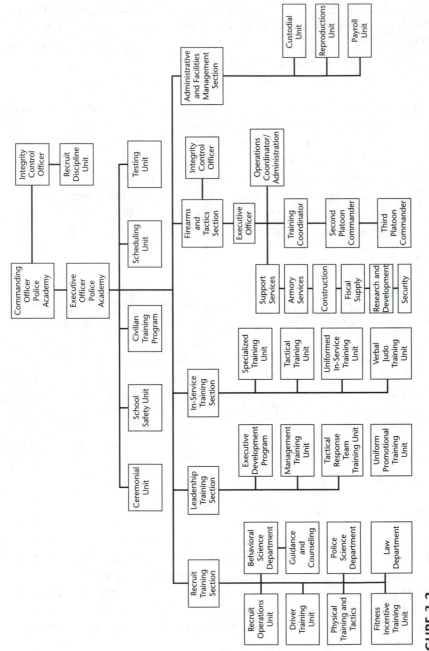

FIGURE 3-2
Service delivery model

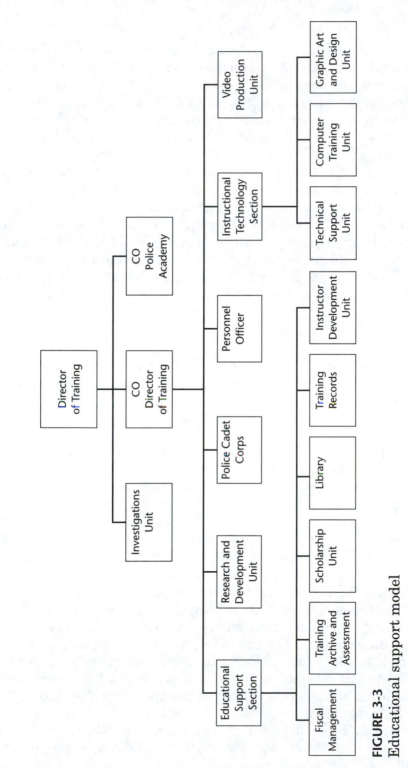

FIGURE 3-3
Educational support model

Since the services provided by support units are usually peripherally related to the actual instruction, and since highly specialized civilians provide most of these services, they can sometimes be organizationally awkward in a law enforcement environment.

Clearly, such an organizational distinction may not be necessary in a small or medium-size police academy where perhaps one individual assumes the responsibilities of a support function, which is simply located within the confines of a service delivery unit. The need for the various approaches to illustrate organizational structure can be adjusted in accordance with the overall size and complexity of an academy. However, whether an academy can properly illustrate its organizational structure in one small chart or many large charts, whether the charts are traditional and hierarchal or circular and flexible, the need for a formal organizational structure is always present.

OPERATIONAL STRUCTURE

The third and final pillar of form and function necessary in a professional police academy operation is the **operational structure**. The operational structure of a police training facility is much the same as the operational structure and practices of any well-run company in the private sector. The classic principles of good management prevail: constant communicating up and down the chain of command and managing the internal environment by empowering staff to make legitimate contributions and to be productive. Managing the external environment by handling political and community inquiries honestly and decisively and generally doing what is necessary to maintain the resources of the command focused on the core functions of education and training are also essential.

In the world of American policing where disaster and a job-wide mobilization of the entire instructional staff (and sometimes even the student officers) are always just one phone call away, maintaining operational consistency and focus can be an extraordinarily difficult task. For the chief of patrol, the chief of detectives, or the chief of special operations, it is relatively simple to decide that "All training is down" and redirect all the personnel and resources normally committed to training toward an emerging crisis. However, since such disasters and operational emergencies are constant, especially in the big cities, this tendency should be carefully considered and reserved for the true emergencies.

Suspending training efforts to respond to a pending emergency is, at the end of the day, risking long-term stability for short-term responsiveness. Unmistakably, there are times when such a trade-off is necessary and, indeed, the only reasonable thing to do.

When done properly, mobilizing training instructors to respond to a genuine police emergency is good for the instructors. It reminds them that they are police officers first and assigned to a detail second. It also reminds the instructional staff of the patrol perspective, a perspective that believes that those who work Monday through Friday with steady day tours in an air-conditioned environment really don't have too much to complain about.

Perhaps the most important operational consideration of managing a police academy is to ensure that the nice, neat organizational boxes and clearly delineated chain of command that exist on the organizational chart are recognized for what they are, a conceptual framework. The nice, neat boxes and clearly delineated lines of responsibility exist for conceptual guidance and administrative convenience; they exist to provide a visual logic scheme to an operation.

But in the rapidly changing real world, an overly rigid organizational structure can also serve to bury constructive ideas, limit timely communications, create distance between a commanding officer and his or her staff, and isolate the bosses from small operational problems until they explode and appear in the morning newspaper. In many insidious ways, a rigid organizational structure, especially in the large agencies, can hamper a well-run education and training operation. Moreover, the more cerebral police officers, the very type who are generally drawn to police academy assignments in the first place, are frequently attracted to such an assignment by the possibility of thinking outside the little boxes, not something that goes on a whole lot in patrol assignments.

Overly structured organizations can, if not managed a little differently, produce an overly structured and fragmented day-to-day operation and become a source of frustration to free thinkers and smart instructors. Some of the essential operational tools normally found in a more academic environment, such as allowing an open and free exchange of ideas, considering typical police problems from different paradigms and perspectives, sharing scarce resources, ensuring curricula consistency and sequencings, and utilizing intellectual property and other rare commodities, can be buried in an overly rigid structure. The very ideas that can make great contributions to a police academy can be lost if the "Yes, sir" mentality is overly enforced.

One of the most vital responsibilities of a training director is to realize and sustain this critical operational balance. A police academy should reflect the semi-military demeanor of the law enforcement agency it is preparing the police recruit to operate within, but without the mindless discipline sometimes associated with it. It should reflect the intellectual curiosity of a university setting without the leisurely presence of students wearing head-phones in the hallway. It should be an intellectual oasis for intelli-gent police officers to enjoy and grow personally and professionally. A well-run police academy can serve as an organizational reminder that being smart and being an excellent police officer are not mutually exclusive!

In the larger picture, and also peripherally related to the issue of operational considerations, is the issue of selecting the best people for police academy assignments. Again, unlike the typical patrol assignment, assignments in specialized details are some-times awarded more for the unique qualities an individual may possess than for the sole consideration of rank. Sometimes lower-ranking police officials are better prepared to run a certain spe-cialized function of a police academy than a higher-ranking, more traditional generalist by virtue of some type of specialized experi-ence or training. These kinds of considerations often emerge in the staffing of some very necessary and important operational func-tions. Some of the following examples of specialized assignments in a police academy illustrate such considerations:

- Assigning a member with a college degree in auditing to the Training Assessment Unit
- Assigning a member with prior experience in internal affairs to the Integrity Control Unit
- Assigning a member who is distinguished in the martial arts to the Physical Fitness Unit
- Assigning a member who is a licensed gunsmith to the Firearms Unit
- Assigning a member who is an attorney to be a law instructor
- Assigning an experienced officer with thousands of felony arrests and low civilian complaints to teach police science

Such special qualities are relatively rare in society, and they are rare within the ranks of sworn police officers. If they are available, they can make important contributions to the professional operations of a police academy, regardless of the rank of the individual. These types of management decisions don't always fit into the highly structured rank-based scheme of a semi-military chain of command, but they do happen and must be addressed operationally, on a case-by-case basis. Although a captain, for example, may have traditionally run the Physical Fitness Unit, it may ultimately be in the best interest of the service to assign as commanding officer a sergeant who happens to possess a black belt in **Aikido** and the proper philosophical perspective of the use of force issue.

Yet another operational consideration, especially in the larger police academies, is the underground emergence of organizational factions within the ranks. Such factions can appear in many different ways, such as "us vs. them," "internal affairs vs. working cops," "sworn personnel vs. civilian personnel," "real cops vs. administrative cops," "younger college-educated officers vs. hair bags," or even "gym instructors vs. academic instructors." There seems to be no limit to the ability of police officers to create distinctions and a pecking order within their ranks.

But regardless of how the lines are drawn, factions will undermine an organization. Moreover, such factions can find shelter in an overly rigid command structure and create an organizational virus capable of infecting an entire culture.

A CASE IN POINT

A police instructor walked into a police academy classroom full of police recruits and respectfully began his lecture on the Internal Affairs function. In accordance with the lesson plan, he began talking about how the Internal Affairs Unit maintains a nonrecorded phone number where members of the service can call up and anonymously report police corruption they have witnessed. However, as the instructor wrote the 800 number on the board, he smiled, winked at the recruits, and said, "Yea, they actually expect you to believe that this line is not recorded and you won't be labeled as a rat for the rest of your career."

In the above case, the instructor did not know that one of the students in that particular class was the son of an Internal Affairs boss and was offended by the instructor's cynical remark. That night, the recruit officer actually called the number that was given out in class and reported the veteran instructor. As it turned out, the line was not recorded, and the individual involved is no longer a police academy instructor.

The point to be made is this: *Any factions allowed to manifest themselves in the police academy instruction become ingrained in the police culture*. If an agency wants to perpetuate such nonsense in its culture, simply allow factions to exist in the police academy. Imagine the potential damage of teaching the officers who will be around for the next twenty years the factions that exist today! If not, then such distinctions must not be allowed to exist, especially when no one is looking.

When they are reflected in the instruction, these distinctions not only become disruptive; more importantly, they can become a part of the organizational culture taught to recruit officers. Make no mistake about it, young police officers pick up on such behavioral patterns and mimic them. Young recruit officers, and even veteran officers, who hear senior instructors constantly refer to any group of people in an unenthusiastic light will perpetuate such feelings in their behavior, if for no other reason than to appear to be one of the guys. *It stands to reason that if the police academy is, in fact, where the police culture begins, then that culture better be as positive and healthy as possible.*

Many other fundamental decisions about the day-to-day operations of a police academy are made by carefully considering the larger operational challenges facing a police agency and working backwards from that point. At the end of the day, a training facility's core function is to produce individuals who are intellectually, physically, morally, and tactically prepared to help an organization meet its goals and objectives. The exact operational strategies utilized to accomplish this will vary from one agency to the next but will almost always include some of the following considerations.

How Will the Police Academy Teach?

Under the parameters of how to teach are many important operational factors to be considered. While the later chapters of this text discuss what to teach, equally important is how to teach it. Instructional methodology decisions are crucially important to a police academy's success, and they have widespread implications.

Obviously, police academy lessons can be taught with the traditional lecture-based methods. Although this is perhaps the easiest format to utilize in assembly-line education, it may not be the most consistent with the way adults learn. Other possible innovative instructional methods should be considered to keep the lessons interesting for the students, to sustain instructor enthusiasm, and to facilitate **knowledge integration** along the way.

Innovative Instructional Methods

- Interactive group exercises
- Interdisciplinary role plays
- Reading assignments and/or homework assignments
- Theater methods (such as reflective team exercises and socio-dramas involving police actions)
- Multisensory oral presentations in class
- Cultural field trips designed to study the community in its environment
- Computer-based tutorials, video-based instruction, and video simulators

While some of these instructional methods do require the advanced development of the instructional staff, such an investment should be made in any case. The application of different and diverse instructional methods keeps the lessons fresh, the students engaged, the instructors on the learning curve, and the educational environment challenging and new.

It is important to note here that the real question to be answered in determining exactly what instructional method should be utilized is what form of instruction is best suited for the particular type of lesson to be learned. Traditional lecture methods have a clear place in basic informational sessions. Theater workshops seem to work very well in the behavioral sciences, and cultural field trips are a powerful method to teach cultural competence and an appreciation of diversity. The various subject matters normally associated with teaching policing vary significantly, and the most appropriate instructional method should be utilized according to the topic at hand.

Another current example of the power of instructional methods can be seen in the use of technology in instruction. Due to the fairly recent advances in video technology, firearms simulators have become an excellent instructional method to teach firearms judgment. Through video simulations and laser technology, significantly better instructional methods have emerged. In firearms instruction, the traditional shooting holes through paper targets a few hundred times will always be a necessary and effective instructional method to teach *how* to shoot. But integrating video simulators into the instructional process has proven to be more effective in teaching the judgment involved in *when* to shoot. Given the scope of most questionable police shootings around the country, marksmanship is rarely the question, but the judgment involved in why it was necessary to shoot at all is usually at issue.

A CASE IN POINT

In New York City, the Firearms and Tactics Unit of the New York City Police Academy began to utilize firearms simulators in its training in 1992. Without a question, the principal focus of that training was on the judgment involved in *when to shoot, not how to shoot*. Since that time, the number of police shootings in New York has been reduced to an all-time low. The total number of shots fired by the police declined from 81 in 1992 to 36 in 2001. The total number of people wounded by police gunfire declined from 56 in 1992 to 26 in 2001, and the number of civilians fatally wounded by police gunfire declined from 25 in 1992 to 10 in 2001. Moreover, these declines in police shootings occurred during a period of record crime reductions and during a time when the N.Y.P.D. had about 9,000 more police officers on the job than it did in 1992.

Significantly more police officers producing significantly more activity and reducing crime to historic levels, and doing so with more restraint than ever before! An astonishing accomplishment realized, at least in part, by the instructional methods used to train New York City police officers.

Structured field training, not the traditional type after graduation from the academy but training while at the police academy, is yet another innovative method to teach an important component of policing: knowledge integration. Experience has demonstrated that sitting in a classroom and learning the materials enough to pass a written exam come fairly easily to most police recruits. However, actually applying that knowledge in an integrated fashion on patrol, in the face of adversity and screaming victims, is another matter. *Police science is, and always will be, an applied discipline.* Assigning recruit officers to patrol for a brief period of time, not after graduation like a traditional field training program but during actual training, is a way to facilitate knowledge integration and to advance the learning curve for police recruits. A uniformed field training experience allows police recruit officers to become comfortable with initially awkward experiences such as wearing a uniform in public, wearing a bullet-resistant vest, listening to the police radio and having a conversation with a partner at the same time, and the many other subtle yet crucial aspects of becoming a real police officer.

The implementation of a visiting professor program is another instructional method that has enjoyed great success in the New York City Police Academy. Inviting a visiting professor from a local college or university appears to be an excellent way to bring an unusual level of expertise and distinction to a police academy and provide that expertise to the student officers. Due to the interdisciplinary nature of policing, a visiting professor from practically any discipline can contribute to the police academy mission; teaching anything from English to the various branches of the behavioral sciences would be appropriate and applicable.

Visiting professors can also help to inspire and encourage police officers to continue their formal education and actually help them with the proper referrals. Even visiting professors, however, should be required to submit lesson plans, examinations, and other appropriate course documentation. In the interest of instructional consistency, the proper progression of knowledge, and other documentation responsibilities, an academic paper trail must be maintained. Local colleges and universities are usually more than willing to provide a visiting professor with a course reduction at the school to allow for an assignment at the police academy. Properly structured, it provides a win-win situation for both institutions.

Other operational issues such as the overall length of the academy, the actual size of the class or company size to maximize learning and interaction, and the reliance on guest speakers should also be carefully considered and reflective of local priorities. In all cases, however, a healthy combination of the various instructional methods should be explored and utilized. Instructional variety is an excellent way to sustain interest in the lessons, enhance the development of the instructors, and properly illustrate the instructional goals of a course.

SHOULD THE POLICE ACADEMY EDUCATE OR TRAIN?

The operational decision as to whether a police academy seeks to educate or train is often the source of confusion and, if left unresolved, can lead to mixed results. Training, by definition, is teaching a subject matter on a perceptual level. Training is usually associated with hands-on instruction, repetition, and preparation for a trade. For example, police academies normally train in the use of firearms, self-defense tactics, use of the police baton, speedcuffing, filling out of proper forms for certain types of offenses, and pursuit driving of a radio car. Clearly, such skills are training-based and best learned by actually practicing the skill over and over again.

Education, on the other hand, is more on the conceptual level and traditionally associated with preparing for a profession. Police academies normally educate in such subjects as the law, law enforcement ethics, integrity, and other behavioral-based subjects that cannot actually be enacted to be learned. An example of this distinction can be illustrated in the educational process itself. Elementary school children typically are trained, at first, to do mathematics: 1 M&M + 1 M&M = 2 M&M's. The children learn the principles of mathematics by physically moving the candies together and actually touching the two M&M's; then they get to eat the candies at the end of the lesson. As the lessons in mathematics progress to higher-level concepts such as algebra and calculus, however, the lessons become more conceptual in nature. At some point, the math students no longer touch anything or eat anything; they simply must learn to do the math in their heads. The same progression is utilized to prepare police officers. A good part of preparing police officers must be done in their heads as well because that is the way it is done in the street.

Such a distinction must be examined because some police academies are prepared and seek to train recruit officers only in the very practical aspects of policing and rely on local colleges or universities to educate the recruits. Others rely on precertification practices or hiring standards that require college hours to accomplish this mission. The larger police academies with more resources usually seek to do both, educate and train the officers.

Generally speaking, this is a much better model if an agency has the necessary faculty, resources, and other support structures and organizational support. The more direct control over an individual's orientation, education, and training an agency has, the better it can build in important considerations such as pride in the department, pride in the shield, and pride in the self. Could one ever imagine a day when the U.S. Marine Corps contracted out its boot camp orientation to a private vendor? If building organizational pride and commitment is an integral aspect of the initial orientation and training process as it should be, why would a police department ever want to delegate that responsibility to a private source?

However, either method is acceptable, as long as it is understood up front exactly who will do what and at the end of a prescribed training period it all comes together to produce a professional police officer. Police academies that claim to be in the education business must also understand that such a position will require significant resources to support such a claim. A library or access to a library, credentialed instructors, research capabilities, college-level instruction and workloads, academic documentation, and some type of state accreditation to validate it all will always be necessary. A police academy that claims to be educating its officers and is not appropriately supported by such resources will easily be attacked by attorneys looking to support failure to train suits and ultimately fail in its mission and expose its members to lawsuits.

Simply speaking, the stakes are too high to underestimate the critical distinction between education and training and all that it implies.

WHAT PRICE IS A DEPARTMENT WILLING TO PAY?

The question of what price a police department is willing to pay to support and institutionalize a professional education and training process is a relative question. On one hand, the only real cost of training to an agency is the cost of the time lost on patrol by the personnel attending and running the training function. In most cases, the personnel are on the payroll already, so there is no direct or additional cost associated with salary, benefits, and the like.

However, there is no disputing that the time the police officers are in training they are not performing the core functions of the agency such as arresting bad guys and writing summonses. Individual agency heads must make a decision about the total number of annual training days they will dedicate to each member of the service. Many agencies around the country will permit police officers to attend at least five days annually, inclusive of their obligation to qualify with their firearms twice a year. Once again, these are decisions that must be made at the local level in compliance with the appropriate state mandates and guidelines.

WHO WILL ENSURE THE QUALITY OF THE CURRICULUM?

Everything that is done in the interest of policing a free society such as the American Republic must be accountable to the citizens—even police training. In a free society, there is a great deal of interest in the police, what they are doing, why they are doing it, and how they are trained to do it. Accordingly, professional police academies *must* build some type of public accountability and/or advisory component into their operations.

There are many forms and structures this accountability can take, but there must be public access and review in some form. If it is, in fact, true that the culture of any police department begins at the police academy, there will always be significant public interest in the content and quality of the instruction.

For internal validity, advice, and accountability, many police academies have implemented some type of **training advisory board**. These advisory boards vary in size and influence, but essentially they are comprised of members of the department from various units, assignments, and ranks. Membership on the board allows the various officers to voice their respective training needs on a regular basis and to hopefully get them addressed in the upcoming annual training agenda. Membership on the board might include the following:

Sample Internal Training Advisory Board

- Chief of patrol
- Chief of detectives
- Chief of personnel
- Chief of special operations
- Five police officers from various sectors around the city
- One police officer union delegate
- Police academy representatives

This internal training advisory board is important because members of an agency who are involved in the many different aspects of policing all have very specific training needs. These training needs change from year to year as operational priorities adapt to changing crime conditions. Without such a board, police academy curricula tend to be disproportionately focused on patrol or administrative issues and updates, often at the expense of crucial investigative, tactical, and police officer safety lessons. Although such boards will often produce conflicting demands on the training agenda, such conflicting demands can usually be prioritized and ultimately worked out to the satisfaction of all involved. Specialized units within a law enforcement agency that are denied an opportunity to influence the official department training agenda to meet the needs of their members will often go off in their own direction and create an unauthorized training process, which will always create problems down the road.

For external validity, advice, and accountability, many police academies have also instituted some type of **citizen advisory board**. Indeed, some states (for example, Texas) have mandated civilian participation in police advisory boards through state law. These advisory boards also vary in size, membership, and influence but are essentially comprised of members of the community, elected officials, representatives of local colleges or universities, and perhaps members of other nonprofit organizations. The purpose of these boards is to supply a mechanism for constant community feedback and accountability.

Citizen advisory boards provide a training director with a constant source of new and exciting information for review and can sometimes provide access to additional resources not normally available through traditional agency budgets. They can also offer political shelter from the inevitable claims of "The police teach the blue wall of silence right in the academy" and other cynical allegations often made against the police when the police are not open and honest about their training practices.

Civilian oversight, input, and accountability are essential components of law enforcement training and must be addressed in the operational plans of a professional and reputable training operation. More often than not, citizens exposed to police academy operations for the first time are pleasantly surprised by the professionalism, dedication, and level of pride and spirit they find.

OPERATIONAL LIMITATIONS

Training directors should be honest and up-front about their commands' limitations. Often in the wake of community and/or political concerns about the police, the capabilities of training and retraining may be overstated. Police academies are an essential component of the personnel and organizational selection and development process. They can make tremendous contributions to an organization's present and future effectiveness. They are not, however, part of the department's disciplinary process, nor do they possess a magic wand that can be waved over the head of a problem officer, suddenly turning him or her into a sensitive and caring human being.

Sometimes veteran police officers can be emotionally or physically worn down by the constant negative feedback normally associated with policing. As a defense mechanism, they may develop rude, disrespectful, and even deviant behavioral patterns. Such behavioral patterns may help an officer to get through the tour, but they are personally and professionally destructive. Police academy directors should not suggest that they are prepared to address such problems with the traditional training methods or courses by allowing these officers to be sent back to the police academy for retraining after an incident.

Police academies are educational and training entities, not reform schools. Veteran members of the service who are repeatedly the subject of civilian complaints for being rude and obnoxious to the public will only be rude and obnoxious to the instructors if they are sent back to the police academy for additional training. There is a fundamental difference between an officer who wants to do a good job but does not know how and an officer who knows how but decides, for whatever reason, not to. One needs additional training and the other needs swift and certain discipline. Agencies that cannot or choose not to make such a distinction run the risk of infecting all the good police officers along the way and undermining the command and control practices of the department.

This is also true of the mandated training often imposed by an outside entity in response to an isolated incident or some type of legal consent decree. As a rule, police officers are very smart and politically astute individuals. They will not respond well, nor should they respond well, to any form of mandated or "cover yourself" training forced on them to make a political problem go away.

Agencies that put their police academies in such a position run the risk of the good officers dismissing an entire training experience as a negative one. *Moral courage is expected of street cops, and it should be expected at the highest levels of an organization as well.* Police officer discipline is a supervisory issue, and it always will be.

CONCLUSION

Based on all the philosophical, organizational, and operational considerations outlined above, it is more than reasonable for a police administrator to ask: Is it necessary, and is it worth it to the agency that makes such a significant commitment of resources that could otherwise be directed toward the core functions of the agency?

The answer to these questions is, Yes, it simply must be done, and it is worth it. National defense spending is expensive, but it is imperative to the existence of the American Republic. Education is expensive, but it is irreplaceable to future success. The importance of professional policing to the American Republic is second only to the importance of a professional and well-trained military. The core principles of freedom, justice, and other key virtues of America are defended abroad by the military, and they are defended domestically by the police. The stakes are equally as high. Indeed, as domestic crime and international terrorism continue to become more and more widespread, even this geographic distinction will begin to blur. It already has in the wake of September 11, 2001. On both fronts, failure is not an option.

Through effective education and training, a police department can produce a police officer who is effectively prepared to become a living personification of the ideals of the American Republic. The police are the gateway to the American criminal justice system, and they stand at the foundation of American social justice. The value of successfully preparing them for their roles and responsibilities should be self-evident.

KEY TERMS

Aikido

Blue Wall of Silence

Citizen Advisory Board

Conceptual Level

Individual Development

Instructional Methodology

Knowledge Integration

Moral Courage

Operational Structure

Organizational Development

Organizational Structure

Perceptual Level

Ring of Gyges

Service Delivery Model

Training Advisory Board

Training Philosophy

Voluntary Compliance

QUESTIONS FOR DISCUSSION

1. What are the three pillars of form and function, and how do they complement each other in terms of overall operations?
2. What additional statements could be added to a training philosophy? Why would they be important?
3. If you had an opportunity to interview the training director of your local police department, what specific questions would you ask?
4. Why is an organizational structure important to a successful organization?
5. What are some of the educational support functions necessary to maintain a professional police academy?
6. What are the major issues associated with a police academy's operational structure?
7. What are the various types of factions that emerge in most police departments?
8. List as many innovative police instructional methods as possible.
9. What is the difference between education and training? Which is more important?
10. How can a law enforcement agency distinguish between an officer who needs training and an officer who needs discipline?

Suggested Readings

Champy, James. (1996). *Reengineering management: The mandate for new leadership*. New York: Harper Business.

Henry, Vincent. (2002). *The compstat paradigm: Management accountability in policing, business, and the public sector*. New York: Loose Leaf Law Publications.

Leonard, V.A. and Harry More. (1987). *Police organization and management*, (7 ed.). Mineola, New York: The Foundation Press.

Sun Tzu. (1989). *The art of war*. Edited and Foreword by James Clauvell. New York: Dell Publishing.

Souryal, Sam. (1977). *Police management and administration*. St. Paul, Minn: West Publishing.

Wilson, O.W. and Roy McLaren. (1977). *Police administration*, (4 ed.). New York: McGraw-Hill.

chapter **4**

EDUCATING AND TRAINING NEW POLICE OFFICERS

Teaching Police Science

"Although I have been a police officer and detective for almost twenty years now, I am still somewhat baffled by exactly what it is that I'm supposed to be doing each day."

—Detective Michael Granton

INTRODUCTION

Perhaps the most fascinating aspect of practicing and teaching police work is its constantly evolving and interdisciplinary nature. To be effective and just in a free society, a **job description** for a police officer must include proficiency in police science, psychology, diplomacy, sociology, law, medicine, martial arts, and, finally, communications. As August Vollmer, one of the first police reformers, once observed:

> The citizens expect police officers to have the wisdom of Solomon, the courage of David, the strength of Samson, the patience of Job, the leadership of Moses, the kindness

of a Good Samaritan, the strategic thinking of Alexander, the faith of Daniel, the diplomacy of Lincoln, the tolerance of the Carpenter of Nazareth, and finally, an intimate knowledge of every branch of natural, biological, and social sciences. If he has all these, he might be a good policeman. (Bain, 1939)

This job description produces quite a training mandate for America's police academies. To even begin to approach such a training mandate, most any and all academic disciplines and/or literature bases that provide some insight into human behavior and the overall human condition can be helpful to police personnel. That is also why many of the best police officers come to American policing from many different income groups, neighborhoods, age groups, cultures, college majors, and prior job experiences. No matter what paradigm or perspective an individual brings to policing, there is an opportunity to make a contribution in such an interdisciplinary occupation. However, since this text is structured to discuss many of these different disciplines one at a time, the principal focus of this chapter is on the teaching of police science.

POLICE SCIENCE

The actual term **police science** is a somewhat old, misunderstood, and outdated label. Throughout history, occupational-specific criminal justice subjects such as police science, penology, and corrections all had their roots in the very practical and procedural agency-oriented programs taught in the 1930s. These programs had a very practical and explicit purpose: They were designed and taught to address the needs of the typical in-service police officer or corrections officer returning to college. In the 1930s, many in-service students turned to the local colleges and universities to learn how to be more effective in controlling their day-to-day work environments and to prepare for promotional opportunities and management roles. Advanced education and training opportunities were not offered by the various departments, so members turned to outside sources to study the newly emerging disciplines and to improve their promotional opportunities.

In fact, some of these police science classes were taught in police academies by ranking police personnel. Specialized colleges and universities did not yet exist for such courses because there was no body of knowledge, no established literature, and certainly no credentialed faculty members. For example, one of the most pre-eminent colleges of criminal justice, John Jay College of Criminal Justice in New York City, originally began by offering police science classes to New York City police officers in the New York City Police Academy.

However, over the years, society got more and more complex. As the problems of society became more complex, so too did the role of the police in controlling them. The historical police function, which traditionally consisted of simple foot patrols and responses to calls for service, became more and more challenging. As society grew more and more complex, the public expectations of the police grew proportionately, and public scrutiny of the police began to intensify.

As the perceived role and public expectations of the police grew and evolved, the larger and more philosophical issues of justice, social justice, restorative justice, and indeed criminal justice began to emerge. It soon became apparent that to effectively address these larger and much more foundational issues and concerns of justice, a more systemwide interdisciplinary body of knowledge would be necessary. In short, it also became clear that to effectively prepare the practitioners for their roles and responsibilities, there had to be a focus on both training and education.

The need for a broader vision of the concerns for overall justice in society led to a more scientific and scholarly examination of the police and the other components of the criminal justice system. Led primarily by attorneys and Ph.D.'s in the various branches of the behavioral sciences, there was a deliberate move away from the overly specific agency orientation of policing and corrections toward a broader and more intellectual focus of the criminal justice system. Somewhere around the 1960s, this systemwide approach became very popular, and the academic discipline of **criminal justice** was born. Criminal justice soon became mainstream at colleges and universities around the country, and terms such as "police science" slowly disappeared.

In 1964, the State University of New York at Albany became the first major criminal justice program in the United States (Duffee, 1990). In 1966, the College of Police Science at the City University of New York was renamed John Jay College of Criminal Justice. Four years later, Michigan State University School of

Police Administration and Public Safety made the transition to the School of Criminal Justice (Duffee, 1990). Today, most colleges and universities have long since replaced their police science and corrections classes with sociology, criminological theory, and/or criminal justice classes. Graduate degrees and even doctorates in criminal justice are available at most of these universities.

The key point to be made here is that the establishment of criminal justice as a legitimate academic discipline is practically and intellectually appropriate at the college or university level. The criminal justice body of knowledge and the literature unmistakably deal with the much broader perspective of justice as well as the underlying philosophical principles from which it was built. Today, hardly a trace of the original police science materials can be found on the campuses teaching criminal justice, and this is as it should be.

But the very occupational-specific, procedurally based body of knowledge originally known as police science still has an imperative place in the education and training of American police officers. Police science, as it has always been known, is the operational cornerstone of police academies all around the country. Indeed, the knowledge once known as police science is still the nuts and bolts of what good police officers are expected to do for a living. While it may indeed be overly specific and procedure-oriented to justify college-level instruction and credits, it remains critical and irreplaceable to a young police recruit preparing to do police work.

A fundamental distinction between a student of criminal justice and a student of police science is that students of criminal justice can learn the issues in the abstract and pass a college course, whereas students of police science must learn their lessons and must then apply those lessons in the real world. The actual application of the knowledge is what separates one discipline from the other. Police science is an applied discipline.

Since the application of the material is at the core of police science, a police science curriculum must be structured and delivered in a fashion that provides a factual and realistic introduction to the actual job of policing. Historical patrol practices that have been discredited by the research, as well as the current police priorities and procedures which appear to be successfully contributing to the reduction of crime, should all be taught and learned by police recruits. Indeed, knowing and following the specific departmental policies and procedures learned in the police academy will be expected of every successful police officer.

In the police science curriculum, the sometimes complex and ever-evolving roles of the patrol officer as well as the procedures and paperwork that they must do in the day-to-day patrol duties are emphasized. It is important to note that the actual lessons and course content of a police science curriculum in a police academy should be based on the roles and responsibilities, policies and procedures, and strategies and tactics that will be expected of officers when they graduate. A police science curriculum that spends too much time on the philosophy or theory of policing and does not prepare student officers to perform the day they enter the street will run the risk of perpetuating the old saying, "Forget what they taught you in the academy, and let me show you how police work is really done." A police science curriculum simply must be based in the current realities of the job and effectively prepare a police recruit for the way the job is really done.

To best accomplish this, a police science unit should be staffed with credible police instructors with as many medals to their credit as possible. Although being an experienced street officer does not, in and of itself, make one a good instructor, the two are certainly not mutually exclusive. This is the one of the few academic disciplines that can, and should, select instructors with proven experience and street valor. If an experienced street officer is available for a teaching assignment in the police academy and also happens to possess a college degree or an advanced academic degree, then the best of both worlds is possible. In American policing today, this type of educated officer is available and should be sought for such an assignment. Police academy instructors are not merely lecturers; they are role models and mentors for the next generation of police officers.

POLICE SCIENCE CURRICULUM

A model police science curriculum would be difficult, if not impossible, to provide. Since the specific lessons must be reflective of local agency traditions and operational priorities and practices, a curriculum would vary greatly from one department and jurisdiction to another. However, as a general rule, the following major topics should be considered for inclusion.

POLICE SCIENCE CURRICULUM

Orientation	Handling Calls for Service
Introduction	Radio Communications
Mission and Values	Department Forms and Reports
Role of the Officer	Preliminary Investigations
Myths of Policing	Department Directives
Managing Crime Scenes	Evidence Preservation
General Regulations	Motor Vehicle Enforcement
Professionalism and Ethics	Ticket Writing
Patrol Operations	Quality-of-Life Enforcement
Patrol Duties and Responsibilities	Community Policing
Strategy-Driven Policing	Use of Force Progression
Handling Property	Overview of Arrests
Special Operations of Department	Support Resources for Patrol

Total = Approximately 100 Hours of Instruction

ROLE OF THE OFFICER

After all the requisite administrative processing and orientation, a thorough and comprehensive police science curriculum should include an analysis of the role of the police officer. This instruction should include the historical role, the current role, and the possible future role of the police. Only then will rookie police officers be able to understand their place in the ongoing operational transformation currently being experienced in American policing. Only then will they be in a position to understand the various patrol styles and personalities they will surely encounter when they hit the streets and begin to formulate their own police personality. This is critical given the fact that the patrol officer's role has varied greatly over the years and continues to vary greatly from time to time, from shift to shift, from bureau to bureau, and from one crime pattern to the next.

Throughout history, the traditional role of the patrol officer has been the basis of the police science curriculum. Historically, from around the turn of the twentieth century through the early 1960s, the vast majority of law enforcement organizations that existed during this period of time were developed in a very traditional way. In that paradigm, the patrol officer was the backbone of the police organization, and this role provided the officer with enormous amounts of individual officer discretion. Depending on the level of specialization, which was very limited during this time, between 60 percent and 70 percent of the sworn personnel were assigned to patrol operations doing random activities (Gourley, 1974).

However, the publication of a number of significant research projects seriously called into question many of the fundamental operating assumptions of traditional policing. Foremost in this regard was the publication of the **Kansas City Preventive Patrol Experiment** (Kelling et al., 1974). An interesting point to note here is that the original idea to question the value of random patrol was generated by patrol officers within the Kansas City Police Department who knew, based on their experience, that random patrol was not a productive use of their time. In Kansas City at that time, to generate some new and innovative patrol strategies, the chief of police formed a number of task forces. The idea to test the validity of preventive patrol was developed by the patrol officers on these task forces and sent up the chain of command for approval as well as research and development.

The Police Foundation in Washington, D.C., which had just received some $30 million from the Ford Foundation for police research, welcomed the opportunity to test the concept. This is an especially appropriate insight because it illustrates how once the patrol officers were given the opportunity to have some input into their roles and responsibilities, their views provoked significant organizational change. For example, the well-publicized Kansas City Preventive Patrol Experiment research undermined two fundamental assumptions of the traditional role of the police officer. In a nutshell, the research first suggested that the police officers performing preventive patrol had no impact on the citizens' overall feelings of safety (Kelling et al., 1974). Second, it suggested that there was no statistically significant difference in the crime rate when random patrol was removed and the officers' time was dedicated to different functions (Kelling et al., 1974).

Primary Functions of Patrol

At that time, the typical role of the patrol officer was divided into two primary functions: **random preventive patrol** and responses to citizens' calls for service. Random preventive patrol was institutionalized based on the assumption that it offered increased police visibility to the community. Further, it was believed that this police visibility would have a positive impact on preventing street crime and enhance rapid response to calls for service. Both of these assumptions were considered essential to the role of the patrolman at the time, and both were seriously called into question by subsequent widely published research (Kelling et al., 1974; Kansas City Police Department, 1977).

The second primary function of the patrol officer, responding to calls for service, often included the need to resolve matters that were both criminal and noncriminal in nature. This diversity of role required a distinct focus in the training of the officers, as very different strategies and tactics resolved criminal and noncriminal matters. As a result of both the way the police officers were trained and the prevailing role they were expected to fill at that time, the police, out of necessity, developed primarily into a reactive, incident-driven organization. Interestingly enough, this reactive role emerged as the main focal point of police science education and in many departments remains so today. Proportionately, more time is spent in police academy training on reacting to crime than on strategies and tactics designed to prevent crime from occurring in the first place. Clearly, little (if any) proactive law enforcement was provided by municipal police departments.

Because the day-to-day activities of the police were reactive in nature, there was simply no need to develop or utilize many of the critical tools that today's police agencies heavily depend on to respond rapidly to changing crime conditions. Foremost in this regard are the patrol planning functions and the utilization of crime analysis support systems. Patrol officers who were simply expected to respond to calls for service and handle whatever they confronted had no need to consider a master patrol plan or to be advised of a developing crime pattern on their respective beats. Moreover, the police academy had no reason to teach critical thinking skills or planning strategies; it was simply unheard of.

Another typical characteristic of the traditional role of the police was the managerial philosophy of control. In retrospect, probably the only logical explanation for a patrol supervisor requiring his or her officers to continuously randomly patrol their sectors or beats in uncommitted patrol time was so that the supervisor could effectively maintain control of the patrol officers' day-to-day activities. Requiring mindless activities that had no actual crime control value but that were easily quantified on a daily work card was typical of the traditional police role and was utilized to keep patrol officers busy.

In all fairness, this control-oriented management style of the patrol function was a natural progression for the times. As police executives sought to regain control of their officers and detectives from the political machines that wanted to control and direct their activities, adopting a strict, impersonal, militaristic organization seemed reasonable (Folgelson, 1977). Additionally, public officials were very concerned about corruption during this period. It was generally believed that the total lack of police discipline and leadership provided a constant temptation for corruption (Folgelson, 1977).

The natural response to these concerns was the installation of a control-oriented management system that utilized strong middle managers to maintain constant control of the patrol officers. Also quite logically, police officers' performance, and indeed job security, was essentially dependent on organizational conformance and a "bean-counting" mentality. In a strict militaristic organization, conformity is critical. Patrol officers knew that unconditional conformity or blind faith in superior officers was necessary because in the heat of a potential gun battle, there would be no time to question authority.

To the traditional patrol officers, this line of reasoning seemed rational for two predominant reasons. First, at that time, their role expectations of the job were primarily based on the law enforcement function. Second, most police officers of this time had significant military experience and were accustomed to such a rank-dominated relationship.

The traditional role for a police officer, as described above, served the police mission well during its time. However, it did produce some serious institutionalized barriers for police agencies that were beginning to become involved in more complex social situations that required more complex police responses. In the traditional role, there was very little room for change or innovation. There was no search for excellence in the traditional organizational model. Recommendations or suggestions for change were probably frequently met with "But we have always done it this way" and "If you don't like it, go work somewhere else" responses. This philosophy extended to the community as well.

For these reasons, the traditional role of the police officer certainly did not recognize or utilize, let alone reward, the types of skills that some of the new police recruits were starting to show up at work with, skills they acquired at the university while studying criminal justice. As police officers began to enter American policing with some college experience, the very real limitation of the traditional curriculum of police science as a discipline became apparent.

As the role of the police grew in complexity, and as the police officers' educational background grew in complexity as well, it marked the beginning of what was perhaps the most significant change in the discipline of police science. More and more operations research was directed at police policies and procedures. The traditional practice of random preventive patrol was not the only time-hardened assumption questioned by the operational research that emerged from this time period. The Kansas City Police Department also conducted some research to test the conventional logic of **rapid response** to citizen calls for police service (Kansas City Police Department, 1977). The police rapidly responding to citizen calls for police service, using lights and sirens, always seemed to make sense, and it was believed to be a valid responsibility. Police science curriculums throughout the country taught this practice. It was believed that a rapid police response to a call for help would obviously increase the police's chances of apprehending the criminal at the scene of the crime. The research focused on essentially two prime issues: first, the time it took citizens to call the police when they became involved in a situation that required police attention; second, the time it took the police to respond to their calls for service.

The findings in this research seriously called into question yet another sacred cow of police science, rapid police response. The findings suggested that the time it took most citizens to get around to actually calling the police exceeded the time it took the patrol unit to respond. Further, these reporting delays frequently rendered rapid response by the police a moot consideration (Kansas City Police Department, 1977). Given these research findings, serious thought had to be given to the existing police science teachings. Police officials began to think that perhaps there was a better way to be practicing police science and looked to the criminal justice literature to find out what that better way might be.

The abundance of police research generated around the traditional role of the police continued to accumulate and undermine traditional operational practices. Additional operational assumptions, such as the effectiveness of field interrogations and the safety of one-officer versus two-officer patrol units, were tested in San Diego (Boydston, 1975, 1977). Needless to say, this research was not very well received by the various police administrators. This was the case not only because it threatened their professional practices but also because the research continued to publish reports stating only what was not working in American policing. In most every case, no operational alternatives were suggested that practitioners might explore. This uncertainty left police administrators wondering exactly what to do next and left those teaching the body of knowledge known as police science tentative about exactly what to teach.

As it turned out, however, all this turmoil was not a bad experience for American policing. Out of the dissatisfaction with random patrol grew additional research that considerably changed the focus of resource allocation and, more importantly, also expanded the roles and responsibilities of the patrol officer. Many police departments began to experiment by using the uncommitted time of the patrol officers in **directed patrol**. Police administrators began to surmise that they could perhaps assign patrol officers specific crime prevention tasks to perform during their uncommitted patrol time. Other changes included the following:

- Abandoning equal shift deployment
- Prioritizing calls to keep the patrol officer in service as much as possible
- Developing crime analysis and directed patrol specifically designed to reduce crime

For example, the city of Wilmington, Delaware, developed and utilized a split force patrol program that was designed to utilize the time previously used for random preventive patrol on more directed activities (Valiente and Nolan, 1975). In that research, approximately one-third of the patrol force was removed from calls for service responsibilities and freed up for the criminal apprehension role full-time. This research was critical because many innovative strategies were developed and tested in the process. In Wilmington, the patrol sergeants utilized crime analysis information as a basis to direct the field activities of the criminal apprehension units with much success.

Along these same lines, the San Diego Police Department began a program called the Community Oriented Policing Program

(COP Program). That program was designed to give the complete responsibility of identifying community problems and solutions to the patrol officers. Realizing that no one in a police agency is better prepared to identify community problems than the local neighborhood cop, the San Diego Police Department administrators began to try and tap into that patrol expertise.

Yet another directed patrol effort worth mentioning was the directed patrol programs in New Haven, Connecticut. Again, patrol officers' uncommitted time was directed based on detailed **crime analysis**. Directed deterrent runs (D-runs) were performed during the time that was previously devoted to random preventive patrol, and once again success was realized in crime reduction.

All of these research efforts are essential to the changing theme of police science because they all involved, for the first time, a significant expansion of the role of the patrol officer. The slow but steady increase in the role of the patrol officer marked the beginning of a police organization that utilized and rewarded the skills of the smart patrol officers and kept them engaged. Police administrators began to realize that perhaps the most valuable tool that a police officer had was not his gun or nightstick, but his brain. Only at this point did the value of teaching police science again become self-evident, and it was under these organizational circumstances that the well-trained patrol officer could begin to be distinguished as an asset to the agency.

The discipline of police science, over time, began to emerge as a continuation of the momentum in organizational change that began in the early 1970s. Rapid organizational change in police agencies was apparent throughout the country. These changes were due, at least in part, to the operational research that continued to gain popularity, as well as the initial success that directed patrol activities enjoyed. The police officers, as well as the police administrators, realized that random patrol produced random results, and it became apparent that sensible law enforcement could certainly aim higher than random results. As time passed, less and less of patrol officers' time was devoted to random preventive patrol and more of it was used in directed patrol activities based on available crime data. As patrol officers' analytical skills increased in value, intelligent, well-trained police officers were needed to fill these positions.

Progressive police science curriculums, as they should be taught today, are based on the new operational expectations and roles that evolved from this experience and research. The role of the police officer today is, in fact, a logical progression from the earlier transitional roles of policing. As productive tactics and strategies developed to better utilize the uncommitted time of the patrol officer, strategies termed "differential police responses" were developed out of necessity. Because it was now realized that previously uncommitted time could effectively be utilized, efforts were made to increase the amount of time that was uncommitted. Building dispatcher strategies designed to manage calls for service from the 911 system better accomplished that. Also, the practices of matching manpower deployment to workload conditions, using **call prioritization** for service, and taking offense reports over the telephone gained in popularity.

ISSUES IN PATROL OPERATIONS

As mentioned earlier, the specific patrol operations vary from department to department, from tour to tour, and even from day to day. Paradoxically, patrol can be routine and boring in some ways and diverse and exciting in many others. It is the responsibility of police science instructors to understand the patrol operations of the agency and communicate that information to the new recruit officers. Detailed instruction must be provided covering the classic patrol activities such as making memo book entries, fulfilling patrol duties and responsibilities, doing traffic enforcement, responding to calls for service, working the police radio, writing reports and tickets, and handling the numerous types of calls a patrol officer is expected to handle.

Officer Safety and Survival

When on patrol, a uniformed member of the service can expect to become involved in many different types of situations. Some will require bravery and a command presence; others need sensitivity and caring. During one tour of duty, a police officer may be called on to act as an enforcer, a father figure, a mediator, a lawyer, a social worker, a psychiatrist, and perhaps even a rescue worker. This being the case, there is much to learn in police science. Regardless of the particular role the police officer may be assuming at the time, he or she must always be aware of the underlying considerations of **officer safety and survival**.

Officer safety is of paramount importance to each and every patrol officer. A true common denominator in the otherwise diverse world of patrol is the mind-set and tactics of police officer safety. Regardless of the type of call for service or self-directed activity, officer safety is always an issue. Whether the location of a job or activity or the location of a suspect is routine or unknown to an officer, police officer safety is always a concern. Police officers *must* learn that they cannot protect and serve the community until or unless they protect and serve themselves first.

For example, young police officers who drive the radio car with reckless abandon to arrive at the scene of an officer who needs assistance don't understand the true nature of patrol yet. They have not figured out that, no matter how noble the intentions, it is impossible to help a fellow officer if you get in a vehicle accident on the way and never arrive at the scene. Older officers who become overweight, out of shape, and overly stressed may have forgotten the fundamental principles of officer safety and survival, and they need to be reinstructed. Recruit officers must learn and practice fundamental officer safety and survival tactics to the point that they are instinctive. Tactics such as speaking to citizens in a way that does not unnecessarily escalate a confrontation, blading their body to speak to and interview suspects, properly placing the radio car to accomplish safe and effective traffic stops, having a constant awareness of body language and always seeing a person's hands, and using the practices of cover and concealment, as well as other fundamental and time-tested strategies, should all be taught and repeatedly stressed to enhance safety and survival.

Despite all of the advances realized in the behavioral sciences, human behavior remains a relative unknown, and professionals who deal with human behavior for a living, usually in negative and dangerous situations, must never forget this. There is no explaining human behavior, and no police officer gets paid enough to get hurt or killed by taking foolish chances.

The Compliance Continuum

Another major area of study and management concern in patrol operations is the appropriate use of force and the **compliance continuum**. Very few considerations are more important to police officer safety, citizen safety, and overall confidence in the police than the ability to obtain voluntary compliance when possible, and the judicious use of force when necessary. In reality, the vast majority of individuals whom the police come in contact with will simply comply with a lawful order given by a uniformed police officer. Thank goodness, that is almost always the case. However, there are some individuals in a free society who simply will never comply, and they must be forced to comply against their will.

The legal authority to use force on an otherwise free citizen is what makes police officers so special and unique, and a primary reason why their education and training are of interest to the community. In a free republic, a police officer can use only the amount of force that is necessary under the circumstances to gain compliance. This decision to use force is one that can have life-and-death consequences and will be reviewed and scrutinized endlessly. Every day, police officers deal with the responsibility of gaining compliance, so the steps in the compliance continuum must also be learned to the point of instinct.

Most police agencies today teach the following six steps for gaining compliance with a lawful order:

Steps in the Compliance Continuum

1. Professional presence
2. Verbal commands
3. Unarmed physical force
4. Nonimpact weapons
5. Impact weapons
6. Deadly physical force

There is an important distinction in teaching the six steps of the compliance continuum that, although it may seem counterinstinctive, is correct. Most law enforcement agencies spend the majority of time teaching their officers to be proficient in the use of the final step—deadly physical force. This seems appropriate because the stakes are the highest there, and it is clearly the most serious. However, it is at least equally important to spend that same amount of time teaching the officers to be effective and proficient in the first two steps—professional presence and verbal commands—because that is the way compliance is gained in the vast majority of cases. But more importantly, the more effective an officer is at communication, the less often he or she will have to go to the next steps to gain compliance.

Once again, the first step in gaining compliance is the effective use of **professional presence**. In the vast majority of cases, this is enough for a police officer to get what is wanted. A professional police officer who responds to a scene and appears in command, dressed in a sharp uniform with a hat and a police radio, can effectively control most situations. People make a preliminary judgment of another person they come in contact with based on that person's initial appearance, and criminal suspects are no exception to this. That is why businesspeople wear expensive suits, and why police officers wear neat and easily identifiable uniforms. Uniformed police officers who wear a portable police radio also present an assumption that plenty of backup is available if a suspect creates a situation where force will be necessary. Even a tough guy who might otherwise consider fighting one police officer should recognize that before it's over, he will be fighting two, three, four, or more police officers.

After professional presence, the effective use of verbal commands is the next step in gaining compliance. Again, most people will do what a police officer tells them if the officer tells them in a clear and nonconfusing way. Professional police hostage negotiators know this, and so do good street cops. Effective requests, commands, and appeals to reason can and do successfully convince most people to comply with a lawful order of the police. Simply telling a suspect in a loud, clear voice, "Sir, please put your hands behind your back so I can put the handcuffs on you," and not just grabbing a suspect, can make an officer's job potentially easier and less confrontational. Effective communication and a small amount of courtesy during enforcement actions cost an officer nothing, but they can convince a suspect to comply while still maintaining his or her dignity in front of friends.

Clearly, the days of telling a perpetrator to do something "because I said so" are over and probably were never that effective to begin with. It is usually in the behavioral sciences curriculum that most of the actual time is devoted to effective communication, but living with the implications of not learning this will manifest itself everywhere.

Unarmed physical force is the third step in gaining compliance from a suspect and also requires a significant commitment to training. Although police critics refuse to admit it, experienced police officers know full well that there are some individuals who simply must be forcefully taken into custody for the safety of the community. In cases where professional presence and effective verbal commands fail, there is, indeed, a right way and a wrong way to put your hands on a criminal perpetrator.

Even in such a situation, instinctively punching another person in the face or swinging the baton in an over-the-head fashion frequently serves only to escalate the fight, enrage community witnesses, and injure the officer. Experienced martial artists, either sworn or civilian, should teach this part of the curriculum. Fundamental open-hand compliance tactics based on pressure points and grappling techniques can and should be taught to patrol officers. This is so critical because uniformed police officers carrying a firearm on their hip cannot afford to lose a street fight and give up their weapon.

Given the inherent dangers of hand-to-hand tactics and the additional concern of protecting the firearm, police officers should not hesitate to progress to the next level, the use of nonimpact weapons. This primarily includes the use of mace or oleoresin capsicum pepper spray (O.C. spray) but also includes the utilization of electronic dart devices, stun gun technologies, high-pressure fire extinguishers, and tear gas and/or capture nets. O.C. spray can be an extremely effective weapon in confrontational situations; it can be used when some type of physical force is appropriate to protect the officer and restrain a perpetrator. Additionally, it is effective against animals, intoxicated individuals, and persons under great emotional strain. Nonimpact weapons provide an effective option to be utilized against resisting perpetrators, but they are not 100 percent effective and cannot be applied in every scenario faced by the patrol officer.

Impact weapons present the next available option to gain compliance, and the typical option in this category is the police baton. Different law enforcement agencies authorize, train with, and deploy different types of batons. They include the PR.24 or handle baton, the straight baton, the expandable baton, and others. It does not include, as a matter of routine, the flashlight, clipboard, or department-issued portable radio. Although anything goes in a fight for survival, these implements are not designed for striking another person and do not typically work well in this fashion.

Originally called a nightstick because officers were only allowed to carry them at night, the police baton is used by almost all law enforcement agencies today. One of the most significant factors that makes the police baton such a valuable weapon is its length. Unlike the shorter "Billy," which used to be called the day stick, a baton allows officers the distance and leverage to protect themselves by keeping their bodies and weapons beyond the reach of a perpetrator.

The final and highest level of force an officer may use to gain compliance with a lawful order is the use of deadly physical force. Clearly, the highest level of training must be dedicated to the potential use of deadly force. In America today, deadly physical force can only be used as an absolute last resort when an officer or another person is in immediate danger of serious injury or death. The use of a firearm is one of the most serious decisions a police officer can ever be asked to make, and the training and practice to acquire and maintain a certain level of proficiency are unequivocally important.

Teaching the use of force, and the actual application of the use of force, is clearly critical and compelling. It requires an officer to immediately consider a complex set of circumstances and decide exactly the level of force he or she can utilize to respond. Through training, a logical progression of steps designed to gain compliance is engrained in an officer. It does not mean, however, that in every situation an officer must progress from step one through step six. A police officer may very well arrive on a scene and be immediately faced with a level of threat that can only be responded to with deadly force. That is why the mark of a professional, well-trained police force is not the number of deadly force cases they are involved with but rather the number of cases they effectively de-escalated at the lower levels and never had to use deadly force to settle. Police confrontations that were resolved with good judgment, not good marksmanship, occur every day in policing, and they should be captured and studied. Although they may be difficult, if not impossible, to capture, they represent the ultimate goal of effective law enforcement training and education.

Written Directives and Department Regulations

Teaching and explaining the various departmental forms that constitute the official departmental written directive system requires a significant segment of a police science curriculum. New police recruits must learn about the various types of written directives, such as department policy, that officially govern their behavior and provide the parameters of acceptable behavior. Department policy also, and equally as importantly, provides the written parameters of protection from criminal and civil liability, for both the department and the individual officer, by establishing exactly what behavior is sanctioned as "official."

Written interim orders are also issued from time to time. Interim orders are essentially partial changes or clarifications of existing department policy statements. The use of interim orders provides a department with an immediate mechanism to distribute changes in department policy because the more formal department policy statements are usually updated only once a year or so.

Operations orders are yet another type of written directive that explains the details of an upcoming special event. Operations orders explain reporting times and locations of the police officers working the assignment, the number and types of officers involved, and the type of detail it is, such as a St. Patrick's Day parade, a marathon, or a Fourth of July celebration.

Other typical written directives include legal bulletins, training bulletins, and other short-term bulletins intended to provide operational details to the members of an agency. The important consideration from a training perspective is that organizationally the police academy must be out in front of all newly issued written directives. The most effective way to actually realize a change in behavior, which is what most written directives call for, is to train the officers on all new directives before they go into effect.

Education and training, not policy alone, change police officer behavior. Police commissioners can sit in their office all day long and issue new policy statements, but due to the proliferation of written directives, police officer behavior will probably not significantly change until they are trained in the new mandates. New written directives issued without a training experience simply become more useless paper on a clipboard at roll call. The more significant the policy statement is, the more important training will be to implement it.

Professionalism and Ethics

Police professionalism and ethics can sometimes be difficult subjects to teach in a police academy. Ethics, which is essentially a philosophical subject, can be difficult to teach in a nonphilosophical, practical manner. Additionally, the practice of ethical decision making is not a simple matter of following department policy, like most other police science subjects. It is, instead, reflective, self-prescribed, and self-governing. What two police officers do at 3:00 A.M. in a dark backyard with a perpetrator in custody after a long and exhaustive struggle is really a matter of their ethics and professionalism more than department policy and/or supervision. Moreover, ethical decision making is manifested in so many different aspects of policing that even if they existed, specific guidelines would not be effective or applicable.

For example, police discretion is a critical component of an individual officer's reaction to situations involving the safeguarding of a perpetrator's rights, an issue which stands at the very foundation of policing a free republic. Other typical ethical dilemmas for police officers include the following:

- Choosing what to do if their patrol partner engages in misconduct such as bribery, corruption, or brutality
- Deciding whether to lie under oath in a court of law if the truth does not serve their personal interests
- Determining if they are willing to lie under oath to back up a story of a partner or coworker

To stand up in a court of law and take an oath to "Swear to God to tell the truth, the whole truth, and nothing but the truth" and then lie (or "testilie," as some police officers call it) creates a significant ethical and moral dilemma for the untrained police officer. Most police academies include in the police science section a comprehensive presentation from the Internal Affairs Unit. This strategy seems to work well because after a comprehensive presentation is made about the right way to behave, an Internal Affairs presentation is usually appropriate to demonstrate the resources that an agency is willing to dedicate to catch you if you choose not to be ethical Some people behave in a certain way because it is the right thing to do, and some because of the fear of getting caught and punished. Either way, this approach seems to be effective. Since most modern Internal Affairs Units have the best resources and investigators assigned to them to safeguard the overall integrity of the agency, this is usually a very compelling and interesting block of instruction.

For example, in the New York City Police Academy, the chief of Internal Affairs does this presentation personally. Requiring an extraordinary commitment of time and dedication to the long-term integrity of the department, this chief shows up in full uniform, and he provides such a professional level of instruction that there is no doubt left about the expected level of behavior in the New York City Police Department.

Preliminary Investigations

Preliminary investigations are a crucial part of patrol officers' responsibilities. This is the case because patrol officers are typically the first to arrive at all crime scenes. Many situations are fairly routine, and some are unusual and potentially complex. A well-trained patrol officer will know when to handle a situation, when to simply establish a perimeter and secure a crime until some specialized unit and/or detectives arrive to handle it, and when to conduct a preliminary investigation and call for a supervisor. Regardless, the first police officer on the scene typically is required to take immediate and decisive action, and this immediate action will almost always have a profound impact on the subsequent ability of a department to solve a case. Actions such as rendering immediate first aid to the injured while calling an ambulance, noting a first impression of the scene and the details in a memo book, and recognizing and separating potential witnesses or suspects are all essential and must be taught during police science instruction.

After the immediate crime scene and the people involved are secured, police officers are sometimes expected to take initial statements from witnesses and secure an inner and outer perimeter of the crime scene (especially from other police officers who like to wander onto the scene to get a look). Establishing a "pen" or gathering area for media; recognizing, collecting, and protecting physical evidence, especially potential DNA samples; and calling specialized units to the scene (as well as other related activities) are all included in the preliminary investigation phase of a criminal case. Almost without exception, these actions are expected of the patrol officers who first respond to a crime scene. Regardless of the level of specialization practiced in a department, the generalist on patrol will probably always be the most critical factor in fighting crime. Patrol officers' roles and responsibilities are at the very heart of police science and demand a significant commitment of instructional time and resources.

Specialized Resources

To be effective in preliminary investigations, as well as in the other typical responsibilities of patrol, an officer must be aware of the scope and types of specialized resources available to him or her. In big-city police departments, as well as most small agencies with mutual aid agreements, the level of specialization and support for patrol can be quite considerable. Patrol officers who find themselves on a scene that seems to be getting worse fast can call for immediate backup from such specialists as Emergency Service Units, S.W.A.T. Units, hostage negotiators, Crime Scene Units, patrol supervisors, Helicopter Units, medical examiners, Harbor Units, K-9 Units, Plainclothes Units, uniformed task forces, etc.

Truly experienced patrol officers know that they are not expected to know everything to be successful on patrol, but they are expected to know who to call to a scene and to act as if they know everything until help arrives. As a general rule, time is on the side of the police officer. A detailed knowledge of what to do at a crime scene, and who and when to call for help, is essential for success and safety on patrol.

COMMUNITY POLICING

Perhaps the most significant characteristics of the changing discipline of police science were the introduction and acceptance of the various community-based programs and the philosophy of community policing in general. This organizational progression effectively paved the way for the upcoming community-oriented policing movement in American policing, and it significantly increased the role of the police officer.

Community policing was also the first strategy of police science that enjoyed a rich philosophical base and was built on the research findings of the past. With the introduction of community-based programs, patrol officers began to emerge as social leaders in their respective beats/neighborhoods. Once again, citizens began to come to their local police officer to discuss concerns about quality-of-life issues in the neighborhoods that may have eventually led to serious criminal activity.

The key focus of these developments was the expansion in the role of the patrol officer. The very qualities that a patrol officer developed through higher education were suddenly in demand. Under the community policing philosophy, college-educated police officers were assigned to the following areas:

- Speaking at community meetings
- Writing community newsletters and departmental policy statements for public distribution
- Thinking through neighborhood problems expressed by the community and providing logical police responses

Clearly, American policing no longer existed as a closed institution but became very much open to the public. Suddenly, the value of a discipline built around the science of policing became clear. In the 1990s, this new trend in police science continued. In this emerging vision, the community policing model became the standard.

The core seeds of this new paradigm continued to grow as police science began to teach the value of community policing as a philosophy, and not as a program. As the fresh philosophical and operational aspects of community-oriented policing materialized, effective training and education became the cornerstones of implementation. The skills needed to practice community policing were taught at the police academy, and the young well-trained patrol officers finally found themselves in an organizational structure that utilizes, appreciates, and actually *rewards* the skills they had spent their time developing.

The police had ultimately realized that they cannot effectively fight crime alone. Accordingly, they must be more responsive to the citizens if they are to be successful in their mission. In the emerging paradigm, the police officers had to begin to develop crime control strategies with the public as partners to combat the crime problem. Joint police–community crime control strategies, such as new legislation, increased enforcement efforts, public educational campaigns, and increased community action, were increasingly utilized.

Based on this realization, numerous police agencies began to institute various community-based programs that ranged from using foot patrol programs to putting the neighborhood cop back on the beat (Moore and Kelling, 1983; Walker, 1984; Trojanowicz, 1985). It is important to note here that the community-oriented movement was also advanced through the problem-oriented approach that appeared in the police literature (Goldstein, 1979; Eck and Spelman, 1987).

Today, the police organization continues to evolve, and police science leads the way by teaching the needed skills and tactics. For example, the emerging model is slowly removing itself from the formal, militaristic organizational structure. Consequently, patrol officers will be encouraged to think about community problems and develop strategies to address them in their uncommitted time. Further, this aspect of the role expansion became possible through the rejection of the traditional duties that used to consume all the patrol officers' time. The emerging model does not contain the traditional elements that have been questioned by research. Traditional practices such as deploying all patrol cars to perform random preventive patrol and placing a high priority on providing a rapid police response to all calls for service have not produced their desired results and should not be perpetuated in the emerging police science curriculums.

In policing today, patrol officers must be well trained to utilize their analytical skills in problem identification, problem analysis, and problem articulation, and they must also possess the ability to develop and propose community-based solutions. A logical extension of this process, the planning function, is another critical component of policing today. For the patrol function to effectively move away from simply being incident-driven, good operational planning is imperative. It will be needed to originate functional tactical action plans and crime analysis information to guide the uncommitted patrol time of the patrol officers. These planning and research activities will also dictate that a police officer possess and utilize logic, analytical, and quantitative skills. The emerging model utilizes the planning function extensively.

Given the organizational transformation of policing, which is still very much in progress, a police science curriculum for the new millennium must be thorough and detailed in the historical lessons of policing. In addition to the appreciation for how the role of the patrol officer has changed over time, specific types of information and skills must still be taught in the police science curriculum to prepare the recruit officers for the day when they graduate.

ORIENTATION TO THE POLICE DEPARTMENT

One of the necessary and important components of a police science curriculum should be a complete and thorough orientation to the law enforcement organization. This is the case because new members of a police agency must, before anything else, quickly begin to learn the essential characteristics that make a police department effective:

- Police officers must trust each other because their lives may depend on it.
- Police officers who work together must establish and sustain **unit cohesion**.
- Police officers should take pride and ownership in themselves, their uniforms, their police shields, and their departments.

This process of ownership and pride begins by teaching respect for the history, traditions, symbols, and beliefs of an agency. For example, new police recruits should visit the police memorial and discuss the individual cases of their brother officers who gave the ultimate sacrifice in the line of duty. Police department traditions and symbols are not just physical traditions and symbols; they are a way of life that other police officers have sacrificed their lives to protect! New police recruits should know those officers' names and their stories. They should understand the saying, "There but for the grace of God go I." They should listen to a panel discussion of police widows and children whose loved ones were killed in the line of duty. They should be exposed to presentations about their agency uniforms, what the symbols on the patch stand for, and the history of their police shields. Finally, new police recruits should visit a police museum and learn the history of their city and agency.

These types of experiences put the day-to-day responsibilities of young patrol officers in the proper historical perspective and start a genuine appreciation of a proud and significant history. Starting a job as a law enforcement officer in America is not the same as assuming an entry-level position in a private-sector company. Police officers cannot expect to make that kind of money, and they cannot expect to be that innovative in their responsibilities. It is, instead, beginning a career that is a continuation of a rich history in which others before them have figured out the best and safest ways to get things done and in which some have sacrificed their lives doing it. *This must be understood.* Police officers without a proper understanding and respect for the history and symbols of their agency will never understand the significance of their role in such a history and thereby be more likely to disrespect it.

Regional and College Police Academies

Providing the necessary orientation to a law enforcement agency can be a special challenge to many police academies because of their structure. Regional police academies or those located within the confines of a local college typically consist of a number of students from various local departments. In such an institution, stressing the history and traditions of a specific department may not be possible, but teaching pride in the profession of law enforcement remains crucial.

STRATEGY-DRIVEN POLICING (COMPSTAT)

A current issue emerging in American policing can be described strategy-driven policing or, as the New York City Police Department calls it, **COMPSTAT**. This issue has important considerations for police science and must be integrated into a contemporary police science curriculum. Essentially, COMPSTAT is a management accountability process. Each week, commanders from all the operational units in a geographic area meet in the N.Y.P.D.'s Command and Control Center. At the meeting, commanders are required to present the activities and conditions of their command and to explain their enforcement activities in the last month to address those activities and conditions. While COMPSTAT is designed to be a management process, it does have operational implications for the patrol officer. COMPSTAT, or whatever management accountability process a department may be using to make timely and accurate deployment decisions, should be explained to the patrol officers. They are the foot soldiers of the fight against crime, and whenever possible and appropriate, they should be advised of the overall plan behind their individual assignments.

A WORD ABOUT INSTRUCTIONAL METHODOLOGY

In all areas of education and training, the instructional methodology is equally as important as, if not more important than, the course content. Add to that the fact that police academies are teaching adults (who, research shows, learn best by doing), and the realization that police science is essentially an applied discipline, and instructional methodology becomes paramount. It is certainly appropriate and acceptable to begin police science instruction with lectures because there is almost always a necessary and proper foundation that must be established. However, as soon as logistically possible, the student officers must be challenged with instructional methods that require them to *apply* their knowledge. Therefore, as much as possible, police science instruction should be provided:

- Utilizing interactive learning strategies such as role plays that actually require the successful completion of all the necessary forms and paperwork.

- Incorporating sociodramas and/or interactive theater techniques that effectively capture the emotion and drama of the calls for service the student officers will face in the streets.
- Applying simulations and/or reflective team exercises that prepare the student officers to work in teams and to communicate with other officers before they arrive at the scene.
- Presenting interdisciplinary workshops that provide an opportunity for instructors from different specialties to debrief the student officers on their ability to integrate knowledge into their policing style.

Toward the end of the training experience, ideally as a component of final testing, the student officers should be required to demonstrate, through a detailed role play, their ability to integrate their knowledge into a safe and effective police response. Then, and only then, are they ready for a patrol assignment.

CONCLUSION

American policing, much like society itself, has historically never stopped changing and evolving. In policing, however, the change and/or progress has been so incremental that most of it has gone relatively unnoticed. It appears that, for a number of reasons, change in American policing has been evolutionary, not revolutionary. Due to the inherent complexity of the police bureaucracy, this incremental process will probably continue.Therefore, it is equally important that the body of knowledge known as police science continues to evolve. Indeed, the one trend that seems to underlie all the changes taking place in policing is the role expansion of the patrol officer.

As the police organization continues to evolve, it is becoming very apparent that any authentic improvement in American policing must be philosophically and organizationally traced to a genuine improvement in the individual police officer. As the role of the individual police officer continues to expand, so will his or her discretion.

Because a police organization cannot possible write policy statements to address every conceivable discretionary situation that a police officer may confront on the streets, all officers must understand the historical, practical, procedural, and ethical limitations of their actions. This understanding always has, and probably always will, go directly back to the quality of the foundation provided by the recruit's police science curriculum. Remember the state-ment made earlier in this text: One cannot train for the police role; one educates for it. Constantly improving the quality of the educa-tion and training provided in police science is not only necessary to improve American policing, but it is critical to preserve the basic freedoms and principles of the American Republic.

Police officers do a lot more than preserve the peace and enforce the laws. They also serve to protect and advance the underlying principles and freedoms of the American system of government. Certainly one could argue that educating the police is not only politically convenient, but it is also a moral imperative.

KEY TERMS

Call Prioritization

Community Policing

Compliance Continuum

COMPSTAT

Crime Analysis

Criminal Justice

Directed Patrol

Job Description

Kansas City Preventive
  Patrol Experiment

Officer Safety and Survival

Police Science

Professional Presence

Random Preventive Patrol

Rapid Response

Unit Cohesion

QUESTIONS FOR DISCUSSION

1. What are some of the most effective instructional methods of teaching law enforcement ethics in a police science curricu-lum? Explain.
2. How can a police science curriculum teach officer safety and survival without making the officers unnecessarily paranoid or overly aggressive?
3. Write a job description for a police officer in your community. What specific job responsibilities are important, and why?
4. What local problems exist in your community that should be included in a police science curriculum?
5. How important is community policing to the lessons included in police science?
6. How is effective crime analysis information incorporated in the deployment of police officers?

7. Do the police in your neighborhood continue to utilize random preventive patrol? What do you think about such a practice?
8. Are the police professionals or tradesmen? What is the difference?
9. Discuss the concept of voluntary compliance in law enforcement. Why is it important?
10. How critical is it to teach the content of written directives and department regulations?

SUGGESTED READINGS

Bain, Read. (1939). The policeman on the beat. *Scientific Monthly* 48: 15.

Boydston, John E. (1975). *San Diego field interrogation: Final report*. Washington, DC: Police Foundation.

Boydston, John E. (1977). *Patrol staffing in San Diego: One or two officer units*. Washington, DC: Police Foundation.

Duffee, David E. (1990). Research in progress: School of Criminal Justice, the University at Albany. *Criminal Justice Research Bulletin* 1:5.

Eck, John and William Spelman. (1987). Who ya gonna call? The police as problem-busters. *Crime and Delinquency* 33, no. 1: 31–52.

Folgelson, R. (1977). *Big city police*. Cambridge, MA: Harvard University Press.

Gourley, G.D. (1974). *Patrol administration*. Chicago, IL: Charles C Thomas Press.

Greenwood, P.W., J.M. Chalken, and J. Pettersillia. (1977). *The criminal investigation process*. Lexington, MA: D.C. Heath and Company.

Kansas City Police Department. (1977). *Response time analysis*. Kansas City, MO: Kansas City Police Department.

Kelling, G.L., T. Pate, and C.E. Brown. (1974). *The Kansas City preventive patrol experiment: A summary report*. Washington, DC: Police Foundation.

Moore, M. and G.L. Kelling. (1983). To serve and protect: Learning from police history. *Public Interest* 70: 49–65.

Trojanowicz, R. (1985). *An evaluation of the neighborhood foot patrol in Flint, Michigan.* East Lansing, MI: Michigan State University Press.

Valiente, N.M. and J.T. Nolan. (1975). *Wilmington split force patrol experiment planning report.* Wilmington, DE: Wilmington Police Department.

Walker, Samuel. (1984). Broken windows and fractured history: The use and misuse of history in recent police patrol analysis. *Justice Quarterly* 1: 75–90.

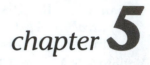
EDUCATING AND TRAINING NEW POLICE OFFICERS

Teaching the Law

"No man is above the law, and no man is below it; nor do we ask any man's permission when we require him to obey it. Obedience to the law is demanded as a right; not as a favor."

—Theodore Roosevelt

INTRODUCTION

The overall goal of teaching a law curriculum in a police academy should be to enable police officers to impartially and effectively enforce the law by providing them with a solid working knowledge of the law. It stands to reason that officers cannot effectively enforce the law if they don't understand the law.

Essentially, however, this is a much more complex responsibility than it may appear to be on the surface. This is the case because lawyers, assistant district attorneys, judges, and those who stand ever ready to judge the police for their actions normally have as much time as they need to consider the facts of a particular situation, refer to the appropriate section of the penal code for guidance, consider legal precedent established in similar cases, and carefully make a calculated determination as to the best course the police should have taken. Police officers, on the other hand, routinely have to make such legal determinations on the street, often when all the actual facts of a situation are not yet clear, and sometimes in the face of imminent danger to themselves and others.

Therefore, teaching the law to police officers can easily become overwhelming because it includes not only studying and learning the actual laws but also appropriately applying such laws to a frequently vague and sometimes perplexing fact pattern. Add to this uncertainty police officer discretion, applicable legal procedures and limitations, and constitutional principles and guidelines, not to mention recent legal opinions, and an officer can easily begin to feel overwhelmed.

LAW CURRICULUM

To successfully prepare a young police officer to enforce the law, the law curriculum of a professional police academy must be comprehensive in scope and thorough in nature.

Much like police science, an exact model law curriculum is difficult to propose because the laws vary so much from one jurisdiction

---

LAW CURRICULUM

Introduction to Law	Legal Issues of Use of Force
U.S. Constitution	Penal Law
Bill of Rights	Limitations of Legal Authority
Sources of the Law	Crimes against Persons
Structure of the Courts	Crimes against Property
Stop, Question, and Frisk	Domestic Violence Laws
Establishing Probable Cause	Bribery-Related Offenses
Laws of Arrest	Vehicle and Traffic Laws
Search and Seizure	Civil Law
Laws of Evidence	Resisting Arrest
Civil Liability and Police Officers	Public Demonstrations

Total = Approximately 100 Hours of Instruction

---

to another. It is possible to propose a basic core curriculum, allowing for adjustments consistent with local and state laws and legal practices.

Introduction to the Law

For modern-day student police officers, an all-inclusive introduction to the law is required. Such an introduction should discuss why the American Republic needs laws, the historical nature and various sources of the law, some of the major legal concepts and definitions of the terms utilized in the study and practice of law, the actual sources of the legal authority of the police, and a review of some of the major court cases.

In the United States of America today, some types of laws are necessary and proper to sustain order. Essentially, laws are simply a set of rules to govern group behavior and to create an orderly society. If there were no laws or rules governing behavior in a society, that society would erode into an existence where "Might makes right," and individual disputes over scarce resources would be resolved by violence and aggression. Without laws, a social structure would emerge where the strong would dominate the weak, the intelligent would take advantage of the not-so-intelligent, the rich would control all the resources and exploit the poor, and any possible notion of equality or justice would be only an illusion.

The law as we know it today in the United States has a rich and significant historical past and was built upon earlier versions of codified behavior. Foremost among them is the **Code of Hammurabi**, the earliest known set of laws that were literally engraved in stone and put forward for everyone to see and obey. The Code of Hammurabi is historically significant because it is the earliest known code of laws designed to govern group behavior by prescribing certain punishments. It provided the first known written guidance in the area of criminal justice and advanced the notion that an orderly society needs written guidelines of group behavior and methods of punishment that fit the crime. The Code of Hammurabi also provided a consistent standard that could be applied across the board based on the violation of the law, not the individual accused.

The **Magna Carta** is another historically significant document that should be studied in the law curriculum. The Magna Carta, officially signed in June 1215, is a major source of modern-day law and procedure and advanced perhaps the most significant legal concept of our time: *due process of law.* The due process clause, and the procedural implications associated with it, is critical to the enforcement arm of the criminal justice system and essential to democratic policing.

Finally, in terms of historical significance, the **U.S. Constitution** is another essential source of modern law and must be acknowledged and reviewed in any police academy preparing police officers to police a free society. New police officers should know that in Philadelphia in 1787, the federalists, who believed in the necessity of a strong central government to keep the thirteen colonies together, and the democrats, who believed in expanded individual freedoms stressed in the New World, met to construct the U.S. Constitution. At that time, the key issues to be resolved in establishing a new and free government included the following:

- How much power should a central government have?
- Should a central government promote mob rule or a pure democracy?
- How could a government resolve the ever-present concerns of minority interests being unfairly suppressed by majority rule?
- How should a national government select a national leader?
- How should a government balance proper governmental representation for the smaller states, which wanted one state to be worth one vote, with the larger states, which wanted the vote to be strictly based on state population?
- How should a government settle the economic concerns of a central government for free citizens who just fought England over taxation without representation?
- Exactly how specific should a government get in regards to individual rights in a written constitution?

All of these philosophically critical issues and others had to be resolved by the Constitutional Convention. The work on the new constitution was philosophically driven and guided by the **Federalist Papers**. The Federalist Papers was a historically great collection of newspaper articles published to explain the federalist position in forming the new government. They argued that adopting a strong central government and ratifying a central constitution would be to the benefit of the large states such as New York. At the time, New York State was a pivotal state to the proposed union due to its deep harbors and strong economic base. In the aggregate, the Federalist Papers claimed:

- Man, left to his own devises, is selfish and greedy.
- In any society, problems will arise and government must be prepared to resolve them peacefully, not through violence.
- To accomplish this peacefully, government must protect liberty and guard against any one faction in society taking advantage of another faction.
- Most importantly, a government must be structured in such a way as to allow it to protect men from each other, people from government, and one branch of government from another branch of government.

Based on such philosophical assumptions published in the Federalist Papers, an attempt was made to construct such a government that would be driven by express written constitutional principles. This is important to know because the police, at some point, would be charged with the enforcement of these constitutional principles.

Even back then, the politicians involved in drafting the new constitution were all reasonably intelligent men, men who fully appreciated the importance of reason over religion in government and therefore provided for the separation of church and state. They understood man's nature, or at least the classical assumptions of man's nature, and therefore provided for a separation of powers by creating three separate branches of government. These three branches, called the judiciary, the executive, and the legislative, were all envisioned and created to provide an unequivocal balance of power in government. Finally, these men fully understood that what they were creating was revolutionary in the world in that it would create a model republic, a society of free and diverse citizens all united by a single common cause: freedom.

An understanding of this history of the law and the genesis of the rule of law is essential to a young person studying to become a police officer in a free republic today because it makes clear the great pains that the American forefathers went through to control and limit government authority and to create individual freedoms. Since a police officer is legally authorized to take away these freedoms, it is essential that the historical and legal significance of such an action is fully understood. As a uniformed representative of government authorized by law to lock an individual up, a police officer simply must understand the significance of that role in the overall scheme of a democracy.

Inevitably, as free and diverse people come together to live, factions will emerge, factions based on geographic distinctions, religious distinctions, and distinctions of race, sexual orientation, income, and many other manifestations of the human condition. To provide the ability and flexibility for a national government to balance all of the involved factions, the U.S. Constitution was carefully and specifically designed to say very little in reference to individual behavioral prohibitions.

Instead, the **Bill of Rights** was attached to the document. The Bill of Rights, or the first ten amendments, was clearly designed to limit the power and authority of law enforcement to take away an individual's freedoms. Collectively, the individual rights guaranteed by the Bill of Rights include the following:

The right to be assumed innocent until proven guilty
The right against unreasonable search and seizure
The right against arrest without probable cause
The right against unreasonable seizure of personal property
The right against self-incrimination
The right to fair questioning by the police
The right to protection from physical harm throughout the justice system
The right to an attorney
The right to a trial by jury
The right to know the nature of any charges
The right to cross-examine prosecution witnesses
The right to speak and present witnesses
The right not to be tried twice for the same offense
The right against cruel and unusual punishment
The right to due process of law
The right to a speedy trial
The right against excessive bail
The right against excessive fines

Clearly, the principles outlined in the Bill of Rights provide an excellent basis for a detailed classroom discussion of the individual rights constitutionally guaranteed to all Americans. They also are an excellent basis for the discussion of their implications for law enforcement. Moreover, they set a solid foundation for a discussion about exactly what differentiates policing in general from policing the American Republic. Any police officers who either never learn these distinctions or choose to ignore them are a danger to themselves, their agency, and the very freedoms that police officers are sworn to protect. To this day, many high-ranking government officials representing emerging democracies from around the globe visit major American municipal police academies to study the way American police officers are trained. It is essentially this section of the law curriculum that emerging democracies are most interested in reviewing. To the entire world, the American rule of law and the principles outlined in the Bill of Rights serve as the backbone of protecting and advancing individual freedoms, and policing them is what separates a democracy from some of the more repressive forms of government currently operating around the world.

For effectively teaching the law, many excellent educational institutions around the country utilize the instructional methodology of rote memory. This is the practice of requiring students to actually memorize certain aspects of a curriculum and recite them instinctively upon demand. The Bill of Rights is an exceptional body of knowledge, one that could be required to be memorized in a law class. A police officer who is required to actually memorize and recite the individual rights articulated in the Bill of Rights will be better prepared to implement them in his or her day-to-day responsibilities of policing a free society.

Sources of Law

Once the philosophical and historical foundations of the law are firmly established, it is a logical progression to begin class instruction on the major sources of laws in the United States and to explain the key distinctions. The four main sources of laws in the United States are:

1. U.S. Constitution
2. English common law
3. Legal statutes
4. Court decisions

Because of its historical importance, the U.S. Constitution acts as the philosophical guide for the creation and interpretation of laws in America. At two separate levels of government—the U.S. Constitution at the federal level and the various state constitutions at the state level—written constitutions provide the foundation for the creation and interpretation of actual laws. In cases where an individual state law is passed that presents a contradiction to the U.S. Constitution, the U.S. Constitution would supplant the individual state law in question.

A second major source of criminal laws in the United States is known as English common law. Common law, or "customary law," comes from the days when the American colonies based their laws on the English common law or customs. Many of the most serious behaviors criminalized in America today are derived from the English common law dealing with such acts as murder, robbery, and arson. Throughout history, such acts were always considered wrong and forbidden, regardless of the presence of actual written laws. Such laws are therefore built on common beliefs or customs.

The third major source of laws is called **statute law**. Statutes are laws actually written by a legislative body. At the federal level, this is the U.S. Congress. Additionally, each state has its own legislative body, which enacts state laws applicable to its particular state. Finally, most municipal governments also have a legislative function typically called the city council, which passes local laws applicable only within that municipality. Collectively, at the various levels, these governmental bodies develop, propose, and pass laws that, when officially approved, become statutory laws.

The fourth major source of laws in the United States derives from the various court decisions. The role of the judiciary in the American Republic is to provide the final interpretation of the laws enacted through any of the other means discussed above. These court decisions or legal interpretations are known as case law. Just as with legal statutes, each level of government has its own court system to review cases. Generally speaking, the U.S. Supreme Court reviews the federal system, and the various state courts review state issues. Because these case decisions can have such a profound impact on the actual limitations of enforcement policies and practices of law enforcement, it is also important for potential police officers to dedicate a significant amount of instructional time reviewing the major court decisions and the case law established by each decision.

Primarily the Fourth and Fifth Amendments of the U.S. Constitution have provided the most significant case law in regard to police operations and behavior. Over the years, case law continues to evolve and further define the parameters of the law, and it is critical for student police officers to be aware of these landmark decisions. As police officers go about their day-to-day responsibilities, their actions are significantly bound by the landmark case law produced by the U.S. Supreme Court and other legal entities. Legal constraints, produced by this case law, govern such crucial procedures as the search and seizure of people and property, arrest procedures, and suspect interrogations. A solid working understanding of these landmark cases is necessary.

For example, case law interpretation of the Fourth Amendment provides significant legal constraints on property collection by officers. Legal concepts such as probable cause, arrest warrant, search warrant, and exclusionary rule must be covered in detail in the recruit's law curriculum. Just as *Weeks* v. *United States* established the exclusionary rule at the federal level, *Mapp* v. *Ohio* made the rule applicable to the various states.

Naturally, as the application of such case law develops, exceptions rise to the surface and require further interpretation by the U.S. Supreme Court. A few examples include *Silverthorn Lumber Co.* v. *United States,* which established the "fruit of the poisoned tree doctrine," and *Robinson* v. *United States,* which indicated that a search of a suspect incidental to a legal arrest did not violate applicable Fourth Amendment protections.

Wilson v. *Arkansas* was a 1995 case where the U.S. Supreme Court ruled that the police must knock and announce their identity before entering a dwelling even when they have a legal search warrant. Then, in 1997, the Supreme Court further ruled in *Richards* v. *Wisconsin* that the police could make a "no knock" entry if announcing their presence might inhibit the safe investigation of the crime.

Harris v. *United States* established that if police officers are in a place that they have a legal right to be in and see illegal property that is in plain view, that property could be seized. *United States* v. *Leon* found that evidence obtained when exercising an illegal search could still be admissible if the officers were acting in good faith. *Terry* v. *Ohio* established the now-famous stop and frisk exception, which states that a person can be briefly detained by a law enforcement officer without probable cause if the officer has a "reasonable suspicion" that that person has committed, or is about to commit, a crime. *Carroll* v. *United States* added that a warrantless search of an automobile is valid if based on probable cause that illegal contraband may be present. *Chimel* v. *California* went one step further to establish that when arresting a suspect, law enforcement officers can search an area in the immediate control of the person to ensure officer safety.

Another key area of law enforcement operations significantly impacted by case law is the Fifth Amendment of the U.S. Constitution and the whole area of suspect interrogations. In this area, *Brown* v. *Mississippi* established that convictions that rest solely on confessions shown to have been extorted by officers through the use of brutality or force are inconsistent with the due process clause and therefore are not allowed.

Miranda v. *Arizona* took the Fifth Amendment one step further and decided that suspects must be informed of their rights prior to any police custodial interrogation. Yet *New York* v. *Quarles* added that a legitimate public safety concern might justify an officer's questioning of a suspect without reading the Miranda warnings. *Illinois* v. *Perkins* established that the Miranda warnings are not needed when a suspect does not believe that he or she is talking to a law enforcement officer. *Escobedo* v. *Illinois* recognized the suspect's right to have legal council present during police interrogation. And finally, in *Arizona* v. *Fulminante*, the Court ruled that a confession was coerced in that specific case but also found that a coerced confession can be "a harmless trial error" if other evidence still proves guilt.

The point to be made is that in the rich history of American jurisprudence, case law can, and does, have a major impact on the day-to-day operational policies and practices of law enforcement. Therefore, as difficult and potentially confusing as it may be, case law *must* be a significant component of the police academy law curriculum.

LEGAL AUTHORITY OF THE POLICE

The police in the American Republic "are granted a great deal of legal authority under a system of government in which legal authority is reluctantly granted, and when granted, sharply curtailed" (Goldstein, 1977). This legal authority is required because the primary role of the police in the American criminal justice system is the initiatory role. That is, by utilizing the powers of arrest, the police can initiate the criminal justice process and instantly transform a free citizen into an incarcerated criminal suspect. Since the freedoms that are directly affected by such an arrest are the very same freedoms that Americans cherish the most—those of freedom, life, and liberty—a number of constitutional guarantees immediately apply once an arrest is made. Foremost in this regard are the guarantees outlined in the Bill of Rights. While the entire first ten amendments protect many of the basic rights and virtues on which a free republic is built, the First, Fourth, Fifth, and Sixth Amendments are the key amendments in regard to the legal authority, and limitations, of the police.

The First Amendment reads "Congress shall make no laws respecting an establishment of religion, or prohibiting the free exercise of; or abridging the freedom of speech, or the press, or of the right of the people to peacefully assemble, and to petition the government for a redress of grievances."

The Fourth Amendment provides that "the right of the people to be secure in their persons, homes, papers, and effects against unreasonable search and seizure, shall not be violated, and no warrants shall be issued but upon probable cause, supported by oath or affirmation, and particularly describing the place to be searched and the persons or things to be seized."

The Fifth Amendment indicates that "no person shall be held to answer for a capital, or other infamous crime, unless on a presentment or indictment of a grand jury, except in cases arising in the land or naval forces, or in the militia, when in actual services of time of war or great public danger; nor shall any person be subject for the same offense twice put in jeopardy of life or limb, nor shall he be compelled in any criminal case to be a witness against himself; nor be deprived of life, liberty or property without due process of law; nor shall private property be taken for public use without just compensation."

The Sixth Amendment requires that "in all criminal prosecutions, the accused will enjoy the right to a speedy and public trial, by an impartial jury of the state and district wherein the crime shall have been committed, which district shall have been previously ascertained by law, and to be informed of the nature and cause of the accusation; to be confronted with the witnesses against him; to have compulsory process for obtaining witnesses in his favor, and to have the assistance of counsel for his defense."

Collectively, these key statements of the Bill of Rights provide the very framework of the legal authority and limitations of the police. While the various states may pass legislation that further restricts the activity and procedures of the police in their respective jurisdictions, the Bill of Rights remains the outside parameter of police legal authority.

A detailed review and lessons on the Bill of Rights are imperative to the proper education of a police student. It establishes both a conceptual framework and the actual source of law enforcement authority. Legal concepts such as due process of law and unreasonable search and seizure are vague by design and subject to different interpretations, yet they are the very essence of actual police action taken on the streets on a daily basis.

Probable Cause

The requirement of **probable cause** for police action in the American legal system is taken exactly from the language found in the Fourth Amendment. While an exact definition of probable cause is difficult, if not impossible, to legally or historically document, perhaps the most widely accepted definition is based on case law. Probable cause exists where the facts and circumstances within the knowledge of the arresting officer, and of which the arresting officer has reasonably trustworthy information, are sufficient in themselves to warrant a person of reasonable caution believing that an offense has been or is being committed, as in the case of an arrest warrant, or that property could be found in a particular place or on a particular person, as in the case of a search warrant (*Carroll* v. *United States,* 1925).

While this definition may seem clear to an attorney or a judge, it may still seem confusing to a student or even an experienced practitioner of law enforcement. A more practical or operational explanation of the legal concept may be simply this: an honest belief of a reasonable man as to the guilt of a suspect. Since such an honest belief will ultimately be tested in a court of law through the review of an affidavit or actual testimony used to justify a warrant, this fairly complex legal concept is actually realized in every arrest made by a police officer. Regardless of whether an arrest is executed with or without a warrant, probable cause must be established for the charges to hold up under judicial scrutiny. In all cases, probable cause must be clearly established before or at the time of an arrest. A legal arrest cannot be justified with facts that turn up after a person is taken into police custody. Because of this, the role of the police academy in educating student officers to recognize the absolutely critical legal concept of probable cause cannot be overstated.

Arrest and Search Warrants

Arrests that are made on the basis of a legal **arrest warrant** are normally very sound. As a practical consideration, arrests that are made with a signed arrest warrant have already established probable cause and usually originate from an investigative section of a police agency. However, patrol officers, due to the reactive nature of their assignments, are normally confronted with the types of cases that do not allow them time to obtain an arrest warrant. Arrests made without an arrest warrant are equally sound, but a bit more risky for the officer.

There are many benefits to obtaining an arrest warrant prior to taking a suspect into police custody. These benefits are unique in that they serve the interests of the police, the citizens of a free society, and the public in general. The first advantage is that a warrant signed by a neutral and detached judge allows an individual somewhat removed from the facts and emotions of a case to make the probable cause determination. Sometimes, police officers investigating a case have what they believe to be enough information to establish probable cause when, in fact, all they have is a small amount of hearsay that would not be allowed in a court of law. As a direct result of this, it is better for law enforcement if a neutral and detached judge reviews a case when it is still in the investigative stage. Further, by conducting an investigation in this manner, the chance of having a case thrown out of court in the end is minimized.

An additional advantage to obtaining an arrest warrant prior to taking police action is the fact that it assures the party who is being arrested of the legal authority of the act. When a police officer executes an arrest and has a signed arrest warrant to show the suspected individual, the actual physical aspects of the arrest are usually much easier. Few suspects will resist arrest or question the authority of the police to carry one out when a signed arrest warrant is presented to them clearly indicating who is to be arrested and what they are to be charged with.

A **search warrant** is equally important and helpful to police officers when they are executing a lawful arrest. An advantage of making an arrest with a search warrant is that after the arrest is executed, a subsequent search can be systematically performed to gather and document additional evidence in a case.

As in the case of the arrest warrant, a neutral and detached judge who can clearly establish probable cause for a search, as well as indicate in advance the proper boundaries of the search, can sign a search warrant. Both arrest and search warrants find their legal authority directly in the Fourth Amendment of the U.S. Constitution. In that amendment, it clearly states, "No warrants shall be issued but upon probable cause, supported by oath or affirmation."

In the case of a search warrant, a sworn affidavit must state precisely what the police will be searching for, where they expect to find it, and what information they possess that leads them to believe the property is there. As in the case of the arrest warrant, a search warrant is also strongly encouraged by the courts. Since it is clearly stated in the Fourth Amendment that there will be no "unreasonable searches and seizures," searches conducted without the benefit of a warrant are carefully reviewed in the judicial system and can sometimes result in key evidence in a criminal trial being disallowed.

The legal advantages of arrest and search warrants must be stressed during police officer training because traditionally police officers have viewed warrants as an obstacle to their job rather than an asset. Through the combination of better education and training of police officers in such legal requirements and the further clarification of the standard by the courts, the issue of warrants is rarely an obstacle for police officers with good intentions. For example, the U.S. Supreme Court has adopted a more flexible "totality of the circumstances test" (*Gates* v. *Illinois*, 1983). This test is utilized to determine the sufficiency of a probable cause statement made in an affidavit for a warrant based on an informant's tip.

This totality of the circumstances test is a little more tolerant than the more difficult "two prong test" that was previously required in the *Aguilar* v. *Texas* and *Spinelli* v. *United States* cases. The two prong test required police officers to prove both the reliability of the information and the reliability of the informant providing such information. This two-pronged standard often required a much more significant amount of investigative time and resources to meet. With the totality of the circumstances test, the two prongs are still there, but an exceptionally strong showing on one can make up for a weak showing on the other.

Further legal clarification of the standard to obtain warrants was also found in the "good faith exception" to the exclusionary rule. Based on such cases as *United States* v. *Leon* and *Massachusetts* v. *Sheppard,* the good faith exception generally established that if an affidavit establishes probable cause that is later determined to be insufficient, or if the format of the warrant is later determined to be invalid, the evidence seized in the case is still valid. While not all states may recognize a good faith exception under state law, all police officers should be aware of the general legal expectation that they must approach all searches and seizures with due regard to such rights.

Finally, another example of legal clarification in the matter of warrants can be found at the National Center for Missing and Exploited Children. The center includes in its training of law enforcement officers a profile of suspects who sexually abuse children or who are involved with child pornography. They believe that by including such character traits in a written affidavit for arrest and search warrants, probable cause can be established not only to arrest a suspect but to completely search the home in an effort to locate additional evidence. This would help the case because the character traits indicate that pedophiles typically collect and save pictures of their victims. If law enforcement officers can recover these types of pictures, their potential value in identification of additional victims and later as evidence can be enormous.

Arrest without a Warrant

The legal authority to arrest without a warrant is based on legislative authority granted by state statute. Accordingly, the exact legal requirements do vary from state to state, and the legal authority covers many separate situations that a police officer may encounter. First, police may make an arrest on the spot, without a warrant, for any offense that is committed in their view. This authority applies to a crime or a breach of the peace, a felony or a misdemeanor. It would apply to a situation where a police officer finds a suspicious person under suspicious circumstances.

If a police officer, based on his or her training, has probable cause to believe that a person has committed a crime, or is about to commit some offense against the law, the officer can make an arrest. Additionally, a police officer may execute an arrest without a warrant in cases where a "credible person" informs the officer that an individual has committed a felony, or when the police officer believes that a crime has been committed, and there is no time to secure a warrant. Again, due to the reactive nature of patrol assignments, police officers most often find themselves in situations that dictate an arrest without a warrant. While this practice is legally sound, it requires a good deal of education and training for the police officers who must make these distinctions on the street.

Police officers must also learn that determinations as to whether an arrest without a warrant, and any subsequent search and seizure, will be admitted in court will be made on a case-by-case basis. A sample of two significant situations that have set the tone for practice in law enforcement offers an illustration of these determinations. For example, it has been established that an "on-view" arrest, made without a warrant in a public place and based on probable cause, and a subsequent search of an automobile did *not* violate the Fourth Amendment requirement (*United States* v. *Watson,* 1976). Further, such an arrest remains valid even if the officers had the time to secure a legal search warrant.

At the other extreme, it was subsequently established that the Fourth and Fourteenth Amendments *did* prohibit the police from making a warrantless, and thus unconstitutional, entry into a suspect's house to make a routine arrest (*Payton* v. *New York,* 1980). The perspective of this case was different because it was in regard to private property, and the Court could not be as generous as in the *Watson* case.

Authority to Detain a Citizen

The temporary detention, or "stop, question, and possibly frisk" (as it is known to police officers), may occur when a police officer has observed a situation where the facts would lead a "reasonable person" to infer that some criminal activity has taken place. The interesting aspect of temporary detentions is that the police officer must observe something, but not necessarily enough to establish probable cause. This is the case because probable cause is required to make an arrest, but the courts have consistently maintained that a temporary detention is not an arrest, so the standard can be lower (see Figure 5-1). In essence, there exist three standards for the police in the United States:

1. There is the lowest standard, a mere suspicion, when an officer has no legal reason to stop a citizen to discuss a crime but may have a common law right of inquiry.
2. There is the situation when a police officer notices something that arouses enough suspicion to look into a situation but not enough to actually establish probable cause to make an arrest. This standard, a reasonable suspicion, is recognized as a result

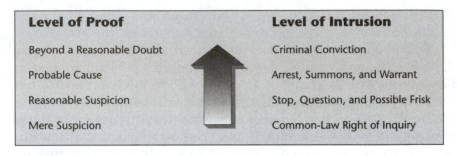

Level of Proof	Level of Intrusion
Beyond a Reasonable Doubt	Criminal Conviction
Probable Cause	Arrest, Summons, and Warrant
Reasonable Suspicion	Stop, Question, and Possible Frisk
Mere Suspicion	Common-Law Right of Inquiry

FIGURE 5-1

of the education, training, and experience of an officer and may result in a temporary stop, question, and possible frisk.

3. The highest standard, probable cause, is when a crime has been committed or is about to be committed. This standard can result in an arrest of a suspect and initiate a full array of constitutional protections that are provided to all citizens.

The original legal authority for temporary detention is based in case law. In the landmark case of *Terry* v. *Ohio* (1968), the U.S. Supreme Court held that the Fourth Amendment right against search and seizure, applied to the states by the Fourteenth Amendment, "protects people, not places." What the Court meant is that the Fourth Amendment applies as much to people on the street as it does to people in their homes. However, it was further stated that the exclusionary rule couldn't be properly invoked to exclude the products of a legitimate and restrained police investigative technique, such as the temporary detention. In this regard, it was clear that where a reasonably prudent police officer is warranted by the circumstances of a given situation to believe that his or her safety, or the safety of others, may be at risk, the officer might make a reasonable effort to search for weapons.

In the *Terry* case, a Cleveland police officer observed Mr. Terry and another man in front of a downtown store, apparently casing the location for a robbery. The officer, fearing that the men might be armed, approached them and identified himself as a police officer. At that time, the officer grabbed Terry, spun him around, and patted down the outside of Terry's clothing. He felt a pistol in the subject's left pocket and tried to reach in and grab it. He then ordered Terry and the other man into the store, removed Terry's coat, and found a .38 caliber revolver. Another gun was found on Terry's companion. Terry was convicted of carrying a concealed weapon and sentenced to the statutorily prescribed term of three years in prison.

After the appeals were dismissed, the U.S. Supreme Court agreed to hear the case to determine if the search and seizure of the pistol violated Terry's Fourth and Fourteenth Amendment rights. The conviction was ultimately affirmed. The applicability of the Fourth Amendment stop, question, and frisk procedures and the approval of a police officer's search of a person for a weapon, regardless of probable cause for a crime, are important to understand. However, such a search must be made with the belief that the officer's safety, or the safety of others, is at imminent risk.

Based on the *Terry* v. *Ohio* decision, police officers in all states must be trained to take certain actions when faced with dangerous circumstances:

- They must clearly and unmistakably identify themselves as police officers.
- They may then ask reasonable questions in regard to the circumstances that suspects have placed themselves in.
- If the initial questions and pat-down of the outer garment dispel the officer's fear for safety, the confrontation is ended.
- If fear for the officer's safety remains, an officer may conduct a carefully limited search of a suspect's outer clothing. Such a search can be conducted in an attempt to discover any weapons. If a weapon is found in this type of search, it may be seized and used as a basis for a lawful arrest.

All of these legal considerations are established in an effort to balance the constitutional protections against unlawful searches on one side with the police officer's safety and survival on the other. They are all based on rather vague legal definitions and require extensive education and training to provide an officer with the ability and confidence to effectively accomplish the mission safely.

Authority to Use Force

Any legal authority granted to the police in a free society to carry out their duties and responsibilities without the corresponding legal authority to effect the amount of force necessary to actually carry out a lawful arrest would be futile. Even given this realization, the use of force authorized and utilized by the police must always be limited to the least amount necessary to end the resistance.

Police officers in a free society must learn and understand that everything changes when you take an oath of office. Unlike John Q. Citizen, police officers have different rules of engagement. As a police officer, even if you win a fight, you lose. Police officers must understand that the purpose of a police confrontation is to end it, not to win it.

They must know that the best kind of compliance in a free society is voluntary compliance. Experienced officers will agree that they simply don't get paid enough money to unnecessarily risk their lives in preventable street confrontations. However, given that the best compliance in a free society is voluntary compliance and given that preventable street confrontations are more trouble to an officer than they are worth, at some point, enforcing the law can ultimately require the use of force. Some bad guys will simply refuse reason and require forcible intervention by a police officer. This point is usually realized in the case of self-defense. Legally, police officers can use the amount of force necessary to protect themselves, or another, against an unlawful attack. In fact, even if the ultimate force, deadly force, is necessary, it may be utilized.

Normally, in cases where deadly force would be used, individual department policy and training requirements are even more restrictive than state law. Clear and compelling proof of this can be found in reading almost any major city police department's patrol guide in regard to the police use of force. Typically, such policies require that an agency investigate a police use of force case the very same way it would investigate any use of force. But police use of force cases are also investigated by the Internal Affairs Division to determine if there were any violations of departmental policy or procedures. They are investigated by a representative of the District Attorney's Office to determine if there were any violations of local or state laws, and sometimes even an investigator from the Federal Bureau of Investigation ascertains if there were any potential civil rights violations involved.

Each of these different and autonomous agencies investigates the same use of force situation to ensure that a police shooting is justified from every possible angle of the law. This extensive and overlapping review of every police use of deadly force is indicative of how serious a free democracy considers the issue. Finally, in jurisdictions where a grand jury exists, many cases of police use of force are automatically referred to the grand jury to provide yet another layer of civilian review.

LIMITATIONS ON THE LEGAL AUTHORITY OF THE POLICE

Clearly, an American Republic that places such a high value on life and freedom must have extensive legal controls, in addition to procedural controls, on the authority granted to the police. These legal controls are of such importance that they can be directly traced to the U.S. Constitution, and they carry with them immense liabilities for violations. Therefore, the police academy must include a comprehensive discussion of these limitations and the implications they carry with them on police behavior. An example of such a limitation is the entrapment defense.

The entrapment defense is philosophically based in the due process clause of the Fourteenth Amendment. The belief is that to entrap a citizen into committing a crime clearly would violate the fundamental fairness doctrine of the due process clause. The rule of law in regard to the entrapment issue was established in the case of *United States* v. *Russell*. In the *Russell* case, two separate standards of entrapment were established: the subjective standard and the objective standard.

The subjective standard and the objective standard are both legally accepted standards. The subjective standard focuses on the behavior of the suspect to determine if he or she is "predisposed to commit crime" (*United States* v. *Russell*). If the suspect's record and/or actions indicate that he or she would have been involved in a particular type of criminal activity regardless of the police intervention, then the entrapment defense will not be successful.

The objective standard focuses on the behavior of the police agent. If the involvement of the police was to an "intolerant degree," then the entrapment defense can be successful (*United States* v. *Russell*). Today, most jurisdictions in this country utilize the subjective standard. That is, once the defense of entrapment is raised in a court of law, the focus of the judicial inquiry will immediately shift to the behavior and actions of the suspect. As the entrapment defense exists, it presents a limitation to how far the police can go to become involved in a criminal enterprise, a limitation that remains intact to constantly maintain the checks and balances inherent in policing a democracy.

Another example of such limitations of police authority is the potential false arrest liability. A false arrest is made by a police officer who, with a claim of official authority under color of law, places the wrong person under arrest. Often confused with a false arrest is the concept of false imprisonment. False imprisonment is an illegal detention made by a civilian with no claim of police authority. A third offense that is often incorrectly confused with illegal detention is kidnapping. A kidnapping, or the holding of a person against his or her consent, can be the same as false imprisonment, but with the additional element of transporting that person to another location. Kidnapping also requires no claim of official authority.

In essence, the legal limitations on the police in regard to arresting the wrong person carry with them the ever-present potential of civil liability. The possibility of a false arrest, and the subsequent civil liability, is a consideration that faces any law enforcement officer who chooses to assert authority without first allowing for the proper probable cause considerations. The proper recognition of probable cause is almost always a direct result of how well the police are trained in this critical area of law. From the government's perspective, perhaps the most effective means of protecting free citizens from police abuse is the redress of civil liability. From the police's perspective, the best means of protecting against police abuse is clear policy guidelines and effective education and training in the law curriculum.

The final and extraordinarily essential consideration in the discussion of the limitations of the legal authority of the police to use force is found in the **Civil Rights Act** (United States Code, Title 42, Section 1983). Claims against the police under the United States Code, Title 42, Section 1983, allow individuals with claims against the police a choice of access to the federal courts or the state courts to have their claims resolved. This can be especially important in federal civil rights cases, where the losing party pays the necessary legal fees for both parties. Thus, an indigent party is not denied judicial relief for a legitimate civil rights claim due to financial status.

There are four basic requirements to bring a United States Code, Title 42, Section 1983, suit to the federal courts:

1. A defendant must be a natural person, not a state government. An individual can sue a local municipal or county agency under Section 1983, but the agency must be below the state level.

2. The local agencies, whether they are a police department or a school district, are usually targeted because agencies normally have deeper pockets than individuals representing the agency, thus creating more room for a potentially large monetary judgment.

3. The defendant must have been acting under color of law. Since most all police officers are considered on duty twenty-four hours a day, seven days a week, this requirement against the police is normally easily established.

4. An alleged violation by the defendant must be of a federal constitutionally protected right. This criterion is also not especially difficult to meet because almost any civil rights violation will usually violate the constitutionally protected rights of "due process of law" or "equal protection of law."

5. The alleged violation must be of constitutional-level severity or simply must be very serious.

Since any case brought against an individual officer and/or his or her agency will have very serious implications, police officers must be educated and trained in the concepts of the United States Code, Title 42, Section 1983, principles. The potential damages to a police officer, the agency, the municipality, an aggrieved citizen, and the overall appearance of justice in the republic can be astonishing if this matter is not effectively covered in the police academy law instruction.

DIFFERENT TYPES OF LAWS

In addition to the various sources of laws and police officer authority to enforce the laws, police officers must study the different types of laws. For the most part, police officers make their living enforcing the least serious type of criminal activities, called offenses or **quality-of-life offenses**. Quality-of-life crimes refer to the less serious crimes such as drinking beer in public, urinating in public, jaywalking, making excessive noise, panhandling, creating graffiti, evading paying fares (for example, jumping over the turnstile in the subway or bus station), littering, and spitting on the sidewalk. The typical police reaction to quality-of-life offenses is to issue a summons and release the suspect. However, young police officers should be taught that enforcing a quality-of-life offense provides an officer with the requisite probable cause to stop and talk to a citizen. These types of interactions can sometimes lead to the discovery of outstanding felony warrants, illegal narcotics and/or illegal firearms, or even an important bit of information the police may be looking for to solve another more serious crime. In fact, the significant reduction in serious crime realized in New York City over the last ten years is due, at least in part, to a focus on the minor infractions usually classified as offenses.

Typically, those individuals who come to the attention of the police by virtue of a minor offense turn out to be wanted for more serious offenses. Therefore, although offenses are the least serious type of criminal activity and it may seem counterintuitive to a young police officer to bother with them, it is simply good police work to pay attention to and enforce them.

A second type of law is the **misdemeanor**. In the American legal system, the misdemeanor is a relatively minor offense that could be punishable by a fine and/or a jail sentence of less than one year in a local jail facility. Normally, misdemeanor offenses are punishable by suspended sentences, community service, and/or fines. Although they may vary state to state, misdemeanor offenses typically include petty thefts, disturbing the peace, disorderly conduct, and other relatively minor criminal offenses.

Finally, the most serious type of crime faced by a police officer is called a **felony**. The felonies are the most serious type of criminal behavior, typically including crimes such as aggravated assault, rape, robbery, arson, and murder. Because of their seriousness, felonies can be punishable by anything from a fine and/or a long prison sentence to the death penalty. A felony is defined as a serious criminal offense that is punishable by incarceration in prison (for a minimum of one year) or, in some cases, death.

Effective Courtroom Testimony

Yet another major consideration for the law curriculum in a professional police academy is the inclusion of class study and actual courtroom practice in the art of giving effective, professional, and credible testimony. When police officers enter the witness stand to give sworn testimony in a criminal case, they are playing a critical role in the criminal justice process. Accordingly, their honesty, professional demeanor, knowledge of the facts of the case, preparation, and credibility are critical to the successful conviction of criminal defendants. Effective testimony is not a simple instinctive skill; it must be learned and practiced.

To be effective, police academy lessons in professional courtroom testimony should openly and honestly discuss the following issues:

Professional Courtroom Testimony

- Reasons a good police officer might lie under oath
- What is at risk if an officer lies under oath
- Importance of preparation before testifying
- Perjury and the possible implications of perjury
- Tampering with evidence issues
- Issues involving eyewitness testimony
- Various rules of evidence and suppression hearings
- Testimony before petit juries versus grand juries

Armed with this knowledge, police recruits must, at some point, actually get up on a witness stand and be cross-examined by an experienced attorney. For the most part, local district attorney offices are more than willing to participate in these training efforts because effective law enforcement is so important to their mission. Many criminal cases are won or lost primarily on the merits of law enforcement testimony. Effective courtroom testimony, when it is done correctly, can be the finishing touch of effective police work. If the testimony is ineffective, however, it can be the deathblow to an effective prosecution.

CONCLUSION

A solid working understanding of the law is, by definition, critical to effective law enforcement. One cannot enforce the law if one does not know and understand the law! Police officers will not respect the law if they were never instructed in the history and purpose of the law in a free society. Although street cops will probably never be required to be lawyers, they are always expected to possess a good working knowledge of the concepts, principles, statutes, and intentions of the legal system. Due to the level of difficulty associated with this responsibility, however, professional police academies should be prepared to dedicate approximately a hundred hours of instruction solely to legal issues for new recruits. They must also be prepared to dedicate significant resources to the ongoing legal education of their members, providing legal updates and briefs as legal concepts and practices change.

Police departments can either pay now for the effective education and training of their police officers or pay significantly more later for the civil judgments imposed on them for the mistakes of their members.

KEY TERMS

Arrest Warrant

Bill of Rights

Civil Rights Act

Code of Hammurabi

Federalist Papers

Felony

Magna Carta

Misdemeanor

Probable Cause

Quality-of-life Offenses

Search Warrant

Statute Law

U.S. Constitution

QUESTIONS FOR DISCUSSION

1. Why is it important for student police officers to study and understand the history of the law?
2. What are the Federalist Papers, and what is their significance to modern-day law enforcement practices?
3. From a legal perspective, what is the source of the major differences in policing a free society and policing in more repressive societies?
4. What are the four sources of law in the United States?
5. Why is it necessary for police officers to possess such a comprehensive knowledge of the various legal issues surrounding their operational responsibilities, and what can be done to keep their knowledge current and accurate?
6. Define probable cause. How can American law enforcement operate on such a vague concept?

7. Define and discuss the legal authority to arrest without an arrest warrant.
8. What are the various levels of proof needed for the police to intrude on the freedoms of a private citizen?
9. In the real world, how can the police balance the need for officer safety and survival against the individual's right to be safe from unreasonable search and seizure?
10. Why is the United States Code, Title 42, Section 1983, important to police education and training? What are the significant issues for the police?

SUGGESTED READINGS

Aguilar v. *Texas* (1964) 378 U.S. 108.

Arizona v. *Fulminante* (1991) 111 S.Ct. 1246.

Brown v. *Mississippi* (1936) 297 U.S. 278.

Carroll v. *United States* (1925) 267 U.S. 132.

Chimel v. *California* (1969) 89 S.Ct. 2034.

Escobedo v. *Illinois* (1994) 378 U.S. 478.

Gates v. *Illinois* (1983) 462 U.S. 213.

Goldstein, Herman. (1977). *Policing a free society.* Cambridge, MA: Ballinger Publishing Company.

Harris v. *United States* (1968) 390 U.S. 234.

Illinois v. *Perkins* (1991) 110 U.S. 2394.

Mapp v. *Ohio* (1961) 367 U.S. 643.

Massachusetts v. *Sheppard* (1984) 82 L.Ed. 2nd 737.

Miranda v. *Arizona* (1966) 384 U.S. 436.

New York v. *Quarles* (1991) 104 S.Ct. 1246.

Payton v. *New York* (1980) 445 U.S. 573.

Richards v. *Wisconsin* (1997) 117 S.Ct. 1416.

Robinson v. *United States* (1973) 414 U.S. 218.

Silverthorn Lumber Company v. *United States* (1920) 251 U.S. 385.

Spinelli v. *United States* (1969) 393 U.S. 410.

Terry v. *Ohio* (1968) 392 U.S. 1.

United States Code, Title 42, Section 1983.

United States Constitution.

United States v. *Leon* (1984) 82 L.Ed. 2nd 677.
United States v. *Russell* (1985) 411 U.S. 423.
United States v. *Watson* (1976) 423 U.S. 411.
Weeks v. *United States* (1914) 232 U.S. 383.
Wilson v. *Arkansas* (1995) 115 S.Ct. 1914.

The Federalist Papers

Federalist Papers I. A general introduction. Alexander Hamilton.
Federalist Papers X. The union as a safeguard against domestic factions and insurrection. James Madison.
Federalist Papers LI. The structures of the government to furnish proper checks and balances between the different departments. Alexander Hamilton and James Madison.
Federalist Papers LXXVIII. The judiciary department. Alexander Hamilton.
Federalist Papers LXXXI. The distribution of judicial authority. Alexander Hamilton.

EDUCATING AND TRAINING NEW POLICE OFFICERS

Teaching the Behavioral Sciences

"The sociological imagination is not merely a fashion. It is a quality of mind that seems most dramatically to promise an understanding of the intimate realities of ourselves in connection with larger social realities."

—C. Wright Mills

INTRODUCTION

Of all the various technical and academic disciplines taught in police academies around the world today, the behavioral sciences are the most overlooked, neglected, and misunderstood. That seems to be the case regardless of the type, size, organizational structure, or geographic location of the academy. This realization is a major issue facing the education and training of American policing because the behavioral sciences are also, without a question, the most important. That's right, the most important!

A solid foundation in the behavioral sciences is a decisive factor in the development of young police officers for so many critical reasons. For example, many, if not most, of the young men and women

113

entering policing bring with them preconceived expectations about exactly what the police do every day. The problem is that these preconceived expectations are based on media images, not reality. The behavioral sciences can correct such preconceived notions early in a career and prevent many problems that traditionally develop down the road as a result of such occupational misconceptions.

The importance of dedicating enough time and methodically teaching the behavioral sciences in a police academy is misunderstood in that many law enforcement instructors and students assume the wrong instructional motives. The behavioral sciences are *not* important to police officers because it is expected that once they "see the light," they too will coddle and pamper a criminal suspect on the street and seek to communicate with a perpetrator's "inner child" instead of making an arrest. There is no danger of that ever happening. The police have always had very little control over the complex sociological factors that contribute to criminality. Ask a criminologist what causes crime, and he or she will offer a long litany of sociological, biological, structural, economic, and philosophical factors. On the other hand, ask a police officer to explain what causes crime, and he or she will simply answer with one word: criminals.

Such a typical police response to the causes of crime is perfectly acceptable and role-appropriate. No reasonable person should ever believe that teaching the behavioral sciences in a police academy environment to people who are preparing to enforce the law for a living could ever change that. Instead, it should be realized that teaching the behavioral sciences in a police academy environment is valuable because it provides young officers with the intellectual and emotional perspectives they need to understand, process, and effectively deal with the constant exposure to the dark side of humanity.

It may very well be that the most appropriate police response to a specific domestic or street disturbance is a law enforcement response: to take command of a scene, offer first aid to the injured, make an arrest, and restore order to the situation. But at the end of the tour, police officers are still human beings, and they still need to go home to their families and process and understand the complexities of human behavior that they are called on to deal with every day. First and foremost, police officers need the behavioral sciences for their own psychological well-being. But beyond that, those who possess the background provided by the behavioral sciences are less likely to process what they see every day through the use of racial stereotypes and racist epithets and more likely to truly comprehend a crime scene for what it is, and to thereby find it in their hearts to apply compassion in their response.

In short, police officers in the American Republic need to possess physical courage, moral courage, bravery, integrity, and the sociological imagination (Mills, 1959). Then, and only then, can the law enforcement part of what the police do for a living make any sense.

THE BEHAVIORAL SCIENCES

Police officers must be educated to view the world with the type of mind that provides a comprehensive perspective and appreciation of diversity. They must know that where you stand depends on where you sit. They must be continuously reminded that the day-to-day troubles that they are called on to reconcile are, in the total scheme of things, isolated human incidents typically representative of a much larger social reality.

Even appreciating the underlying conservative slant and preference for personal responsibility that most police officers bring to the job by virtue of their backgrounds, it must still be acknowledged that, to a certain extent, human beings are the product of their life experiences. Such life experiences, especially in a multicultural society built on various waves of immigration, can be very different, repressive, intimidating, and overwhelming.

Accordingly, when the police answer a 911 call for service in response to a public disturbance, all of this historical baggage is waiting for them at the scene. Like it or not, the uniformed police represent the most visible form of government, and they must at least be aware of all the various sociological factors involved in their job responsibilities. These factors affect what the officers expect to find at a scene when they are called, the way they actually react when they arrive, the manner in which they interpret what is said and what is done, and ultimately the way they view officer safety and survival.

TEACHING THE BEHAVIORAL SCIENCES

Philosophically, intellectually, practically, and even from an instructional perspective, this is not easily accomplished. Before newly hired police recruits begin to study at a police academy, they almost always expect to spend a good deal of time learning police science. Every new police officer seems to anxiously anticipate going to the firearms range and learning firearms proficiency and the appropriate use of force options. Naturally, a police recruit expects to study the law because it is immediately apparent that one cannot enforce the law unless one knows the law. New police recruits even expect to attend the gym each day to build their strength and establish the necessary physical shape for the rigors of police work. Indeed, new recruits expect all of these law enforcement subjects because they are perfectly consistent with the preconceived notions and expectations they bring to the job as they begin an exciting new career in American law enforcement.

However, in this day and age, newly hired police recruits (and to a lesser extent, even veteran officers returning for in-service instruction) are confronted with extensive blocks of instruction in such topics as social structure, culture, cultural conflict, prejudice, the nature and causes of prejudice, myths that cause prejudice, both blatant and subtle discrimination, social issues of power as they relate to governmental powers, the need for equal justice, the family in crisis, effective communication, deviance and criminality, various religious beliefs and their associated behaviors, **victimology**, tolerance, sensitivity, and many other classic subjects in the behavioral sciences.

Nationwide, police officers are called on to maintain order at public demonstrations where the chants of "No justice, no peace" can be heard. Videotapes appear on the national news networks from Los Angeles, Inglewood, Oklahoma City, and other cities raising questions about how the police are trained. An effective behavioral sciences curriculum can at least expose officers to the genesis of these chants and these concerns. Whether the police agree with them or not, the sentiments are real, and if such concerns are not addressed in police training, they will explode into public violence.

It can be very challenging to teach such subjects at a police academy for a number of reasons. The study of sociology, psychology, and other classic behavioral sciences is expected at a university, but not normally at a police academy. Yet, every agency must develop some sort of integrated approach to manage the role of the university and the role of the police academy in this critical area.

Additionally, these blocks of instruction are usually uncomfortable and unappreciated by police officers at all levels of experience for a number of reasons. First, they are typically taken out of their proper context. Instruction in the behavioral sciences should never consist of an isolated presentation about "the need to be sensitive." Instead, the instruction must have some practical value and should be linked to the larger picture. Once the relevance is properly established, a specific topic such as victimology or immigration can be appropriately discussed as a component of that larger sociological picture.

BEHAVIORAL SCIENCES CURRICULUM

Effective Communications
Police Officer Demeanor
Myths about Policing
Attitudes, Perceptions,
  and Myths
Racism, Sexism, and
  Homophobia
Hate Crimes
Immigration, Migration,
  and Diversity
Lesbian, Gay, Bisexual, and
  Transgender Communities
Authority and Ethics
Factors in Human Behavior
Poverty
Victimology
Homelessness
Student Presentations on
  Their Family
Dealing with the Elderly
Culture and Cultural Conflict

African American Community
Latino Community
Special Populations in the Community
Caribbean Community
Asian and Arab Communities
Russian Community
Religious Diversity
Professional Discretion
Police and the Media
Stress and Distress
Mental Illness
Crisis Intervention
Death and Dying
Issues in Suicide
Psychological Wellness
Juvenile Justice
Social Structure

Total = Approximately 125 Hours of Instruction

Consider the subjects outlined below in the sample behavioral sciences curriculum. Collectively, they represent many of the typical subject matters police officers should be taught during their training. However, any one of these subjects taken out of the proper context and presented at the beginning of a firearms session, or during a twenty-minute roll-call briefing at a precinct, would run the risk of appearing to be more administrative gibberish by the officers and easily dismissed.

Perhaps one of the biggest mistakes a police academy can make in the instruction of the behavioral sciences is to simply affix a block of instruction in one of these matters between other blocks of instruction involving more exciting police tactical considerations. Any behavioral sciences subject presented in isolation from the larger context will run the risk of seeming silly and a necessary evil to student police officers who are, rightfully, more concerned with information that will save them from getting physically injured, administratively fired, or criminally indicted.

Secondly, the behavioral sciences subjects are matters that require more advanced and time-consuming instructional methods of education, not just training. They are conceptual in nature, not perceptual. They are value-driven, reflective, and relative, not simply a matter of what is right and what is wrong. Police officers cannot always see or feel the need to discuss sociological matters as clearly as they can the need to hold a firearm or fill out a form in police science. Unfortunately, these discussions tend to be very theoretical in nature and touchy-feely in content, not a traditional strength of police officers or police academies.

Thirdly, newly hired police recruits are typically young and often simply do not yet have many of the adult experiences of life, let alone the practical street experiences of a veteran police officer. Without these experiences, it is difficult for them to possess the necessary perspective to properly understand how such matters can impact their ability to effectively do their job. Contrary to popular opinion, creating police officer sensitivity—creating the **sociological imagination**—is not simply a matter of telling officers information; it is, instead, a matter of creating the necessary perspective for them to fully comprehend the information.

Creating the Sociological Imagination

- How can one possibly understand the psychological trauma involved in being the victim of a violent crime if one has never been a victim, experienced a loved one being a victim, or even met a real-life crime victim?

- How can a police academy instructor inspire police recruits to take care of crime victims and secondary crime victims (such as husbands and mothers) if the police recruit is a twenty-two-year-old who still lives at home with his parents and has not yet learned how to take care of himself?

- How can recruits judge the actions of an immigrant who runs afoul of the law if they were never told that, just a few short generations ago, their great-grandparents might have been in the same boat?

- How can a higher sense of empathy or compassion be instilled in a police officer who has never considered the proverb "There but for the grace of God go I"?

Finally, teaching the behavioral sciences can be awkward because it requires the discussion and examination of some very fundamental cultural beliefs that can be uncomfortable for people to openly discuss. In this age of political correctness, many young adults are reluctant to participate in a group discussion with a multicultural collection of classmates and openly discuss their most personal feelings in regard to race, culture, sexual orientation, and other issues so deeply rooted in their upbringing.

In spite of all these legitimate reasons, however, a police academy is exactly the kind of venue where such discussions and interactions are essential. They are essential not because of some desire for political correctness or political expediency but because of the unique position of power and authority police officers hold in a free society. And because of this unique position of power and authority, police officers are expected to enforce the law in a manner that is as impartial as humanly possible and in a way that advances freedom and social justice. To do that, police officers must be prepared to accept the fact that they will constantly be held to a higher standard than an average citizen. When police officers act under color of law, they are, in effect, a living personification of the American Republic.

Risks Involved

It is important to note that while the establishment of a cutting-edge, progressive behavioral sciences curriculum is critically important to the development of law enforcement officers, it is also not without risk. Open discussions of topics such as culture, race, and sexual orientation carry with them a certain risk to a law enforcement agency, an academy director or commanding officer, and police academy instructors. Conversations that take place in the classroom can be taken out of context and appear in the morning newspapers.

Comments made by one officer may be offensive to another and, if not properly managed, can lead to classroom confrontations. Sometimes the best-intentioned lessons of the behavioral sciences can be potentially explosive and paint an instructor as a racist, which, paradoxically, is exactly the opposite of what is being attempted. Discussions about profiling as a law enforcement tool can quickly degenerate into discussions about racial profiling and offend student officers. Indeed, in many ways, instruction in the behavioral sciences can be risky business.

An excellent tool for teaching these subjects is to invite certain members of the community in to lecture recruit officers on their particular community. Many departments invite guest speakers from certain minority communities and/or agencies that work with the police. It is an effective learning strategy to allow certain groups to appear at the police academy and to speak and represent themselves. But some speakers invited to the police academy to speak from a minority community may go off topic and say something offensive or controversial or use the opportunity to advance a personal extremist agenda.

In some cases, just the mere presence of some controversial public figures in a police facility can be seen as providing them with official credibility and create a political controversy. In many ways, teaching a state-of-the-art behavioral sciences curriculum can be a political land mine for an academy director. The long-established practice of academic freedom enjoyed in the university is unheard of in most law enforcement training facilities.

Creating an ideological controversy based on a matter of diversity can make one a folk hero in the American university. Creating the same intellectual controversy in a law enforcement academy, however, can easily serve to facilitate one's retirement! But it still must be done. The only thing worse than doing a poor job of teaching the behavioral sciences in a police academy is trying to ignore the entire matter and hoping it will never come up in public debate. Any police officer or police academy director who is looking for a risk-free occupation should be doing something different for a living anyway!

Myths about Policing

Real police work involves effectively dealing with people. It involves dealing with all types of people in all types of circumstances. Therefore, a firm and comprehensive understanding of human behavior is essential to effective policing in a free society. While there will be instances when the police are required to engage in a high-speed vehicle pursuit, chase a bad guy through a neighborhood, and even fight a suspect all the way to jail, an experienced police officer will eventually come to understand that the most effective strategy to do the job of reducing crime and disorder is to work with the community; the entire community.

An experienced police officer will soon come to understand that true officer safety and survival are advanced not only through defensive tactics and the use of force but also through effective communication skills and **cultural competence**. Once officers fully understand the importance of dealing with people in a respectful manner and integrate that into their professional demeanor, they become more effective and safer. Unfortunately, some police officers never fully accept this and their work records reflect it, usually in the form of a disproportionate number of civilian complaints, an unusually high number of resisting arrest collars, many use of force complaints, and a general lack of community trust or support in their sector.

Police officers who come to understand the importance of the community go through their day-to-day operations avoiding verbal and physical confrontations and rarely, if ever, receive civilian complaints. American law enforcement agencies are full of experienced police officers who are high-activity cops with good arrest numbers and very few civilian complaints. Being a high-activity cop and being respected in the community are not mutually exclusive goals.

Yet, history has demonstrated how years of good police work, positive community relations, and even significant violent crime reductions can literally be destroyed overnight by one major allegation of police abuse. This reality was made unequivocally clear

to the New York City Police Department after the 1997 brutaliza-
tion of Abner Louima. Clearly, one incident of police abuse of
authority can, and does, destroy years of social capital and community trust in a law enforcement agency for decades to come.

The reality of police work is that it is a people business. Effective police work is about dealing with people, usually in adverse
conditions and negative situations. There should be no doubt that
this is a difficult mandate. But to accomplish such a mandate,
police officers must study migration, immigration, and diversity;
cultures, subcultures, cultural socialization, and cultural conflict;
neighborhoods, communities, power, and the relationships
between these communities and power as they strive for scarce
resources and social mobility; **oppression**, the history of oppression, and the attitudes, myths, and prejudice oppression generates.
All of these factors, in addition to how these factors interact with
their role as law enforcement officers, must be studied by police
officers. How could a police officer in a free republic even consider
doing that job without a working knowledge of such issues?

To meet this responsibility, a professional behavioral sciences curriculum must dispel the prevailing myths about what
police officers do and concentrate on the real business of dealing
with people.

ROLE OF THE POLICE

The American criminal justice system is a collection of three different, autonomous, and diverse components: the police department, the judiciary, and the department of corrections. This is an
important distinction for police officers to learn and understand,
truly understand. It is essential because each component of the
system has a very clear role, mandate, and responsibility.

Police recruits must learn that it is the role of the police
department to serve the public interest, enforce the law, and
arrest an individual if they have probable cause to believe that
the individual has committed a criminal offense. It is the role of
the judiciary to adjudicate such criminal allegations against an
individual, and to do so within the complex array of procedural,
legal, and constitutional due process requirements. Finally, the
role of the department of corrections is to punish those adjudi-
cated and found to be guilty through the various capacities of
incarceration, deterrence, and/or rehabilitation. While a much

more detailed explanation of the criminal justice system could be provided in another venue, for the purposes of a discussion about the role of the police, this suffices.

Trouble for the police often begins when police officers lose sight of their role in the criminal justice system. As stated earlier, the role of a police officer is to bring an accused into the criminal justice system and let the other components of the system do their jobs. Very simply, there is absolutely no operational capacity or legal authority in the criminal justice system for the police to be involved in punishment. When police officers lose sight of their role limitations, trouble will follow. Discussions about "noble cause corruption" and other scenarios where police officers are accused of stretching the rules to get a bad guy off the street or doing the wrong thing for the right reasons will not be necessary if a firm and thorough understanding of the role of the police is established early in an officer's career. Historically, too many otherwise good police officers have been fired, have been indicted, have been made to "wear a wire," have committed suicide, and have even been incarcerated for simply losing sight of their proper role in the criminal justice system. Effective education in this matter right from the start can prevent such tragedies.

Real-life examples of police officers who lost sight of their roles in the criminal justice system are not difficult to find. Compelling evidence of such role confusion does not have to be imagined; it can be found in the New York City Police Department's experience in the Frank Serpico case, the Prince of the City case, and the 77th Precinct corruption scandal "Buddy Boys" case, just to name a few. And unfortunately, each city has its own local examples.

In all of these high-profile cases, otherwise "good stand-up cops" decided to take the law into their own hands and assume the punishment role of the justice system. Perhaps they never heard the lecture about the myths of policing and actually believed the media version of their role. Role confusion leads to these types of mistakes by officers and can only lead to trouble, criminal behavior on the part of officers, and a blurred line between legal and illegal behaviors.

Role confusion almost always leads to personal tragedy for the officer and great public embarrassment for the department. In the wake of such incidents, public officials always ingenuously ask the question, "What turned a good police officer and a good family man into a corrupt officer?" The answer to this question usually is,

"A good heart and bad training about the role of the police in the criminal justice system." This is another major issue in American policing that can be effectively addressed through education and training.

Crime Fighter versus Service Provider

Another key distinction regarding the role of the police that must be addressed in the education and training of police officers is the apparent **dichotomy** between their role as a crime fighter and their role as a service provider. Traditionally, most police officers begin their career expecting to perform their role as a crime fighter. The media accentuates this role, many recruitment advertisements stress this role, and even the initial training police officers are provided prepares them disproportionately for this role. Very early in the training, officers are issued uniforms, guns, shields, handcuffs, and other visible manifestations of the crime fighter role.

But some police academies are not as comprehensive in the education and training they provide to prepare the police recruits for their role as service providers. The police responsibilities as service providers include providing traffic enforcement and helping disabled motorists, searching for missing children, giving directions to lost citizens, generally interacting with the community in a proactive and positive fashion, doing foot patrol in a busy neighborhood, keeping the peace, dealing with various local emergencies in the neighborhoods, and preventing crimes as well as other service practices. As a matter of routine, effectively providing such services requires and utilizes a very different set of skills and abilities than fighting crime. Sometimes, compassion is appropriate instead of decisiveness, suggestions work better than commands, and an officer's experiences as a parent or spouse are more helpful than experiences as a street cop.

It is at these times that education and training in the behavioral sciences are helpful, and it is therefore imperative that such distinctions are made clear in the behavioral sciences curriculum.

CULTURAL COMPETENCE

The United States of America is typically characterized as a place of many different and diverse cultures, races, and ethnicities. This is true in any city, county, or state throughout the land. It is also true of most police agencies. But as this country, and the various public service agencies that serve it, becomes more racially, ethnically, and religiously diverse, the challenges for policing will grow proportionately.

These various cultural differences manifest themselves as diverse standards or styles of living, celebrations, languages, foods, music, hairstyles, religious observations, and sexual orientation. These differences can present themselves in society both in lawful and beautiful ways and in unlawful and deviant ways. The challenge to American law enforcement is both to recognize and appreciate the beautiful diversity and to police the unlawful diversity. In either case, the police are perhaps the first, and the most likely, form of government to encounter these differences.

Modern-day police officers with responsibilities to enforce the law and provide services to all the various communities must be knowledgeable about the larger sociological considerations of these various groups. Accordingly, the behavioral sciences component of the curriculum must present an overview of such concepts. Many factors shape the paradigms of individuals, and this is true of immigrants, citizens, and police officers alike. In fact, about the American Republic it has been said:

> America has always been a country at war with itself. Our history is one of self-conflict. Perhaps our most profound wars have been our cultural wars—the ones fought for the soul of our nation. Perhaps we are, at once, the most generous nation to have ever existed—and the most selfish. We are the most inclusive society that the world has ever known, and at the same time we have become the most exclusive in our attitudes towards others. We are a kaleidoscope of cultures. (Houston, 1996)

To prepare to police such a society, police officers must constantly stay abreast of the ever-changing cultural picture in American society. In addition to this ever-changing cultural picture, however, police officers must also be prepared to effectively understand and deal with the inevitable result of cultural diversity: **cultural conflict**. Essentially, all people are social animals. Their behavior is, at least to some extent, a result of their social environment. As these social environments come together, especially in the inner cities and urban areas, cultural conflict will result. When it does, it will become the responsibility of the police to resolve such conflict.

Such conflict has been extensively studied in the sociological literature (Wirth, 1925; Sutherland, 1929; Cressey, 1938; Sellin, 1938; Matza, 1969; Short, 1971; Shasta, 2002). Based on the literature, there is a consensus that culture is a predominant factor in human behavior. However, certain groups, essentially the ones with the historical and political power, use their cultural assumptions to define what behaviors are allowed and what behaviors are criminal. If a smaller subculture within the larger society participates in a certain behavior that is not recognized by the dominant culture, cultural conflict will arise. When it does, the police are called in to resolve such problems. With all the potential implications for law enforcement and the protection of the public order, police officers must be aware of the theory of cultural conflict and provided with information to recognize and resolve such disputes in the street.

EFFECTIVE COMMUNICATION

As police officers are called on to resolve these disputes, perhaps the most effective weapon at their disposal is their ability to communicate. As they go through the day, police officers communicate for a living. It is therefore in the best interest of everyone involved in a free society to invest in officers' education and training in effective communication skills.

Effective communication is essential to all people. But police officers face extraordinary challenges in the process of their communication. These challenges include ensuring the basics of all communication, such as the effective transmission of information from one person to another. But police officers must accomplish this objective in the presence of emotion, excitement, violence, and often language barriers. Due to the nature of their job, police officers do have a disproportionate amount of negative communication. While the vast majority of people who live and work in any city are probably good and decent people, most of a police officer's day involves the other, smaller number of them who are in some form of crisis and need police intervention.

Due to the sensitivity of the law enforcement mission, police officers must be trained to communicate on many different and distinct levels. For example, officers not only should learn the intricacies of verbal communication skills but also should master the practices of nonverbal communication—body language, tone of voice, voice inflections—and even the potentially daunting impact their command presence can have on others. All of these considerations should have a significant place in the behavioral sciences educational practices of a progressive police academy.

Dealing with Emotionally Disturbed Persons

Under the best of circumstances, communication can be a difficult and challenging proposition. Unfortunately, law enforcement is rarely called on to be involved in the best of circumstances. Normally, police officers are called on to intervene and resolve situations involving the worst of circumstances, frequently involving an emotionally disturbed individual. There are many different circumstances when the police are forced to come in contact with an emotionally disturbed individual.

Contrary to popular belief, emotional outbursts that require the intervention of the police are not just limited to situations and/or individuals who suffer from some type of mental illness. There are many ways that otherwise normal individuals can become involved in situations that cause extreme emotional distress. Situations such as vehicle accidents causing serious physical injury to a family member, loved ones becoming a crime victim, accidents in the home causing serious personal injury, or any type of unexpected violence or injury can drive otherwise reasonable and healthy individuals to extreme emotional outbursts. In such situations, law enforcement officers can find themselves in a crisis that requires extraordinary communication and counseling skills to resolve. Special communication skills and extraordinary patience are needed to resolve such encounters without unnecessarily escalating the level of distress.

Police officers may be called on to resolve an emotional crisis on the part of a victim of a crime, typically involving serious physical assaults, sexual assaults, vehicle accidents, or deaths. They may also be called on to resolve an emotional crisis on the part of a perpetrator, such as a barricaded suspect, a hostage situation, a suicide threat, or a cornered robbery suspect involved in a violent confrontation with the police. Finally, the police may become involved with an emotionally upset individual who happens to be another police officer. It is not unusual for police officers involved in long and sustained foot or vehicle pursuits to be distressed at the conclusion of the pursuit. If another officer is not on hand to intervene, this distress can sometimes lead to serious consequences for an officer. Some of these situations have been videotaped and televised nationwide.

For all of these reasons, significant time and effort should be dedicated to communication skills and the special considerations of communicating with emotionally disturbed individuals, no matter who they are.

PROFESSIONAL ETHICS

Whether it was in the behavioral sciences section of the police academy curriculum or someplace else, in some form or fashion, police academies around the country have been teaching law enforcement ethics for a long time. Unfortunately, most officers would agree that law enforcement ethics has rarely been taught well. Some police academies teach law enforcement ethics as a philosophical subject. While ethics is a philosophical matter, it is difficult to teach philosophy to police officers. Theoretical **ethical dilemmas** and even more theoretical potential solutions to such dilemmas are probably not the best way to prepare police officers for the sometimes difficult, yet always very real, choices they will face on patrol.

Still other academies have tried to teach law enforcement ethics by ignoring the large areas of gray normally associated with ethical dilemmas resulting from discretion in law enforcement and simply insisting on a right and a wrong way of doing everything in patrol. These academies distribute an official "law enforcement code of ethics" to the student officers and insist on compliance. To go one step further, law enforcement instructors utilizing this method usually follow up the lecture on ethics with a lecture on the investigative capabilities of the Internal Affairs Division and stress the probability of being caught if one acts in the wrong way.

This approach to teaching law enforcement ethics is very traditional and usually well accepted by police officers because it is, like everything else in policing, practical and full of threats. But the traditional approach to teaching ethics is almost always immediately dismissed by the student officers. It is too easy for the officers to dismiss it as "The department is just covering itself by officially telling us about ethics." In the police world, ethical discussions focused on simple right versus wrong judgments emerge as unapplicable to the realities of the street. Regardless of the reason, ethical lessons that are not taken seriously by student officers fail to actually change behavior.

Once on the street, police officers quickly realize their role is not a simple matter of black and white but is in fact mostly gray. Surviving on the street and providing justice sometimes require a fairly sophisticated sense of what's right and what's wrong, and the specific procedures found in a patrol guide can't always provide the necessary guidance in this regard. In law enforcement, the area of police officer discretion is enormous, and the proper utilization of discretion requires a good sense of ethical awareness.

Over the last couple of years, however, enormous progress has been made in developing law enforcement curriculum to teach ethical awareness and moral courage. While the possible numbers of situations an officer may encounter while on patrol are endless, the underlying ethical principles needed to navigate them are not. So a police academy *can* teach certain principles of ethical awareness and illustrate them with practical and appropriate law enforcement scenarios. These highly specific and realistic law enforcement examples can significantly improve the ethical guidance needed for police officers. The principle of **moral courage**, for example, is proving to be an effective ethical strategy for police officers. In law enforcement, physical courage has always been a personality trait that is considered to be imperative and highly regarded. No police officer will work with a coward. With all the uncertainties of patrol, an officer must be able to count on the physical courage of a partner to be there to help in dangerous situations.

While law enforcement has always recognized and placed an enormous value on physical courage, the idea of teaching and promoting moral courage, or the moral strength and integrity to make moral decisions, is a relatively new concept. In many police academies, police officers now learn both, the physical courage to survive physically on the street and the moral courage to survive morally on the street and to effectively face the tough moral decisions.

Sooner or later, almost all police officers will be challenged physically and/or morally. Either way, police agencies that expect their officers to be prepared to deal with the unique challenges normally associated with significant discretion, undercover police work, use of force and deadly force decisions, and even questions of loyalty to other officers and to self must commit the necessary time and resources to effectively teach ethical awareness.

THE POLICE PERSONALITY

From one perspective, the vast majority of recruit training programs do an astonishing job in their core mission, assuming that their core mission is to take a newly hired civilian and transform that civilian into a professional police officer. This is a complex transformation that requires development on a physical, tactical, intellectual, moral, and, perhaps most importantly, instinctive level. The difference between a newly hired civilian and an experienced police officer is that an experienced police officer has the confidence, education, training, and ability to take decisive police action in the street in the face of an emergency. By virtue of their experience and training, good cops become very capable at such things as knowing how to recognize a problem developing, taking immediate command at the scene of a problem, knowing how to identify who is probably at fault in any given situation, recognizing if an individual is trying to be deceptive, and especially knowing how to attach blame.

In fact, at the graduation ceremonies, police academies rightfully take great pride in the successful transformation of their graduates. Family members often compliment academy directors on the noticeable change in their sons and daughters. In many ways, this is the same type of transformation a martial artist experiences. The difference between a student of the martial arts and a warrior is that a warrior, if suddenly attacked, will instinctively use his or her skills. This transformation comes only from sustained education and training in the art.

This transformation of the human spirit, however, is not without its costs. While any self-respecting professional police academy must be very effective at teaching the transformation from civilian to professional police officer, how many of them are equally effective at teaching an officer how to turn it off at the end of the tour? How many police academies have considered the following questions:

- Is it possible that the **police mind-set** so painstakingly taught at the police academy to keep the police safe on the street is the very same police mind-set that causes the officers problems at home?
- Is it possible that the emotional indifference, the assertive communication style, the propensity to take command of situations, and the automatic presumption that someone will

hurt you if you can't see his or her hands are not the most constructive personality traits for a spouse or parent?

- Does the strongly developed capacity of veteran police officers to diagnose what is wrong with any situation prepare them to go home and find what might be wrong with their homes, their spouses, or their children?

- Do the appalling divorce, alcoholism, and suicide rates in American policing suggest that police officers are so accomplished at the skills of policing that they might be "policing" their families instead of loving them?

- After the successful transformation of recruits into police officers at the police academy, have any academies considered also providing training to help the officers retain their own personal traits, the traits their families loved and admired before they became police officers?

These questions are, of course, all rhetorical. The literature, the research, the way police officers are portrayed in the popular media, and personal experiences are all clear on this: Police officers are struggling in their personal lives.

A CASE IN POINT

When one is preparing to take off on a commercial airline, the pilot always comes on the speaker and advises passengers that if they hit turbulence during flight and suddenly lose altitude, the oxygen masks located above each seat will fall. Passengers who are traveling with children or others who may need assistance should put their oxygen masks on first and then assist the other passengers.

This makes sense. Individuals cannot take care of someone else if they do not take care of themselves first, if they can't breathe. American policing dedicates significant time and effort to the transformation of civilians to police officers. Yet, very little time is spent preparing the officers to become civilians again when they go home. Police officers are generally not taught how to take care of themselves first so that they will be able to take care of others.

Since the behavioral sciences instructors in most police academies are the most suited to teach human behavior, they should always remember to finish the job by reminding officers of the importance of becoming human again at the end of the tour. To use the airline analogy, police officers cannot effectively protect the American Republic for any sustained period of time if they can't "breathe" themselves!

FAMILY DAY AT THE POLICE ACADEMY

A final consideration for every police academy is the development of some type of Family Day. This is important because as newly hired police officers go through the transformation from civilian to police officer, they typically experience enormous growth and may begin to experiment with many behavioral changes. In response to all the stress and demands normally experienced in police training, behavioral changes may occur swiftly, and these changes will be noticed by friends, family, and loved ones.

A CASE IN POINT

A parent of a young police recruit called the commanding officer of the New York City Police Academy one day exceedingly distressed. She stated that she was very worried about her son, who was a police recruit, because he was suddenly behaving oddly. When asked to explain, the mother indicated that her son insisted on referring to his father as sir, and every night her son would come home from the police academy, lock himself in the bathroom, and continuously yell in the mirror, "POLICE! DON'T MOVE!" The parent wanted to know if the department had a psychiatrist available to interview her son "to make him normal again."

A police Family Day is a first-rate opportunity for an agency to invite the families and friends of the student officers in for a day. It allows academy instructors to speak to family members and to explain what the recruit officers will be experiencing. It creates an occasion for the police commissioner and other high-ranking members of the service to meet the recruit officers and welcome them to the police family. Informal seminars can be hosted to explain how critical family support is in a law enforcement career. Family Day can also be fun for all involved. The department can provide demonstrations of the police helicopter, police vehicles, police dogs, the bomb squad, the police marching band, and other exciting "buff stuff."

Regardless of the form, an opportunity should be provided for the family and friends of recruit officers to be a part of the process. Throughout a police career, few things will be as important to officers' success as family support, and that should be made clear from the very beginning. It can also help officers through a fairly difficult time as they begin to develop their own individual policing styles.

CONCLUSION

In every academic discipline, in every case, instructional methodology is critical to the learning process. The instructional methods utilized to teach adults are, in many ways, equally as important as the message. However, this is especially the case in the behavioral sciences. Due to the subject matter typically involved, extra effort should be made to move away from the standard-issue lecture-based instruction and to integrate more advanced instructional methodologies.

The types of subjects discussed in this chapter are well suited to specially designed role plays, guest lecturers, sociodramas, simulations, and reflective team exercises. In the behavioral sciences, the student officers should be encouraged to be active participants in the learning process. Through student officers' participation in the learning, many peripheral lessons may be learned along with the core instructional objectives. Unintended lessons in patience, understanding, and mutual respect often emerge from reflective team exercises. Since policing is an applied discipline, knowledge integration will always be an important consideration, and it can be facilitated through innovative instructional methods.

KEY TERMS

Cultural Competence

Cultural Conflict

Dichotomy

Ethical Dilemma

Moral Courage

Oppression

Police Mind-Set

Sociological Imagination

Victimology

Questions for Discussion

1. Discuss the various reasons that the behavioral sciences are important for police officers to study in the police academy.

2. What are some of the classic myths about policing that should be addressed in recruit training?

3. How important is an understanding of culture and cultural conflict to the police? How can such an understanding make their job easier?

4. When recruit officers make presentations to the class on a specific culture, is it better to have them present their own culture or a different culture that they have recently studied? Why?

5. Is it important for recruit officers to study racism, sexism, and homophobia in the police academy? Why would a police officer be concerned with such social issues?

6. What are the various special populations in the community? List as many as possible, and discuss in class why they should be included in the curriculum.

7. What should be the minimum age to become a police officer? Why is maturity so important to the job responsibilities?

8. Are the police primarily crime fighters or service providers? How is the education and the training different in preparation for these two police roles?

9. What is the most appropriate role for the police in a free society?

10. What does the chapter mean by the "transformation of the human spirit"? Explain and discuss.

Suggested Readings

Cressey, Paul. (1938). Population succession in Chicago: 1898–1930. *American Journal of Sociology* 44: 59–69.

Houston, Paul. (1996). For whom the bell tolls. *Phi Delta Kappa*.

Matza, David. (1969). *Becoming deviant.* Englewood Cliffs, NJ: Prentice-Hall.

McAlary, Mike. (1987). *Buddy boys...When good cops turn bad.* New York: G.P. Putnam's Sons.

McAlary, Mike. (1994). *Good cop, bad cop.* New York: Pocket Books.

Mills, C. Wright. (1959). *The sociological imagination.* New York: Oxford University Press.

Sellin, Thorsten. (1938). *Culture conflict and crime.* New York: Social Science Research Council.

Short, James. (1971). *The social fabric of the metropolis: Contributions of the Chicago School of Urban Sociology.* Chicago: University of Chicago Press.

Shusta, Robert, Deena Levine, Philip Harris, and Herbert Wong. (2002). *Multicultural law enforcement: Strategies for peacekeeping in a diverse society,* 2nd edition. Upper Saddle River, NJ: Prentice-Hall.

Sutherland, Edwin. (1929). Crime and the conflict process. *Journal of Juvenile Research* 13: 38–48.

Wirth, Louis. (1925). Culture conflicts in the immigrant family. Master's thesis, Sociology Department, University of Chicago.

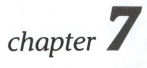

EDUCATING AND TRAINING NEW POLICE OFFICERS

Teaching Physical Education

"Upon these fields of friendly strife are sown the seeds that upon other fields on other days will bear the fruits of victory."
—General Douglas MacArthur,
U.S. Military Academy

INTRODUCTION

The above quote by General Douglas MacArthur is especially appropriate when talking about the significance of physical education and training and the police, at all levels. Newly hired police recruits, experienced in-service officers, experienced supervisors and managers, and even chiefs and civilian executives should constantly be exposed to the virtues of physical wellness, diet, and nutrition.

A properly structured police academy physical fitness curriculum places the student officers in learning situations where they are forced to work together, rely on each other, sweat together, develop together, and build **unit cohesion** and teamwork. Physical education, much like police work itself, is the rare combination of individual achievement and collective effort. Done properly, rigorous physical fitness training in the gym provides a structured format for officers to compete with themselves, and each other, in a protected environment.

It provides an effective instructional method for the officers to post a personal best or perhaps to win a game. However, the more important purpose of such physical training is to prepare the officers for the physical rigors of the street where, at any given moment, they can find themselves in much more grave competition, competing not to win a game but to protect their very lives, the life of their partner, or the life of an innocent citizen. In such street encounters, failure is not an option. The officers who have trained hard over time will survive, and those who have not will get people hurt. What lessons in the entire police academy curriculum are more compelling than that?

However, if the officers are to "bear the fruits of victory" on patrol, their physical fitness training must be real, challenging, passionate, job-related, and intense. It must provide the officers with the confidence and competence to act today as well as stress the importance of a lifelong commitment to physical fitness.

PHYSICAL EDUCATION INSTRUCTION

The job of a police officer is, in many ways, diverse and challenging. Therefore, the educational environment and instructional expectations of a police academy designed to prepare them for the job must be the same. For example, in the academic disciplines of police science, behavioral sciences, and the law, an educational atmosphere of intellectual reflecting, problem-solving, independently thinking, and questioning conventional practices should be created and encouraged. However, in the gym, the exact opposite is true. Every day, when an officer enters the gym to participate in physical education and training, there should be a noticeable difference in the atmosphere.

Physical fitness classes should be highly controlled and structured in strict military protocols. Instructor rank and all other formalities should be observed throughout the lesson. Compliance to all orders given during class must be immediate and precise. Physical fitness standards must be carved in stone for everyone to meet, with incremental workouts designed to help everyone ultimately meet them.

The physical education and training curriculum is no place for informality and congeniality. Police officers who are weak in the police academy gym and drop out of the lesson will be weak in the street. Police officers who consistently lose the friendly competitions of their physical fitness training will get another officer killed on patrol. At the recruit training level, the physical fitness training is the place to separate those who have the physical courage for police work from those who should be doing something else for a living. At the in-service level, it is the place to constantly remind officers of the importance of physical wellness and a sustained commitment to staying in shape.

All things being equal, most people typically do not enjoy the rigors of physical fitness training. While many police officers will naturally show an interest and a propensity to participate in weight training and strength building, maintaining a proper diet, running, and following other cardiovascular routines are often less popular. Such natural propensities are exaggerated by other occupational factors such as shift work, unpredictable overtime, constant access to the best food in the sector, and sitting in a radio car for eight hours a tour.

This is true in spite of the fact that the medical research clearly indicates, and experienced police officers know intuitively, that significantly high rates of cancer, stress and distress, suicide, and death from heart disease are related to police occupational factors and the accompanying lifestyle (Violanti et al., 1986).

This is probably the case, in least in part, because it may *not* be made immediately clear to police officers that there is a compelling relationship between the necessity of training hard now and the ability to perform decisively at some critical time in the street later. In fact, the propensity to become out of shape due to the routine of sitting in a radio car for eight hours a day and eating fast food sometimes becomes a running joke and a source of amusement to veteran officers. Rookie police officers sometimes deliberately spill Bavarian cream on their uniforms to look more like the veteran officers.

Learned Behavior Through Training

In his quote, General MacArthur was surely referring to the "friendly strife" of competition and the discipline it instills in military soldiers. In the battlefield, behaviors learned through discipline, which become instinctive through the repetition of training, can be a lifesaver at some later time during the heat of battle. Clearly, however, the same is true for police officers. The day-to-day responsibilities of a police officer regularly involve, and can at any moment invoke, significant physical activities (Hoffman, 1996). Therefore, sufficient levels of physical fitness are essential to be able to perform these responsibilities safely and properly. For example, no police officer would ever want to pursue a violent perpetrator up three flights of stairs in the housing projects and end up in a violent struggle, only to find out that his or her partner is not in good enough physical condition to make it up the stairs and assist!

Due to the unpredictable nature of the job, staying in good physical condition through physical training now can prepare an officer for a completely unexpected armed confrontation later. In police work, an unexpected physical confrontation is not only a possibility but a probability; both on and off duty. It is not a question of if but a question of when. Because of this realization, ongoing, sustained physical training *must* be an important component of a police officer's life.

Such a lifestyle typically begins with instruction in the police academy and should be constantly reinforced at all levels throughout a police officer's career. Some type of physical training is an important and consistent component of virtually every police academy in the country with regard to recruit officer training, but there is a significant drop-off at the in-service level.

For police officers, physical fitness is essentially defined as the ability to function effectively physically, intellectually, and emotionally in the patrol environment. It provides the ability to effectively and safely carry out the routine functions necessary to be successful and safe in a law enforcement role. Therefore, the overall goal of teaching physical education in a police academy must be threefold:

1. It is essentially to teach and to test general physical fitness standards to recruit officers and to provide them with the proper foundation and habits for a lifetime of physical wellness.

2. It is equally important to provide more specific and immediate physical education opportunities for recruit officers to prepare them for the rigors of the typical physical encounters they will experience on patrol, such as handcuffing a violent perpetrator, chasing down a suspected burglar, or physically containing an emotionally disturbed person.

3. Basic physical fitness and wellness standards must also be taught and sustained through in-service training to encourage officers to stay prepared for the unexpected confrontations and to stay healthy. The time has come for law enforcement to stop joking about physical wellness and start taking it seriously.

At the recruit level, clearly **cardiovascular endurance**, flexibility, muscular strength, **anaerobic power**, stamina, agility, and overall fitness must be taught and mastered in training. However, to enhance the operations of a police academy in terms of covering all relevant subjects, the best physical fitness programs also include the related physical tactics used by patrol officers: basic self-defense, fundamentals of boxing, basic military formations and drills, proper stance to assume when questioning a perpetrator in the street, and other related physical movements.

Teaching and practicing these skills during the physical training component of the police academy training makes the training interesting, keeps the recruit officers actively involved in the learning, and also illustrates the direct relationship between physical fitness and officer safety and survival. Listed below is what might be included in a typical physical training curriculum:

PHYSICAL TRAINING CURRICULUM

Fitness Preassessment	Team Tactics
Introduction to Military Drills	Gun Disarming Techniques
Military Formations	Effective Weapon Retention
Crowd Control Strategies	CPR—Defibrillator
Introduction to Calisthenics	Self-Defense—Practical Exam
Calisthenics—Every Day	Police Baton
Basic Self-Defense	CPR—Practice
Self-Defense—Boxing	CPR—Practical Exam
Self-Defense—Falls	Basic Water Safety
Three-Mile Run	Speed-Cuffing Techniques
Self-Defense—Grappling	Diet, Nutrition, and Stress

Total = Approximately 130 Hours of Instruction

The above subject areas are a few of the key examples of the major physical education topics to be covered in police academy training. At first glance, the total hours of instruction recommended in the curriculum may seem elevated. This is the case because some of the subjects should be integrated into the various lessons every day. Unlike academic lessons, in the interest of time, physical training cannot be crammed or condensed. Because of the physical limitation of the muscles to grow and appropriately recover, physical training must be completed incrementally over a period of time. To best accomplish the mission and maximize the benefits of the training time allowed, certain components such as calisthenics and three-mile runs must be slowly and gradually integrated and increased in the instruction.

Fitness Preassessment

Any responsible and professional physical fitness regimen must begin with an individual comprehensive **fitness assessment**. Each recruit officer must be individually reviewed in terms of determining his or her current fitness capacity prior to training. Although most police departments require a prehiring physical examination from a medical doctor, the physical education staff must still conduct additional prehiring fitness assessments. This important step must be completed prior to academy training. Complete and accurate medical records must be recorded in terms of pretraining ability, flexibility, body fat composition, and other relevant physical and medical characteristics. In addition to establishing the necessary documentation for all training records, it also provides a statistical baseline for later comparison to posttest performance data and allows a training staff to demonstrate a recruit officer's progress.

Stress and Nutrition

Any comprehensive curriculum on physical fitness in law enforcement simply must include a discussion of the related issues of **stress** and **distress**, diet, nutrition, and overall physical wellness. Stress is probably a major trigger that contributes to the overall poor eating habits, lifestyles, and behaviors of police officers and their accompanying illnesses. This, coupled with the inherent stress associated with police work, makes a review of stress and nutrition a critical foundation to physical fitness.

But perhaps more important than learning about stress itself are the lessons to be learned about stress reduction techniques and decompression practices. The potential behavioral manifestations of not learning very early in a law enforcement career to effectively deal with stress and use stress reduction techniques can be devastating to officers. Indeed, resulting from the stress and distress normally associated with law enforcement are the self-destructive behaviors that have plagued policing for generations: the problems of cynicism, job-related emotional scarring, policing the family instead of loving them, alcoholism, divorce, and ultimately police suicide.

Moreover, as if the relationship between policing and suicide was not compelling enough, there also exists a relationship between policing and alcoholism (Wagner and Brzeczek, 1983). This relationship is well established in the literature of policing and recognized by experienced police officers everywhere. To deal with the emotional distress of the job, police officers sometimes choose to go to the pub and drink alcohol. The drinking is generally done with other police officers as a way to socialize and relax. Such behavior, sooner or later, effectively leads to undermining the police family and can lead an officer down the path of self-destruction, all stemming from stress and/or distress. Since the ultimate purpose of police academy training is to prepare officers to do the job safely, how can a physical fitness program not address these red flags in a very direct and comprehensible fashion?

Police recruits and experienced officers must learn that many of the responsibilities of a patrol officer are very stressful. Police officers will face operational stress, organizational stress, role conflicts, family stress, and many other types of stressors. In many ways, just the job of enforcing the law in a free society is stressful in itself. People who live in a free society don't want to be policed.

A career as a law enforcement officer in a free republic is such a contradiction in terms that it is inherently stressful. Moreover, police recruits must also learn that not all stress is bad; there is such a thing as positive stress. Properly applied, a little stress can push an individual to be more productive on patrol and more aware of safety and survival considerations. But too much stress or sustained exposure to stress can quickly and unexpectedly turn to distress and become exceedingly destructive to physical wellness, the human spirit, and the human body.

For all of these reasons, strategies and tactics specifically designed to effectively deal with stress and distress should be included in every physical training curriculum. To some, this recommendation may seem obvious and self-evident. But for some reason, strategies to deal with the stress/distress of law enforcement have not been traditionally recognized as an important subject in preparing to be a police officer. A police academy physical fitness program, at all levels, must teach stress recognition, stress management, and stress reduction techniques. Effectively dealing with the stresses of policing can profoundly impact police officers' ability to perform on the job, to be happy at home, to sustain a marriage and a family, and, indeed, to sustain their own life. Police officers have to be reminded that they cannot take care of everyone else if they don't take care of themselves first. Providing detailed information on diet and nutrition, physical exercise, and the importance of maintaining a life outside of police work is perhaps one of the most important safety and survival lessons an officer will ever learn.

One way or another, police departments must begin to take the fitness challenge very seriously, and, as usual, the police academy and training officers should be at the forefront of this charge. *Police officers' lives depend on it!*

A CASE IN POINT

The New York City Police Department has implemented the N.Y.P.D. Cardiovascular Fitness Program. This model program provides all department personnel, both civilian and sworn, with access to state-of-the-art exercise equipment and expert instruction and advice. A number of fitness centers are staffed with professional trainers and located at various police facilities around the city. All personnel are encouraged to visit these centers on a regular basis to exercise.

In addition to the exercise equipment, the N.Y.P.D. fitness centers also offer nutritional guidance and stress management tips to any and all members who are interested, and this information is incorporated into the training at all levels.

Calisthenics, Three-Mile Runs, and Military Formation

Daily **calisthenics** and three-mile runs are critical in a police academy to enhance the overall cardiovascular conditioning of recruit officers and to prepare them for the rigors of patrol. While it is generally recognized that patrol can be very routine and slow-moving for hours at a time, it is also recognized that, at a moment's notice, a physical challenge or confrontation can occur.

To prepare for such challenges, daily calisthenics and three-mile runs are excellent methods to build and sustain cardiovascular conditioning in police officers. Moreover, as long as daily stretching, running, and exercising are to be done, an effective instructional method to accomplish them is to conduct the exercises and runs in a **military formation** with official company sergeants leading the formation and using official military commands, company flags, and company symbols.

This way, in addition to the self-evident cardiovascular benefits of the runs, the student officers can also practice moving from one location to another in military formation. This practice teaches and reinforces in the officers the value and importance of following orders and other verbal commands from a sergeant, unit cohesion, teamwork and responsibility for a partner, and other key operational skills that will "bear the fruits of victory" on other days. These are the exact skills that will come in handy later at the scene of civil unrest, a terrorist attack, or some other type of mass police action.

Over the last few years, some police academy administrators have begun to move away from many of the military aspects of training. This is especially true in the departments that have moved toward community policing and away from the traditional bureaucratic semi-military organization. However, each training administrator should be cautioned, especially in this day and age, that every law enforcement organization may still be called on to respond in a timely and organized fashion to a critical incident. It remains the responsibility of the training director, regardless of the organizational policing philosophy, to sustain such organizational expertise through training.

Recruit officers should be clearly instructed that the purpose of the run each day is not simply to develop the ability to run three miles. Any experienced police officer will tell you that a criminal

A CASE IN POINT

On September 11, 2001, minutes before the south tower collapsed at the World Trade Center, police helicopters hovered near the remaining tower to check its condition. "About fifteen floors down from the top, it looks like it's glowing red; it's inevitable," the pilot of Aviation 14 reported at 10:07 A.M. Seconds later, another pilot reported, "I don't think this has too much longer to go. I would evacuate all people within the area of that second building." These warnings, captured on police radio tapes, were transmitted twenty-one minutes before the building fell. Police officials said the warnings were relayed to the officers, most of whom managed to escaped. These officers escaped because, in a moment's notice, based on changing conditions, the police department's command and control ordered an evacuation. Because of the initial training provided at the police academy, the response to these orders was immediate and instinctive, the discipline was tight, and police officers' and civilians' lives were saved.

suspect who is not caught in the first ten steps will probably get away. Instead, a three-mile run at the academy is designed to provide the recruits with the cardiovascular ability to conduct a sustained police action that may very well include jumping out of a radio car, running into a building, going up a few flights of stairs, and then struggling with a bad guy.

This type of scenario on patrol is not at all unusual and can create a situation where a victim's life, a partner's life, or the officer's own life can depend on the officer's physical conditioning. As unpleasant as a three-mile run may be to some, any recruit who is not sufficiently motivated by such a realization, or incapable of completing such an exercise, should be fired from an agency at once.

Military Traditions and Protocol

The presence of military traditions and **military protocol** in American policing is extensive and built on strong tactical reasoning, as illustrated in the above Case in Point. For example, as a practical matter, the military salute, elaborate uniform and use of insignia, rank structure, use of military time, and many other examples of military traditions are visually apparent and operationally helpful. But of all the military traditions and protocol utilized in policing, perhaps the abilities to drill and to quickly and efficiently fall in to military-type formations are the most important. Aside from roll calls, the day-to-day practices of a patrol officer seldom require the military precision taught in drill.

There are times, however, when such skills are absolutely necessary and crucial to police operations. Moreover, these times tend to be the most critical and urgent faced by police officers. For example, if a riot suddenly breaks out on the northeast corner of 42nd Street and 8th Avenue, it will become a public safety imperative that the responding police know exactly how to form up quickly and respond en masse to military-type commands.

These formations and commands must be taught and mastered at the police academy during physical training to prepare the recruit officer for such a situation because when these actions are necessary, there is no time for training or reinstruction.

Perpetrator Frisks and Speed Cuffing

While the substantial legal issues that surround stop, question, and frisk and handcuffing are covered in detail in the law curriculum, the actual physical techniques for doing so are demonstrated and practiced in the physical fitness component of training. The importance of teaching the proper way to frisk and cuff a perpetrator cannot be overemphasized.

The safety and survival of an officer can be significantly enhanced by practicing proper techniques such as taking cover, utilizing effective verbal commands ("Police! Turn around slowly and keep your hands where I can see them!"), and using a solid tactical approach. The safe application of the tactics of handcuffing, such as stabilizing a perpetrator, using a wristlock, and applying the handcuffs, must be practiced repeatedly in physical education training on the mats.

Basics of Self-Defense

The importance of teaching the basics of self-defense in a police academy is, for the most part, self-evident. It is, however, an interesting topic in American policing today. Every police academy in

America teaches some form of self-defense to the recruit officers. Essentially this is accomplished by teaching the basics of body mechanics, ways to blade the body when speaking to a suspect, basic boxing techniques, and perhaps some basic grappling and/or ground fighting techniques. Clearly, such topics are appropriate and necessary for a police recruit, and given the time usually allowed for the subject of self-defense, they are probably minimally effective.

However, some of the most crucial topics, which ought to be taught at the same time to all police recruits in a free republic, are frequently overlooked. These topics include the ultimate goal of voluntary compliance in law enforcement, the compliance continuum (discussed in police science), and the proper context of any police use of force.

These topics may seem a bit philosophical perhaps, but nevertheless appropriate and necessary in a physical fitness component of a police academy. In a free society, the use of force, *any* use of force, especially by a police officer, is philosophically inconsistent with the purpose of government and potentially problematic. Any conversation in training about the police use of force should begin with a realization that in a free society, even if the police win a fight, they lose. Therefore, the most important aspect of teaching self-defense in a police academy is not necessarily the actual techniques of self-defense but the decision to use force at all, as well as the development of the advanced communication and tactical skills necessary to avoid it.

There is a very subtle, but very important, philosophical shift that occurs when one becomes a police officer. The officer must, at that point, understand that the goal of law enforcement is **voluntary compliance**. If voluntary compliance is not possible, any and all force options must be minimally applied and progressively utilized. Finally, the context of force in law enforcement is essentially different than it is in the street where most individuals learn such a notion. When most people are young and growing up, they are taught that the purpose of a physical confrontation is to win it. This lesson is typically reinforced by participating in organized sports, watching professional sporting events, watching criminal trials on television, or simply going through the various trials and tribulations of growing up in most urban areas. To win is emphasized in all things throughout childhood.

But once an individual becomes a police officer and thereby a uniformed representative of a free society, the purpose of an on-duty confrontation becomes to end it, not to win it. This is a fundamental distinction to be taught, and one that is not immediately apparent to many officers. Additionally, police officers must also learn that even if you win a confrontation, ultimately you lose. By the time an officer gets through physically healing, not to mention the various media, community, departmental, civil, and possibly even criminal evaluations, any feeling of "winning" anything is somehow very quickly lost. Ask any police officers who have been tried and convicted by the media, without any regard to due process of law, if they feel like they have "won" anything. This realization necessitates a very different tactical approach and also requires a very different mind-set, a mind-set that is established and reinforced through ongoing training.

This is why some of the most progressive police academies in this country, and most of the police training facilities in Asia, are teaching recruit officers some discipline in the martial arts. Most martial arts disciplines, unlike the American sports of boxing and wrestling, are firmly rooted in a philosophical foundation of honor, respect, restraint, restoring of harmony, discipline—a **warrior code**.

More importantly, such character traits are normally instilled *before* any physical techniques of striking or aggression are taught, producing an individual who understands the big picture of using only the amount of force necessary to end a threat. To continue teaching police officers the techniques of force before they fully appreciate the consequences of them is a formula for disaster in America. In a confrontation, using force designed only to restore some sense of harmony or balance to the environment is quite a different approach from entering a confrontation to win it (Westbrook and Ratti, 1970). Police officers must understand such a distinction, and the physical training unit must teach it to them.

Such a warrior code applies perfectly to policing a free society and to preparing a young police recruit to integrate the warrior code's principles for a life of peace. The philosophy of the martial arts, coupled with the physical proficiency it teaches, prepares a recruit student to approach the inevitable confrontations of police work with the proper desire for a peaceful resolution, not an ego-driven victory.

Consider the discipline of **Aikido**, which has been referred to as the gentleman's form of martial arts. Aikido is a graceful method of teaching self-defense that can be effectively used against any form of physical attack. But in addition to its devastating physical techniques, Aikido also teaches an underlying philosophy of harmonizing all of man's vital powers to restore order. There are no attacks taught in traditional Aikido, and there are no competitions. The goal is to merely neutralize an attack and render an attacker harmless. Clearly, to do this requires the same skill, practice, and commitment as other American contact sports. But it includes a more important philosophy, and in a free society, that is the critical difference. Once again, it is said, "Philosophy matters in all things, even policing—especially policing."

Unfortunately, with all the pressures facing American police academies today to get the student officers out on the street as soon as possible, most police academies could not possibly allot the necessary time and resources to teach the recruits a martial arts discipline such as Aikido to an acceptable level of proficiency. But, perhaps given the apparently constant issue of police brutality and abuse of authority cases that present themselves, the academies can no longer afford not to.

Allowing the necessary time to study the martial arts is a classic example of how a completely integrated career approach to police officer training could be initiated. Recruit officers could begin to study the discipline as recruits, and police agencies could then offer ongoing classes once or twice a week for free to the officers who wish to continue their studies. Officers could attend the classes on their own time, and the department could pay for the instruction. Proactively training the officers to a level of proficiency in Aikido would be cheaper in the long run than reactively paying the substantial legal fees normally associated with defending the typical police brutality case. History has shown that when officers improperly apply force, they can be subjected to significant departmental, civil, and criminal investigations. Even worse, an allegation of abuse of force and the surrounding publicity further break down community trust and confidence in the entire law enforcement agency, a trust that is essential to effective policing. The choice seems easy!

USE OF THE POLICE BATON

As an officer strives to gain voluntary compliance, at some point a professional presence and effective verbal commands may not work. In these cases, police officers are issued and trained in the use of the straight baton. Basically, there are two types of police batons: the straight baton and the side-handle baton. Although the side-handle baton was very popular for a while, it appears that many agencies are either sticking with or returning to the traditional straight baton.

The classic straight baton is made of either wood or, more recently, polycarbonate plastic. Straight batons are approximately twenty-six inches in length, one and one-fourth inches in diameter, and about twenty-one and one-half ounces in weight. With the proper training, they can serve as very effective tools for everything from keeping a suspect at a distance to controlling vicious dogs and/or various crowd formations. Comprehensive straight baton training curriculum includes the demonstrating and practicing of various jabs, one- and two-hand striking blows, one- and two-hand blocking techniques, "come along techniques," and the most effective and defensible parts of the human body to target for strikes. No jabbing or striking blows with the straight baton or the side-handle baton are ever designed to be delivered above the shoulder area or to the head. Instead, what are called primary target areas, such as the collarbone, knee joint, elbow joint, rib cage, and groin area, are taught. Blows to these parts of the human body tend to bring about suspect compliance and cause temporary trauma and pain, but they normally do not result in serious physical injury. Teaching and practicing the effective use of the straight baton is an important element of the overall physical fitness training program.

MEDICAL EMERGENCIES

An imperative aspect of a police officer's responsibilities is to respond to and effectively handle medical emergencies on the street. Sometimes, the police will respond to a scene initially and simply have to isolate and control crowds at the scene and secure a victim or victims long enough for an ambulance to arrive. But sometimes, the nature of an injury or a medical situation may dictate immediate and decisive medical attention. Accordingly, an important component of the physical fitness training curriculum must deal with responding to and handling medical emergencies.

Police officers must be appropriately trained to recognize and diagnose medical emergencies, recognize the difference between a life-threatening emergency and a non-life-threatening emergency, and provide assistance, if needed, until medical emergency workers can respond. Normally, a regional medical services council such as the American Red Cross or the American Heart Association carefully governs most of the medical emergency training standards offered to police officers. Most of the training-related materials and levels of proficiency can, and should be, purchased directly from these reputable health organizations. Because these standards do vary from city to city and because they can be the source of civil liability, it is best to adhere to official medical training guidelines. Within the parameters of these official manuals, police officers are trained to administer C.P.R. as individuals or in teams, to utilize safety masks (such as the mouth-to-mouth ventilation masks), and to recognize and treat the common signs of shock, seizures, and various head injuries. The actual amount of time in the curriculum normally dedicated to such activities is carefully prescribed by the governing agency and should always be observed.

CROWD CONTROL FORMATIONS

Crowd control formations and tactics are yet another critical component of the overall physical training plan. Although the considerable managerial and operational planning functions in response to crowds, both planned and ad hoc, are necessary to review and teach, the actual physical formations and verbal commands must be practiced in physical fitness training.

It is important to present the basics of crowd control formations and progress through the various formations and group movements employed by the police as they are presented in the respective agencies' patrol guides. Everything from the basic platoon formation of one lieutenant to five sergeants to forty police officers should be practiced over and over again. After recruit school graduation, there probably will be very little time, space, and inclination to teach a police officer a refresher course in crowd control matters. When crowd control formations are called for in an unexpected mobilization, there is little time for instruction or uncertainty. In the physical fitness program of a police academy, the formations should begin with an actual platoon commander requiring the officers to form up and count off. During this training, platoon commanders can practice platoon alignment, forming a basic wedge formation with general support, forming a wedge formation with lateral support, and forming a wedge formation with close support.

The duties of police officers, both individually and collectively, in times of crowd control or any type of civil disorder are to preserve human life, protect property, and restore law and order. A thorough working knowledge of the purpose and actual applications of the basic military formations is critical to this duty and must be mastered at the recruit officer level.

CONCLUSION

In a professional police academy, the physical fitness curriculum should establish the clear and compelling relationship between good physical and mental conditioning and officer safety and survival. In short, nothing could be more compelling and important for a young officer in training. Physical training and ongoing physical wellness are an important part of adult life, and an important part of policing. Since policing is, at the end of the day, an applied science, officers must prepare on the "fields of friendly strife" right from the first day of police academy training. Instructional blocks in physical training should be conducted every day, they should be intense, and they should be treated very seriously. A recruit officer who fails to perform at the expected level of proficiency in any and all of the established skill areas taught in the physical training department is no more prepared to be a police officer than a student who fails the law curriculum. A legal clarification can almost always be looked up, but a physical confrontation can occur immediately and requires an instinctive response from an officer. Very few things taught at the police academy are a matter of life and death, but physical training is one of them.

KEY TERMS

Aikido

Anaerobic Power

Calisthenics

Cardiovascular Endurance

Distress

Fitness Assessment

Military Formation

Military Protocol

Stress

Unit Cohesion

Voluntary Compliance

Warrior Code

Questions for Discussion

1. What did General Douglas MacArthur mean in his quote by the words "Upon these fields of friendly strife"?
2. What are the major causes of concern in regards to overweight police officers?
3. What are the major occupational factors associated with law enforcement that can contribute to poor physical conditioning? List and discuss each.
4. How can police officers be encouraged to adhere to a lifelong commitment to physical wellness?
5. What types of examinations should be included in a comprehensive preassessment fitness examination?
6. How strong is the relationship between physical fitness, stress, and proper nutrition?
7. What are the various types of self-destructive behaviors that are associated with stress?
8. How elaborate should a police academy curriculum be in the matter of self-defense?
9. Should some form of the martial arts be taught to American law enforcement? What are the advantages and disadvantages of each argument?
10. Is the premise "The purpose of a police confrontation is to end it, not to win it" acceptable for American policing?

Suggested Readings

Dietrich, J., and J. Smith. (1986). Non-medical use of drugs and alcohol by police. *Journal of Police Science and Administration* 14: 300–306.

Friedman, P. (1967). Suicide among police. In E. Schneidman (ed.), *Essays in self-destruction.* New York: Science House.

Hill, K., and M. Clawson. (1988). The health hazards of street level bureaucracy: Morality among the police. *Journal of Police Science and Administration* 16: 243–248.

Hoffman, B. (1996). How today's law enforcement officers rank. *Muscle and Fitness Magazine,* pp. 76–79.

Labovitz, S., and R. Hagehorn. (1971). An analysis of suicide rates among occupational categories. *Sociological Inquiries* 41: 67–72.

McCreedy, K. (1983). Entry-level police training. *Police Chief* 50: 22–58.

Morgan, Forrest E. (1992). *Living the martial way. A manual for the way a modern warrior should think.* Fort Lee, NJ: Barricade Books.

National FOP looks at police suicide and how to prevent it. (1995). *Law Enforcement News* 21 (422): 1, 8.

New York City Police Department. (1993). Office of the Chief of Personnel, Physical Fitness Incentive Program.

Southward, N. (1990). Taking the job home. *FBI Law Enforcement Bulletin*, pp. 19–23.

Violanti, J. (1984). Police suicide on the rise. *New York Trooper*, January, pp. 18–19.

Violanti, J. (1986). The mystery within: Understanding police suicides. *Law Enforcement Bulletin* 64: 19–23.

Violanti, J., J. Vena, and J. Marshall. (1986). Disease, risk and mortality among police officers: New evidence and contributing factors. *Journal of Police Science and Administration* 14: 17–23.

Wagner, M., and R.J. Brzeczek. (1983). Alcoholism and suicide: A fatal connection. *FBI Law Enforcement Bulletin*, pp. 8–15.

Westbrook, A., and O. Ratti. (1970). *Aikido and the dynamic sphere: An illustrated introduction.* Tokyo, Japan: Charles E. Tuttle Company.

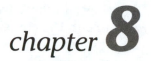

EDUCATING AND TRAINING NEW POLICE OFFICERS

Teaching the Use of Force and Firearms

"The capacity to use coercive force lends thematic unity to all police activity in the same sense in which the capacity to cure illness lends unity to everything that is ordinarily done in the field of medical practice."

—Egon Bittner

INTRODUCTION

From Plato and his *Republic* to modern-day elected officials of the American Republic, philosophers, politicians, scholars, and citizens alike have all participated in an ongoing debate about the best way to establish government-sanctioned use of force in a free republic. As discussed earlier in this text, such a massive intellectual and practical undertaking requires the reconciliation of some very central, fundamental, and essential questions:

- Who should rule?
- Who should possess the power to enforce the decisions of the ruler?

- How can those who are authorized to use force remain accountable to the citizens?
- How should those who are authorized to use force be educated and trained?

Inevitably, such fundamental social questions soon lead to a discussion about the notion of power in a free society. Within the context of a social structure, the notion of power presents itself on many fronts: political power, financial power, administrative power, intellectual power, legal power, and, ultimately, pure physical power. Because pure physical power is precisely the type of power the social contract was designed to protect free citizens against, and because it is typically the type the police find themselves authorized to utilize, the conflict persists.

Throughout history, one of the most fundamental and important functions of a government is to provide and sustain a social structure in which might does not make right. But to provide such a balance, official decisions must be made to determine who should be allowed to possess such pure physical power and exactly how that physical power should be applied to free citizens. Those in power must also institute comprehensive systems of checks and balances to closely monitor and ensure compliance. Perhaps most importantly, a great deal of attention must be paid to the education and training of those who are officially sanctioned by the government to apply physical force and demand compliance, such as the military and law enforcement.

Historically, these have always been very complicated philosophical issues to resolve. Today, these issues are no less complicated, and elected officials continue to engage in public policy debates involving the U.S. military, civilian law enforcement, and the use of force. Most recently, the challenge of domestic terrorism has served to activate the entire debate.

JUDICIOUS USE OF MILITARY FORCE

In a major U.S. military action waged against international terrorism in Afghanistan, representatives of the U.S. government engaged in incessant debates about not only if a war was morally permitted but if it was morally necessary—even in direct response to one of the most violent and deadly acts of hatred and terrorism ever launched against Americans, the attacks of September 11, 2001. Moreover, once the moral questions involving the use of force were resolved and the decision was made to respond, the debates continued to further decide the most appropriate and humane tactics to fight the war. Following the debates, military strategies and tactics were then authorized that were specifically designed to allow the U.S. military to cautiously drop technologically advanced smart bombs on the Taliban, thereby minimizing the amount of force utilized. Moreover, as an additional sign of the national reluctance to use force, at the same time as the bombing, international food drops for starving civilians in Afghanistan were coordinated and implemented.

The point to be made is that, even in the practice of war, Americans' reluctance to use force and their collective values of peace, restraint, and justice are apparent. In fact, these values are so intrinsic and fundamental to the American way of life that these values passionately sustained themselves and moved to the forefront, even during a time of war.

JUDICIOUS USE OF FORCE IN LAW ENFORCEMENT

The presence of the American values of peace, restraint, and justice is equally as evident in the domestic uses of force, such as civilian law enforcement. For example, in July 1998, the New York City Police Department announced its intention to require its 40,000 uniformed members of the service to switch to the use of **hollow-point ammunition** and to move away from the more traditional fully jacketed **ball ammunition**. The decision to switch to the new hollow-point bullet was proposed by the police academy firearms experts and moved forward in the wake of significant operations research, considerable technical advice from experts around the world, and an overall desire to utilize a bullet that was safer for the community and the police. It was well established that the hollow-point bullet was specifically designed to expand and actually slow down when it hits bone and flesh, meaning it is less likely to ricochet and injure innocent bystanders and more likely to bring about the necessary trauma to end a violent attack as quickly as possible.

Traditional Ball Ammunition

- Penetrates more than hollow-point bullets
- Travels completely through objects such as walls, car doors, and human bodies
- Imparts less energy to an object due to increased penetration

- Ricochets more than hollow-point bullets
- Penetrates body armor more effectively
- Is significantly less expansive
- Is significantly less effective than hollow-point bullets

Hollow-Point Ammunition

- Penetrates less than ball ammunition
- Is less likely to travel completely through objects
- Imparts more energy to an object due to reduced penetration
- Ricochets less than ball ammunition
- Penetrates body armor less effectively
- Is significantly more expansive
- Is significantly more effective than ball ammunition

The policy decision to change ammunition was considered to be in the best interest of restraint, and a fairly routine administrative decision well within the parameters of a police commissioner. It was further believed that such a move would illustrate that, even in the direst circumstances of a deadly confrontation, the police were still interested in using the least amount of force necessary to safely accomplish their mission.

Yet, in spite of significant professional, technical, scientific, and even moral support for the change in ammunition, considerable public apprehension erupted over the proposal, driven by unrelenting media coverage. The **Civilian Complaint Review Board** of New York City was commissioned to do a comprehensive study and to make its findings public through policy recommendations. The **American Civil Liberties Union** called for public hearings and demanded that the New York City Police Department explain such a decision. Various community leaders immediately spoke out, based on myths and war stories they had heard, and claimed that the police were switching to "exploding bullets" and "armor-piercing cop killer bullets" and even accused the police of wanting to "use a bullet with sharp metal hooks that tears through human tissue and causes massive bleeding and damage." Even the *New York Times* published an editorial opinion claiming "the hollow-point bullets, which expand when they enter the flesh, are banned as inhumane in warfare by the Geneva Convention" (*New York Times*, 1998).

For weeks, the major print and television media in New York City were actually engaged in a raging public debate over police bullets. It was a public debate, however, that entirely missed the real issues in the police use of force and instead centered on the erroneous assumption that there actually is a humane way to shoot someone.

In the end, after vast amounts of time and resources were dedicated solely to defending the decision to use less force, members of the New York City Police Department very routinely began to be issued and to train with the hollow-point bullets. It was a policy change initiated by the training division in good faith that, in the end, turned out to be one of the most humane and restraining use of force decisions a law enforcement agency could ever make.

There are important lessons to be learned from the U.S. military action in Afghanistan and the New York City hollow-point bullet experience. They are but two examples of how any decision, even a good faith decision made with the best intentions, that involves the use of force in a free society will be subjected to considerable public debate, substantial community emotion, and overwhelming public and political scrutiny. Clearly, the use of force, and the power that it represents, plays a significant role in all social relationships. Any government-supported use of physical force to gain compliance, coupled with the natural reluctance of free people to accept it, creates the power struggle normally associated with a democratic government. This struggle can have enormous implications for social control and the public belief in restraint and justice.

CONFLICT THEORY AND FORCE

Police officers should be informed that there is an entire faction in American society that believes the day-to-day operations of formal social control agents, such as the police, are nothing more than the tools with which those who control the ability to use force in society maintain their social advantage. Such positions range from social **anarchism** (Tifft, 1979) through Marxism (Chambliss, 1975; Spitzer, 1975; Quinney, 1977) to value of diversity (Pepinsky and Jesilow, 1985). Many elected officials in America today admit that the genesis of their beliefs about the use of force in society can be directly traced to the writings of Karl Marx. In his political philosophy, Marx saw conflict in society as being due to a scarcity of resources and an historical inequality in the distribution of those resources, most notably power.

For all of these reasons, it seems clear that from the time of Plato's *Republic* to the American Republic, there remains a constant and relentless struggle to balance the relationship between formal social control, government power, and the use of force in any way, both foreign and domestic. From the time of Plato's *Republic* to today's American Republic, it remains a constant endeavor to build a sense of equilibrium between power, the use of force, and issues of equality and justice.

This premise is essential to the education and training of police officers in the use of force because, more often than not, all of these issues will come to a head because of a split-second decision made by a twenty-five-year-old police officer working alone on some street corner at 3 A.M. Moreover, when the public scrutiny of such a shooting begins, it will almost always come knocking on the door of the police academy first, to determine exactly how that individual was educated and trained to make such a determination.

There is tremendous public concern and relentless governmental and civilian oversight in a free society about the issues of power, the use of force, and the equal application of these principles. *There should be!* The authority to use force in the line of duty is one of the most controversial components of police work, and it probably always will be. Justifiable use of force by the police always initiates great public interest. Questionable use of force by a police officer can have tragic consequences for all the individuals involved as well as a community, a city, and a nation.

Therefore, police departments must act quickly and decisively to take proactive measures to prevent such situations from occurring and to effectively defend against them when they do occur. Only through the judicious use of force will the community's confidence in a police department be sustained. Only then will the necessary bond between the police and the community they serve be strong. Community concerns over questionable police shootings in St. Petersburg, Florida; Miami, Florida; New York City; Cincinnati, Ohio; and most every other major city at one time or another can attest to this.

TRAINING IN THE APPLICATION OF FORCE

Due to the social complexity involved in the police use of force, resolving a simple street dispute, one of the core functions of a police officer, runs the potential of becoming a cultural, social, and political issue. For example, a uniformed police officer called to the scene of a public disturbance becomes a visible representation of the government. Depending on the actions of the combatants, an officer may decide to mediate the dispute at the scene and take no further formal action. Conversely, an officer may decide to classify that dispute as an assault or disorderly conduct and arrest the individuals involved. To simply assume that the relative power and influence of the individuals involved in the dispute are not a factor in such a determination would be an oversimplification. Power and the use of force and the implications these issues have for the perception of fairness and justice in a society are impossible to overstate. They are, therefore, absolutely critical to the education and training of a young police officer.

In fact, the Community Relations Service of the U.S. Department of Justice maintains that "Training can have a significant impact on all aspects of police service delivery and is of critical importance in the control of police-community violence."

Teaching Policy Guidelines

The reality persists that, in a free society, the sometimes-abstract notions of power and government are only as fair and judicious as the individual police officer who applies them in his or her day-to-day interactions. Over the years, various administrative, policy, procedural, legal, and educational strategies have been employed in an attempt to manage the use of force by police officers. Police departments publish administrative policies and procedures, legal opinions, training memorandums, and other forms of written directives specifically directed toward controlling the use of force. Exactly how restrictive they are, however, is a product of the philosophy of the local chief of police and the community the police serve.

Guidance on the parameters involved in the police use of force can be found at many levels. On the federal level, the U.S. Supreme Court has considered the issue of the police use of force and ruled that the shooting of unarmed, fleeing felons actually violates the Fourth Amendment of the U.S. Constitution (*Tennessee* v. *Garner*, 1985).

A U.S. Supreme Court decision has also made it much less difficult for a citizen to file a lawsuit and ultimately collect damages as a result of a police use of force action (*Monell* v. *Department of Social Services*, 1979). Yet, many law enforcement agencies continue to allow the use of force to apprehend a fleeing felon who is armed with a deadly weapon and has committed a serious crime. In fact, only four state legislatures took action to change their respective use of force statutes in the five-year period that followed the *Tennessee* v. *Garner* ruling (Fyfe and Walker, 1990).

Additionally, some of the more progressive departments, particularly big-city police departments, train their members to much more restrictive standards in the use of deadly force. More restrictive standards that are strongly governed by state law, and even further constrained by the stipulations of the Standards of the Commission on Law Enforcement Accreditation, elaborate both department policy and extensive education and training curriculums.

In New York State, Article 35.05 of the New York State Penal Law states that force is justifiable and is not criminal when these situations exist:

- When force is required or authorized by law or by judicial decree or is performed by a public servant in the reasonable exercise of the public servant's official duties or functions
- When it is necessary in time of emergency to avoid imminent public or private injury and it clearly outweighs the criminal conduct involved

New York City police officers, for example, are trained in the requirements of Article 35 of the New York State Penal Code. But, they are also held accountable to, and trained in, the more restrictive departmental policy. In this regard, the New York City Police Department policy clearly states:

- The minimum amount of force will be used that is consistent with the accomplishment of a lawful mission. Firearms are to be used as a last resort, and then only to protect life.
- Firing of warning shots is prohibited.
- Discharging a firearm to summon assistance is prohibited.
- Discharging a firearm from or at a moving vehicle is prohibited, unless the occupants are using deadly physical force against an officer or another vehicle.
- Discharging a firearm at dogs or other animals is prohibited unless there is no other reasonable means to eliminate the threat.
- Firearms shall not be cocked, double action at all times.
- Deadly physical force shall not be used against another unless officers must protect themselves or another from imminent death or serious physical injury.
- Some warning (such as a verbal command, "Police! Don't Move!") must be given, where feasible.
- Deadly physical force shall not be used against a fleeing felon who presents no threat of imminent death or serious physical injury to others.

- Deadly physical force shall not be used in defense of property.
- Deadly physical force shall not be used when doing so will endanger innocent persons.

These are all typical examples found in New York City departmental policy statements that are much more restrictive than federal or state law, and they must be comprehensively covered in the police academy training curriculum. This is the case because regardless of case law, state statutes, or policy directives, police officer behavior, especially behavior resulting from a split-second decision about the use of force, is instinctive. Instinctive behavior is best controlled through the repetition of training and a firm understanding of tactical awareness, not through written directives.

It is also important to note that the legal precedent exists to expect that the training provided to police officers effectively integrates all departmental responsibilities, even those that may be mandated under directives or policies other than the deadly force policy, such as the vehicle pursuit policy (Alpert and Fridell, 1992). To best provide such a comprehensive and integrated approach to use of force training, the following topics should be included in a core curriculum:

BASIC FIREARMS CURRICULUM

Roll Call Inspection	Officer Safety and Survival
Basic Firearms Safety	Mass Reflexive Response
Compliance Continuum	Dog Encounters
Shooting Fundamentals	Off-Duty Incidents
Malfunction Clearing Drills	I.D. of Plainclothes Officers
Department Policy on Use of Force	Tactical Reloading
Live Fire Range Exercises	Firearms Simulator
Live Fire (Approximately 500 Rounds)	Exertion Course
Shooting from Cover/Concealment	Postshooting Tactics
Cleaning and Maintaining Firearms	Weapon Retention
Introduction to Long Guns	Unintentional Discharges
Firearms Qualifications	Judgment Exercises

Total = Approximately 80 Hours of Instruction

Teaching the Compliance Continuum

Most people think they know about the police use of force because they see it every day on television and in the movies. On television, police officers fight with suspects, engage in wild high-speed vehicle pursuits, and get involved in shoot-outs on a daily basis. The popular media, however, never has to follow through and show the significant implications for all involved.

In the real world, however, preparing a new police officer for the potential use of force is a much more important and intricate process. In regard to the use of force, especially deadly force, the education and training of police officers must be based on a progressive and comprehensive continuum of use of force options. The training to gain compliance from a suspect must begin with police presence and run the full spectrum of force options available, depending on the level of threat a police officer is faced with. Critically related issues, such as the effective use of verbal commands, the principles of cover and concealment or isolation and containment, and the tactical advantage, must be integrated into all aspects of use of force training.

In short, through their training, police officers must "prepare for the worst and hope for the best." Due to the complex issues surrounding the use of force and firearms, both the conceptual aspects of education and the perceptual components of training are unequivocally necessary. The essentially intellectual lessons of placing the use of force in a proper social context and knowing when to use force are important. Naturally, the hands-on repetition of the actual **marksmanship** involved in how to use force is equally required. Accordingly, most comprehensive police curriculums begin with a detailed discussion of the compliance continuum and the progression of force options.

The **compliance continuum** simply provides for a discussion of six progressive steps to gain compliance. These steps include professional presence, verbal communication, unarmed open-hand or hand-to-hand tactics, nonimpact weapons, impact weapons, and finally, as a last resort, deadly physical force.

Interestingly enough, teaching the use of force this way also teaches young officers that the level of force utilized by a police officer is dictated by the actions of the citizen, not the officer. This is a critically important distinction often lost in public debate about the police use of force. Police officers are actually taught that they are allowed to react to the threat they are confronted with by

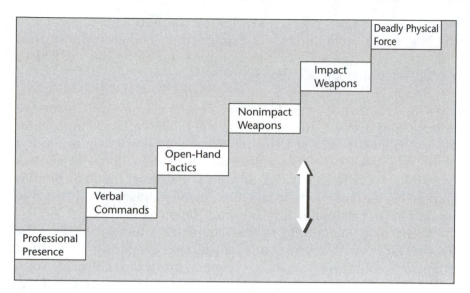

FIGURE 8-1
Compliance continuum

responding with the appropriate level of force. This approach to training is a great complement to the fundamental premise of American police officer training, not to mention the bravery and skill of the officers who must implement it in the face of physical danger.

　The first step that an officer is taught in order to gain compliance with a lawful request is to utilize their **professional presence**. In most cases, this is convincing enough for citizens to comply. If a police officer arrives on the scene of a public disturbance and projects a sense of competency and confidence through personal demeanor, most people in a proper state of mind will not challenge the commands of the officer. The vast majority of community members bring with them an understanding of the legal authority a uniformed police officer represents, and most also understand that a request made by a police officer can be forcibly enforced, if necessary.

　The overwhelming majority of citizen interactions can be effectively resolved by professional presence and effective communication by an officer. In some cases, however, the individuals involved in a dispute are emotionally involved and angry. In such situations, the mere presence of a uniformed police officer may not immediately bring about a peaceful resolution to the conflict.

In such cases, police officers are instructed and taught to utilize effective verbal commands. As discussed in Chapter Six on the behavioral sciences, effective communication skills are critical to an officer's ability to be effective.

Recently the Christopher Commission in Los Angeles looked at police recruit academy training, field training, and in-service training and agreed. In its report, the Christopher Commission stated, "In each phase of training, additional emphasis is needed on the use of verbal skills rather than physical force to control potentially volatile situations and on the development of human relationship skills to better serve Los Angeles's increasingly diverse population" (Christopher Commission Report, 1991).

Clear and compelling verbal commands have proven to be effective for everything from a police–citizen encounter on a street corner to a potentially explosive hostage situation. Effective communication takes time, but time will almost always work to the advantage of a peaceful resolution. Clear verbal commands requesting compliance, along with an occasional appeal to reason, can convince emotionally disturbed individuals to comply with the police. In this regard, police officers must be taught to explain to suspects, whenever possible, what will happen to them when and if they surrender. Time and time again, experienced police officers have realized that communicating with people and allowing them a way out of a confrontation that also allows them to retain their dignity can diffuse a potentially violent situation. This is especially true in a street situation where the police confront a suspect in front of other people.

In some cases, however, professional presence and verbal commands will not be enough to gain compliance from a highly emotional suspect. From a police officer's and a community's perspective, these are potentially very dangerous encounters. Any time a police officer has to use force, the social balance and peace are shattered, and society as a whole loses something. Therefore, experienced police officers are often reluctant to get to the point where they have to actually put their hands on a suspect. As discussed in Chapter Seven on physical training and tactics, because police officers carry firearms, any physical encounter is dangerous. All police officers carry guns, and any hand-to-hand struggle puts them in an extremely complicated situation because they have to defend themselves and also defend against a suspect taking their weapon and using it against them. To make matters worse, officers never know precisely whom they are dealing with in a street encounter and could conceivably run into a highly trained fighter. No good can come from this, and experienced officers know that.

Police officers are trained to actually put their hands on a suspect only when it is immediately necessary for safety reasons or when they are reasonably sure that their strength and skills are sufficient to handle the possible responses. Realizing the inherent danger involved with any hand-to-hand confrontation, and as a result of much thought and research into the matter of nonimpact weapons for American police, most officers are armed with effective alternatives to force.

The most popular nonimpact weapon available to American law enforcement is **oleoresin capsicum cayenne pepper spray (O.C. spray)**. O.C. spray can be used when physical force is required to protect the officer, another person, or even the suspect but only when there is no threat of immediate physical danger. O.C. spray, when used properly, can be sprayed at the eyes of a suspect to distract him or her long enough for police to move in.

O.C. spray does, however, have its limitations. It is not 100 percent effective against everybody, and it does require certain tactical considerations to be effective. Factors such as the physical area involved in the scene and even the wind direction should be considered in the use of O.C. spray. It has also been shown to be effective against dangerous dogs and other animals to deter an attack or to prevent injury.

Finally, many police departments also provide their officers with access to additional force options such as electronic stun devices, high-pressure water fire extinguishers, rubber bullets, beanbag rounds, and capture nets. All are appropriate alternatives to the use of physical force in the right situations, and all are extensively utilized to avoid physical confrontations with the public.

As the force progression moves up in response to the actions of a suspect, impact weapons are an option to gain control of a person and a scene. The most popular of the impact weapons is the straight baton. The straight baton is carried by police officers on patrol and is an important option available to them. A great deal of training is provided to officers before they are qualified to carry the baton because the baton is capable of causing deadly physical force. But, like most police weapons, the baton is specifically designed for less lethal force.

The final and most serious step in the compliance continuum is the use of deadly physical force. Deadly physical force in a free society, no matter what the method, is only to be used as a last resort when an officer or another person is in immediate danger of serious physical injury or death and any other reasonable means to stop the aggressor will not work. Preparing for such an eventuality requires many components of training, and the circumstances must be comprehensive and compelling.

Teaching Officer Safety and Survival

As police officers learn the actual skills of firearms marksmanship, they should also be taught the basic tactical considerations often associated with police gunfights because most actual police gunfights are not especially reflective of the skills normally learned by target practice. Police gunfights occur very quickly, they are over in approximately two seconds, they occur in very close quarters, and they rarely involve the skills of aiming through the barrel sights and slowly squeezing the trigger. More often, they are exceptionally quick and close, and the officer's behavior is purely instinctive. That is why the repetition experienced during target shooting remains critical but must be associated with effective **tactical awareness**.

Police officers must master the basic lessons of tactical awareness by learning to communicate with their partner *before* they arrive on a scene and agreeing to a tactical plan. Regular partners who work together every day often get very comfortable with their respective roles in tactical plans, but officers who are working together for the first time should take the time to discuss tactical considerations.

For example, officers should be taught to discuss and agree in advance on these important tactical considerations:

- How they will park the radio car at the scene so it provides the best possible cover and concealment
- Who will give the verbal commands at the scene (if both officers shout commands at a suspect, it can get confusing and contradictory)
- What possible cover and concealment items are available in a particular sector
- What the officers will do if there are multiple suspects, and what they will do if the suspects flee in different directions when they approach

- Who will call for backup if it's needed
- Whether there are any circumstances when two partners will split up in pursuit of multiple fleeing suspects
- What type of firearm each officer carries and how to work out safety and other important factors
- What type of long gun is in the trunk of the radio car, and where the extra ammunition is
- What code word can be utilized if one officer spots a gun and wants to warn another officer without yelling "He's got a gun"
- Whether there have been other calls for service at the same location, and what the call history of that location is
- Whether there are any active warrants or a protection order in effect for violent behavior for someone living at that location

Training police officers to establish and communicate such a tactical plan with their partners in advance can provide significant tactical advantages and ultimately serve to de-escalate some law enforcement encounters. These tactical advantages will then serve to control the initial decisions made at a scene and can ultimately limit the escalation of force in any given situation by leaving as many options open as possible.

Tactical awareness and preventive tactics specifically designed to minimize the use of force by the police can be applied to many situations normally encountered by the police. For example, tactical awareness has often been applied to the area of high-speed vehicle pursuits. High-speed vehicle pursuits, by their very nature, present a multitude of legal, procedural, tactical, officer safety, and even philosophical dilemmas for the police. Perhaps the essence of this problem lies in the realization that the pursuit of wanted suspects unlawfully fleeing from the police is a very emotional issue to police officers. Many police officers consider a fleeing suspect to be not only a violation of the law but also an insult to them personally and to the profession.

But the issue of police vehicle pursuits is also an emotional issue for the community because high-speed police pursuits, by their very nature, are dangerous. The decision to become involved in a high-speed vehicle pursuit is potentially a deadly force decision. Clearly, the risk of serious injury to the officers involved, the suspects involved, and even innocent citizens in the path of a pursuit makes it such.

On the one hand, the police officers have a sworn obligation to apprehend criminals. However, criminals do not always want to peacefully surrender to the police and go to jail. On the other hand, citizens have a reasonable expectation to be safe in the streets and in their private vehicles—safe from criminals as well as safe from police officers who may be recklessly pursuing criminals.

As the overall practice of the police engaging in vehicle pursuits has gained more and more legal notoriety by classifying vehicles as potential deadly force instruments, training has once again emerged as the primary target of inquiry (O'Keefe, 1990; Alpert and Fridell, 1992). Effective policy guidance and proactive tactical awareness training in this area are absolutely essential. In fact, results of current police litigation stress that courts look not only to the existence of training but also to its sufficiency. The findings in cases such as *City of Canton* v. *Harris* (1989) demonstrate that the management of police pursuit risks requires detailed analysis of the essential elements of the pursuit. Due to such developments, police academies are now well advised to teach the appropriate mandates governing police vehicle pursuits under the title of "deadly force training."

Teaching Marksmanship

There is no replacement or shortcut to the necessity of teaching proper police marksmanship! The mechanics of how to safely handle, point, fire, and maintain a firearm remain essential. Although the actual instructional method of standing on the line at the firing range and slowly squeezing off rounds is somewhat artificial and not related to most actual gunfights on the street, it is still effective in teaching proper marksmanship. At some point, police recruits must practice at a live fire range. Their hands-on instruction should cover such topics as the following:

- Firearms safety
- Shooting fundamentals
- Ammunition
- **Nomenclature**
- Clearing of pistol malfunctions, the use of sights and target acquisition, and proper breathing techniques
- Unintentional discharges
- Live fire exercises with revolvers, pistols, and assorted long guns
- General firearms proficiency
- **Firearms clearing drills**
- Actual firearms qualification

Many small police departments around the country might struggle with such requirements. Live fire exercises can be time-consuming, very expensive, logistically awkward, and potentially dangerous, and they require facilities not immediately available to every law enforcement agency in the country. But they are absolutely mandatory and should receive a training commitment of at least ten firearms range days involving hundreds of rounds fired by each and every recruit. Simply lecturing a recruit on the practical application of using a firearm will no more produce a police officer than lecturing a young person on the application of ballet dancing will produce a professional ballet dancer. It just doesn't work that way.

Teaching Firearms Judgment

While teaching the mechanics of firearms marksmanship has essentially remained the same over the years, teaching the related judgment issues of when to use force has advanced rapidly. It is in teaching judgment in firearms training that significant contributions to the use of force issue can be realized. Noteworthy progress in controlling the police use of force can be, and has been, made through this aspect of law enforcement training.

Progressive police agencies are currently utilizing laser-guided scenario-based technology to teach judgment, paint ball weapons to illustrate principles of cover and concealment, actual tactical villages to demonstrate principles of tactical awareness, and scenario-based debriefings to discuss actual police shootings. Such advancements in technology and instructional methodologies have facilitated significant progress in the area of law enforcement use of force training. These changes in training, more than any other strategy of controlling the use of force, offer an opportunity for real progress. Negative press clippings, increased exposure to civil and/or criminal liability, additional departmental policy statements, community outrage, and even U.S. Supreme Court decisions simply do not help the problem. However, building a more comprehensive training experience that utilizes emerging technology and re-creates actual street conditions designed to prepare law enforcement officers to "prepare for the worst and hope for the best" will. Education and training, not written directives that police officers rarely even read, change instinctive police behavior.

Teaching Logic versus Emotion

Another effective strategy for teaching the effective use of force to police officers is to discuss the difference between logic and emotion. Human beings in general, and especially police officers, make their best decisions when their mind is clear and they are working from a logical perspective. However, when an individual becomes personally involved in a high-stress situation and emotions run high, these emotions can sometimes cloud judgment and hinder a person from making sound choices. Emotions can work to hinder the judgment process, and they are almost always involved in a police use of force decision. Imagine the emotions involved when an individual pulls out a loaded firearm and points it at a police officer or another person. Imagine the emotions involved when police officers are involved in a high-speed vehicle pursuit for a sustained period of time and finally get their hands on a fleeing suspect. Imaging how bad it looks for an individual officer, as well as an entire police department, when an emotional overreaction is captured on videotape and played on the evening news.

Behavior that may seem appropriate at the time to an emotionally charged person appears as a blatant overreaction in retrospect when the emotions go away. This is especially true for a police officer. Since emotions will almost always run high in a use of force situation, it is important that officers are made aware of this limitation through the training process and learn to factor it into their decision-making process. While emotions can never be completely removed from a police officer's reactions, recognizing them can be an important step toward controlling them and not allowing them to become a factor in the decision-making process. Weeks later, when a grand jury reviews the facts of a case and emotions are factored out of the equation, emotional decisions can appear as overreactions and, thus, unjustified use of force.

Teaching Knowledge Integration

Once again, it is important to acknowledge that police science is an applied discipline. Therefore, at some point, it is necessary to utilize an instructional methodology that requires the student officers to demonstrate the ability to integrate their use of force knowledge and apply it to the street. Training police officers in a tactical house or a tactical village is an excellent way to meet this requirement. However, any type of location where actual interdisciplinary scenarios can be provided, the physical and emotional realities of patrol can be replicated, and the student officers' reactions can be assessed in use of force situations will do. Some small police departments simply utilize an isolated street corner in the community, secure the perimeters, and run such role plays at that location. The Federal Bureau of Investigation (F.B.I.) Academy, the Houston Police Department, and the New York City Police Department have tactical villages that are excellent for such a purpose.

In any case, it is valuable for the student officers to actually have an opportunity to apply classroom learning to everything from receiving an actual call for service through using the various tactical plans and marksmanship learned for the use of force. During the role plays, it is fairly easy to re-create the stress normally associated with taking police action, and how the student officers handle the stress can be evaluated in the important area of knowledge integration. Repetition of the scenarios will be required and mistakes will be made, so plenty of time should be allocated for interdisciplinary debriefings.

CONCLUSION

According to research conducted by the National Law Enforcement Officers Memorial Fund, more than 12,500 law enforcement officers have been killed in the line of duty in the history of the United States (Clark, 1992). The F.B.I. reports that 3,280 law enforcement officers were killed between 1973 and 1994, including 1,945 who were killed feloniously (F.B.I., 1971–1994, 1992). The threat to officers is real, and the training director has no more important responsibility than to provide for officer safety and survival through effective education and training.

There is a great deal a professional law enforcement agency can do to administratively manage the use of force in its agency, but the cornerstone of keeping the officers safe will always reside in the way they are educated and trained. Effective recruitment and selection, excellent and comprehensive education and training, the use of force monitoring programs and early warning systems, and strict investigation and accountability can all collectively contribute to the management of the use of force issue in American policing. But no matter how these factors are listed, the cornerstone of officer safety and survival is excellent education and training.

By utilizing the most current instructional materials, methods, and technology, police officers can indeed be restrained yet be decisive and safe in the application of force. With so much at stake, it simply must be realized that there are no shortcuts to a professional firearms educational process and no excuse for a police academy to not provide such a service.

KEY TERMS

American Civil Liberties Union
Anarchism
Ball Ammunition
Civilian Complaint Review Board
Compliance Continuum
Exertion Course
Firearms Clearing Drills
Firearms Simulator

Hollow-Point Ammunition
Marksmanship
Mass Reflexive Response
Nomenclature
Oleoresin Capsicum Cayenne
    Pepper Spray (O.C. spray)
Professional Presence
Tactical Awareness

QUESTIONS FOR DISCUSSION

1. Does it matter what type of ammunition police officers carry in their firearms? What other considerations should also be included in a discussion on police firearms?
2. Do you agree with the position that the police are simply instruments of social control, authorized to use force to advance the interests of those in power?
3. What steps should be taken by the public to hold the police accountable for the use of force?
4. Should department policy be more restrictive than state law when it comes to the use of force by law enforcement? What are the advantages and disadvantages of such an approach?
5. Should warning shots be prohibited?
6. How do police officers learn to distinguish between bad guys and undercover police officers in the street?
7. Can the police use deadly force to protect very valuable property?
8. Where on the compliance continuum are most law enforcement encounters resolved? Why?

9. What are the various nonimpact weapons available to the police to protect the public?
10. How effective are tactical plans in the real world in resolving violent confrontations?

SUGGESTED READINGS

Alpert, Geoffrey. (1984). *Police use of deadly force: The Miami experience.* Miami, FL: Center for the Study of Law and Society, University of Miami.

Alpert, Geoffrey, and Lorie A. Fridell. (1992). *Police vehicles and firearms: Instruments of deadly force.* Prospect Heights, IL: Waveland Press.

Chambliss, William B. (1975). Toward a political economy of crime. *Theory and Society* 2: 152–153.

City of Canton v. *Harris.* (1989). 109 S.Ct. 1197.

Clark, C. (1992). *The making of a memorial: The people behind the National Law Enforcement Officers Memorial Fund.* Washington, DC: National Law Enforcement Officers Memorial Fund.

Dallas Police Department. (1974). *Report on police shootings.* Dallas, TX: Center for Police Development, Southern Methodist University.

Federal Bureau of Investigation. (1971–1994). *Uniformed crime reports: Law enforcement officers killed and assaulted.* Washington, DC: U.S. Department of Justice.

Federal Bureau of Investigation. (1992). *Killed in the line of duty: A study of selected felonious killings of law enforcement officers.* Washington, DC: Uniformed Crime Reports Section, Federal Bureau of Investigation, U.S. Department of Justice.

Fyfe, James J. (1988). Police use of deadly force: Research and reform. *Justice Quarterly* 5 (2): 165–205.

Fyfe, James J., and Jeffery T. Walker. (1990). Garner plus five years: An examination of Supreme Court intervention into police discretion and legislative prerogatives. *American Journal of Criminal Justice* 14 (2): 167–188.

Geller, William A., and Michael Scott. (1992). *Deadly force: What we know.* Washington, DC: Police Executive Research Forum.

Los Angeles Christopher Commission Report, City of Los Angeles. (1991).

Monell v. *Department of Social Services.* (1979). 436 U.S. 658.

Navarro, Mireya. (1996). State of emergency declared after rioting in Florida. *New York Times*, October, p. 26.

O'Keefe, James. (1990). *An empirical analysis of high speed police pursuits: The Houston Police Department's experience.* Ann Arbor, MI: University Microfilms International.

Pepinsky, Harold E., and Paul Jesilow. (1985). *Myths that cause crime*, 2nd edition. Cabin John, MD: Seven Locks Press.

Quinney, Richard. (1977). *Class, state and crime: On the theory and practice of criminal justice.* New York: McKay Press.

Scheingold, Stuart A. (1984). *The politics of law and order: Street crime and public policy.* New York: Longman Press.

Spitzer, Stephen. (1975). Toward a Marxian theory of deviance. *Social Problems* 22: 638–651.

Tennessee v. *Garner.* (1985). 105 S.Ct. 1694.

Tifft, Larry L. (1979). The coming redefinition of crime: An anarchist perspective. *Social Problems* 26: 392–402.

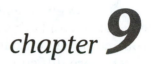

A Field Training Model for New Police Officers

"We should be careful to get out of an experience only the wisdom that is in it—and stop there. Lest we be like the cat that sits down on a hot stove lid. She will never sit down on a hot stove lid again—and that is well; but also she will never sit down on a cold one anymore."

—Mark Twain

Introduction

The above quote by Mark Twain is especially applicable to the learning process of becoming an experienced police officer. Due to the practical on-the-job instructional format of field training, the learning curve for rookie officers is typically very accelerated. While it is essential that young inexperienced patrol officers not be allowed to make a mistake that will get them or someone else hurt, it is equally important that they be allowed to make some mistakes and learn from them in a way that will not prevent them from being afraid to ever take police action again.

177

In law enforcement, being too aggressive in the community can get you and/or your partner hurt. It can unnecessarily escalate routine citizen encounters and can make the job of a police officer much more difficult than it has to be. But being too timid can be just as destructive for a rookie officer and is equally as dangerous.

The delicate balance that an experienced officer achieves can only be learned through practical hands-on experience. The real challenge in preparing young men and women for a career in law enforcement lies in the fundamental realization that it is an applied discipline. Although there is a body of conceptual knowledge large enough to justify spending the first six months or so in a classroom environment, at some point a prospective law enforcement officer has to be able to integrate a great deal of knowledge and demonstrate competency by applying that knowledge on the street. Learning the academic lessons in the law curriculum is important, but so is the ability to demonstrate physical and moral courage, the ability to work with the community, and many other practical knock-around types of skills.

Preparing to become a law enforcement officer by passively listening to lecture-based materials is essentially the same as preparing to become a dynamic public speaker by reading a book on the subject. It is necessary and helpful, and it can provide a certain foundation to build on for the future. But at some point, a student must stand up in front of an audience and apply the knowledge in a very real way.

KNOWLEDGE INTEGRATION

A professional field training program is the ultimate instructional methodology for teaching knowledge integration, and knowledge integration is the cornerstone of becoming a professional police officer. A recruit police officer is, in many ways, like a student of the martial arts. They both begin by learning a series of apparently unrelated techniques associated with the discipline they are attempting to learn. At first, they both perform a series of isolated techniques over and over again, as if the techniques are completely unrelated and remote. At some point, however, these isolated techniques begin to come together, and they collectively form an integrated pattern of movements and behavior. When this integrated pattern subtly becomes an integral part of the personality, instinctive and not rehearsed, the student has become a practitioner.

In both law enforcement and the martial arts, this change can only happen through a sustained commitment to education and training. In both cases, practice makes permanent, not perfect. In the martial arts, this transition happens when the student reaches a level of proficiency that allows him or her to begin to compete with other martial artists, when a student's response to an imminent threat is fight as opposed to flight. At that point, the student becomes a practitioner. In the case of police work, the field training program is the critical point where the student becomes the practitioner. Finally, in both disciplines, the successful application of the knowledge and skills may very well be a matter of life and death, and that is what makes them so compellingly different from most other occupations or disciplines.

In most other occupations, a senior coworker can simply correct a mistake. In law enforcement, however, from the moment young police officers graduate from the police academy, they put on the same uniform as a veteran officer. Rookie police officers sit in the same radio car and respond to the same calls for service, so there is a natural and immediate assumption from the citizens they serve that they are experienced police officers prepared for any eventuality.

Although an experienced partner can somewhat control the nature of the calls for service a rookie officer responds to, there are no guarantees that a serious situation might not occur on the first tour of duty. Accordingly, experience has shown law enforcement that in order to produce a truly experienced police officer who can successfully build on the solid foundation built by the police academy, a middle ground had to exist between the safe confines of the police academy and the potentially brutal realities of patrol. That middle ground, as it is known today, is a professionally structured field training program.

FIELD TRAINING PROGRAMS

The quote by Mark Twain is applicable to law enforcement training because prior to the existence of well-structured field training programs, young police officers who had recently graduated from the police academy would typically make one of two classic mistakes:

1. Most rookies were shy and reserved on patrol and reluctant to engage in simple routine tasks such as picking up the police

radio or volunteering for a call for service in their sector. This approach was both unproductive and unsafe. It was not only unsafe for the individual officer involved but also unsafe for the more experienced officers in neighboring sectors who relied on the rookie officer for backup and support. It also significantly increased the time normally associated with the learning curve to become a confident and safe law enforcement officer.

2. Some rookie officers were at the other behavioral extreme. They graduated from the police academy full of excitement and believed that they were fully prepared to fight crime and/or evil. These officers wanted to respond to every "gun run" that came over the radio or put handcuffs on every citizen they came in contact with, which was equally as dangerous and counterproductive. This approach to patrol can land a young rookie officer in situations way over their head very quickly. This approach can very easily end a career in law enforcement before it barely begins. Even if overenthusiastic rookies are fortunate enough to not get themselves or their partner hurt, it is still not a professional or safe way to learn what can be a fairly complex job.

In either case, rookie police officers were traditionally left to their own devices to learn the job. Some law enforcement agencies still do this today. They provide no structured and safe opportunity to effectively learn the job in a somewhat controlled environment. In today's surroundings, the old on-the-job approach simply leads to the development of lifelong bad habits, not to mention potentially huge exposure to criminal and civil liability for mistakes. The solution to the challenge of testing not only young officers' knowledge but also their ability to apply it was found in the creation of a structured field training and evaluation program.

Their Genesis

The idea of utilizing well-structured field training programs to provide a mechanism for knowledge integration in American policing is not new. It is also not an idea that was specifically designed for and developed by law enforcement alone. In 1965, the **President's Commission on Law Enforcement and Administration** made a number of recommendations to improve the practices of police departments. One of these recommendations was the creation of supervised field training programs.

In 1973, the **National Advisory Commission on Criminal Justice Standards and Goals** recommended that a minimum of four months of field training be included as a regular component of all recruit training. Additionally, in 1983, the **Commission on Accreditation for Law Enforcement Agencies** required field training as a standard in the comprehensive accreditation process for police agencies. The accreditation manual outlined forty-five different standards for training, one of which specifically required every agency seeking accreditation to have a formal field training program for all officers. These requirements were reviewed and endorsed by the Police Executive Research Forum, the International Association of Chiefs of Police, the National Sheriffs' Association, and the National Association of Black Law Enforcement Executives.

Their Structure

The formal structure of an effective field training program is perhaps its most essential element. In American policing today, this means the San Jose Field Training and Evaluation Program. The **San Jose model** was established by the San Jose Police Department in 1972. Today, many variations of the original San Jose model exist in progressive police agencies such as Houston, Texas; Boulder, Colorado; Newport News, Virginia; Largo, Florida; Washington, D.C.; and New York City. However, the basic field training and evaluation format remains the same.

In this format, experienced patrol officers are selected to serve as **field training officers (FTOs)** for the rookie officers. These FTOs receive additional training and compensation to prepare them for this task. Since they are already experienced patrol officers, the additional training often includes specific training and mentoring techniques, effective evaluation methods, the **adult learning process**, and proper behavior documentation strategies. This additional training is absolutely essential to the program's success and must be provided. A program for field training officers might be structured as follows:

Fourteen-Week FTO Program Structure

First block: Includes three weeks of training on the day shift with the first FTO and one week in transition before moving to a new shift

Second block: Includes three weeks of training on the evening shift with a different FTO and one week of transition before moving to a new shift

Third block: Includes three weeks of field training on the midnight shift with a third FTO and one week of transition before moving to a new shift

Fourth block: Includes two final weeks of pure evaluation and no training, with evaluation conducted by an experienced evaluator who was *not* one of the student's training officers

Their Implementation

Once a group of outstanding FTOs is selected, trained, and pre-pared, the implementation of a field training program can begin to take shape and structure. Most programs are fourteen weeks in duration. As illustrated above, this includes three weeks of train-ing under the direct supervision and direction of an FTO on the day shift, three weeks more with a different FTO on the evening shift; and a final three weeks of training with a third FTO on the midnight shift. During these twelve weeks of field training, every effort is made to expose the rookie officer to as many different types of calls for service as possible. But also during this time, every action of the rookie officer is carefully watched, critiqued, and meticulously documented.

The final two weeks are perhaps the most important because they are dedicated exclusively to evaluation. Such a program structure works extremely well for at least three reasons:

1. It exposes a rookie officer to at least three different FTOs dur-ing the training period. This is helpful because all veteran police officers develop their own style of policing consistent with their personality. Exposing a rookie to three different FTOs allows a rookie officer to observe essentially three dif-ferent styles of policing. One is not necessarily better or worse than the others, just different. A rookie police officer can then copy the best personal traits (and ignore the worst traits) of each FTO and incorporate them into his or her own personal policing style.
2. The schedule exposes a young officer to the three different shifts of police work. This is important because each shift car-ries with it unique working conditions, types of calls for service,

workloads, and types of citizens typical of that shift. In many ways, working the midnight shift is a very different type of policing than working during the day, and rookie officers need to experience both.

3. The changes expose young police officers to very different sectors and beats within the city. This is especially important in big-city police departments where the various neighborhoods are noticeably different and call for noticeably different policing styles.

In its entirety, the practice of rotating shifts and rotating partners can be very difficult for a rookie officer to adjust to and yet perform well. That is why the fourth, or transition, week is built into the training schedule. The actual learning process is so realistic that many officers will experience a great deal of stress and distress during the process. The extra nontraining week is essential for the rookie officer's psychological and physical well-being during the training. But for a police agency, the highly stressful yet structured field training process provides a very effective way to judge a young officer's ability to adjust to and perform the various job responsibilities. Most importantly, this assessment can be completed before an officer's probationary period expires, still allowing the department the option of termination before the sometimes burdensome civil service protections become applicable.

The final two weeks of field training, the evaluation phase, are critical to the overall assessment process. During the evaluation phase, the rookie officer is assigned to a **field training evaluator**, usually an FTO who is specifically trained to perform rookie evaluations and not personally involved in their training. This field training evaluator status provides the veteran officer with the autonomy to be critical of a student officer's performance. During the evaluation phase, the rookie officer is expected to operate as a single officer unit and handle any calls for service that come over the police radio.

Although the experienced evaluator is right beside the rookie as he or she works, the evaluator will only intervene in a situation where a rookie officer is about to get hurt or a scene is about to get out of control. In the evaluation phase of training, the field training evaluator is essentially an observer whose job is to assess and document the ability of the rookie officer to perform on his or her own. Some field training programs allow an evaluating officer to perform in plainclothes, removing the normal tendency of citizens to direct their attention to the older, more experienced-looking officer at a scene.

LAW ENFORCEMENT SUBCULTURE

By the end of the field training experience, rookie officers are expected to be able to demonstrate the ability to integrate a great deal of academic knowledge and its practical applications to police work. They are expected to be knowledgeable, brave, and confident on patrol. They are expected to be able to look like a police officer and act like a police officer. In fact, field training programs are designed to be the pinnacle not only of a comprehensive adult learning process but of the **socialization process** as well.

In addition to knowing the skills of policing, rookie officers are being evaluated for acceptance into the police subculture. Like all occupational subcultures, the law enforcement subculture requires certain personality traits that may not necessarily be captured in police academy test scores. During the training, rookie officers are evaluated and critiqued on the personality and behavioral aspects expected of a police officer. FTOs engage rookie officers in apparently idle conversations in the radio car designed to determine if the rookie officers have a "cop personality." Rookie officers are subtly evaluated on several personality traits:

- Bravery and physical courage to back up other officers in times of danger
- Character and moral courage to do the right thing, even if it is not the easiest course of behavior
- Loyalty to the department and to their fellow officers
- Healthy cynicism toward people and situations that present potential threats to officer safety
- Willingness to use force, even deadly force, if the situation warrants such a response
- Ability to hold their ego in check in the face of verbal abuse or other mistreatment from the public

The field training program's incremental approach to applying academic lessons learned in the academy is time-tested, and it works. It provides a systematic and safe approach to learning the sometimes-complex job of a police officer. It allows time for rookie officers to develop an individual law enforcement style that is consistent with their personality and that is also within the established guidelines of an organization and a free society. Finally, it is a proven way for a police department to ensure that rookie police officers have learned the critical skills necessary to perform the responsibilities of the job in a safe and defensible way.

ORGANIZATIONAL COMMITMENT

A professional and well-structured field training and evaluation program in policing is critical to closing the gap between academic lessons and practical application. It is essential to a professional law enforcement agency in preparing its young patrol officers. But, like all important things in life, it is not without costs and does require a significant organizational commitment to succeed.

The major required organizational commitments include the following:

- The officers selected to serve as FTOs and field training evaluators simply *must* be the best and the brightest of the agency. The FTOs must be the living personification of the values, behaviors, and qualities an agency wants to teach to the next generation of police officers. An organization must be willing to dedicate the time and efforts of the best veteran officers for this task.
- Some type of reward system (in the way of extra pay or extra compensatory time) should be provided to reward the best officers for serving as role models. Serving as an FTO is a time-consuming responsibility and requires the total commitment of veteran officers. When training, veteran officers do not work with their regular partners, often work different shifts with different days off, and make many other sacrifices.
- Opportunities to serve as an FTO or a field training evaluator are an excellent way for an organization to provide an extra option in the career path for officers who demonstrate leadership and/or supervisory abilities. Experience as an FTO should be considered in promotional decisions, if at all possible.
- The organization must provide considerable support to the FTOs in the way of specialized training. Rookie officers will not respect an FTO who is not current on their training process and knows less than they, as rookies, do about new policies and procedures. Moreover, the skills that make someone

an excellent police officer are completely different than the skills that make someone a teacher, a coach, and a mentor. FTOs have to be provided with the skills they need to facilitate adult learning and guide rookie officers through a difficult learning process.

- Organizational support must be apparent by the placement of the field training and evaluation program. Organizationally, this normally means that the program should work out of the patrol bureau or the office of chief of patrol, not the police academy. Police academies are the department's training experts and they should be involved, but they do not control the logistical and operational factors necessary to make the assignments in a field training and evaluation program work effectively.

- In each precinct, district, or remote location, a full-time field training and evaluation administrator should be selected and assigned. When the program is up and running, the effective scheduling and coordination responsibilities are a full-time job. In between recruit classes, the ongoing training and professional development of the existing FTOs remain a full-time job responsibility.

- Every member of a police agency must know that the field training program has the complete support and commitment of the command staff. During a standard six-month police academy, a significant investment is made in every recruit officer. However, if a rookie police officer is fully trained and evaluated and the consensus of the FTOs is that a particular officer has failed the evaluation phase, that rookie officer must be fired. Regardless of the significant organizational investment made to reach that point, or any other factor under consideration, the field training and evaluation standard must not be compromised.

Agency Size

It is important to note that different police departments require different training mandates. Smaller departments that train only a few new police officers every year in regional academies may not need such a highly structured program. Within reason, the instructional parameters of the field training program format may be adjusted. Smaller agencies may not require a full fourteen-week commitment or may not have the resources to expose a new recruit to three different FTOs during the training cycle.

The real utility of the field training model lies in its flexibility to accomplish the training mission. The process works, whether it is used on a large scale or a small scale. Law enforcement agencies interested in establishing a field training program should consult other departments of their size for the specifics and tools involved. In the actual implementation phase of a program, many additional considerations must be considered. In part, these considerations include such factors as standardized forms, performance rating systems, proper performance documentation, and internal and external validity of the instruments as well as many other operational aspects.

CONCLUSION

Much is expected of a police officer in a free society. Police departments that make the significant organizational commitment to the proper education and training of their recruits will enjoy dividends for many years to come. Conversely, police departments that constantly seek shortcuts to save a few dollars in the short run will ultimately pay more in the long run.

The successful transformation of a young person from a civilian to an experienced police officer is a time-consuming and expensive process. Experience has demonstrated that of all the emotions and desires experienced by a new police recruit, the most overwhelming desire is the desire to fit in, to look like just another veteran police officer. From an organizational perspective, it is absolutely essential that fitting in means copying the behaviors and attitudes of the handpicked FTOs. That will translate into a new generation of positive, well-adjusted professional police officers.

Without a field training program, a department runs the substantial risk of a rookie officer presupposing that fitting in and looking like the other veteran officers simply means being a negative, cynical "air bag." If this happens, the psychological erosion normally experienced by veteran street officers at around the five-year mark will begin to appear immediately in the rookie, and all the time invested at the police academy will be wiped out. Ultimately, the department will continue to produce problem officers and never accomplish the level of professionalism the community expects.

The field training process is an expensive and time-consuming process. But it is a necessary process because the core American virtues of freedom and justice are at stake. If America has learned anything in the wake of September 11, 2001, it is that the American way of life does not come cheaply.

KEY TERMS

Adult Learning Process
Commission on Accreditation
   for Law Enforcement Agencies
Field Training Evaluator
Field Training Officer (FTO)
National Advisory Commission
   on Criminal Justice Standards
   and Goals

President's Commission on
   Law Enforcement and
   Administration
San Jose Model
Socialization Process

QUESTIONS FOR DISCUSSION

1. Why is it important for rookie police officers to actually work all three shifts during their training process?
2. Compare and contrast the typical calls for service a police officer would experience on a day shift with the typical night shift calls for service.
3. Is it possible for a rookie police officer to perform very well academically in the police academy and perform poorly in the field training program? In what ways are the behavioral indicators different?
4. What are the dangers involved with rookie police officers being too aggressive on patrol? How can these dangers be avoided?
5. What are the dangers associated with rookie officers being too passive on patrol? How can these dangers be avoided?
6. What types of specialized training should be provided for the FTOs in a field training program?
7. List any unusual dangers associated with the evaluation phase of a field training program and discuss them.

8. What types of safeguards can be established in the evaluation phase of a program to protect against personality conflicts or more serious EEO concerns?
9. What are the drawbacks of providing a second chance to a rookie officer who fails the final evaluation phase of the field training program?
10. List and describe the characteristics that should be required to be an FTO.

SUGGESTED READINGS

Commission on Accreditation for Law Enforcement Agencies, Inc. (1983). *The standards for law enforcement agencies.* Fairfax, VA: CALEA.

Kaminski, Glenn F. (2002). *The field training concept in criminal justice agencies.* Upper Saddle River, NJ: Prentice-Hall.

National Advisory Commission on Standards and Goals. (1973). *Report of the Commission: Report on the police.* Washington, DC: U.S. Government Printing Office.

President's Commission on Law Enforcement and Administration of Justice. (1965). *Task force report: The police.* Washington, DC: U.S. Government Printing Office.

chapter *10*

EDUCATING AND TRAINING IN-SERVICE POLICE OFFICERS

Building an In-Service Model

"If I ever go to the doctor and I am told that I only have one week to live—I am immediately going to work and signing up for five days of in-service training. That way, I can be sure it will be the longest week of my life."

—A police officer overheard waiting for his training day to begin

INTRODUCTION

Most police departments are excellent at many different aspects of enforcing the law. This excellence includes the ability to deal with such complexities as ending potentially explosive and violent confrontations peacefully, safely controlling the peaceful movements and activities of large crowds at major public events, finding and arresting violent felons and taking them off the streets, saving lives, and emerging as true heroes in emergency situations, just to name a few. A professional police officer is a true American hero in every sense of the word.

But historically, **professional development** of the individual simply has not been a top priority of American policing.

Unfortunately, the quote at the beginning of this chapter essentially personifies the way most police officers feel about their annual in-service training experience each year. This is true, at least in part, because most police departments have not invested the necessary time and effort to make annual in-service training what it could be, or should be, for the officers. Everyone agrees that in-service training is important, but not everyone dedicates the resources to make it seem that way to the target audience.

In-service training simply has not been a high priority for a number of reasons, and most of them are absolutely valid. The current state of professional development in policing remains a low priority because the vast majority of police agencies have not realized the critical relationship that exists between individual career development and overall organizational success. Customarily, police administrators have believed that career development is accomplished simply by providing an opportunity to take a promotional exam on Saturday morning. On its own merits, there is nothing wrong with this belief. But in the larger context of professional development, it is just too narrow a perspective for everyone involved.

Civil service promotional exams *do* provide a fair and equal opportunity for all ambitious and career-minded police officers to get to the next rank and advance their careers. However, they also reward officers for what they have done off duty (study and take examinations) with little regard for what they have accomplished on duty. Additionally, promotions frequently serve to promote the best and the brightest out of patrol services, precisely where the talent is needed most. Finally, if getting promoted to the next rank is the only way for officers to earn more money, some officers will take a promotional exam for the wrong reason. If an officer does not want to be a supervisor and does not want the additional responsibility of managing other people, taking a promotional examination simply for the pay raise does not constitute professional development. If promotional examinations are the principal mechanism for professional development, the perceived value of working as a police officer in a patrol assignment will always be diminished.

PROFESSIONAL DEVELOPMENT AS CAREER DEVELOPMENT

Most police departments of all sizes have no problem dedicating significant time and resources to the professional development of their officers in the way of recruit training. They will assign a newly hired recruit officer at full pay to the police academy for a full six months before he or she ever performs one tour of duty for the agency. Such a commitment to education and training is necessary and proper.

Yet, in the very same agency, dedicating three or four days annually for veteran patrol officers to attend in-service training or qualify with their weapons continues to be seen as just another silly support function that needlessly takes more police officers off patrol. Such a view is understandable from a patrol sergeant's perspective. The dual responsibility of controlling regular days off, vacation time, and sick time and of providing adequate police services for every sector, covering fixed posts, and responding to calls for services can be challenging. But allowing officer in-service training to drop too far down on the priority list is shortsighted, counterproductive, and against the long-term interests of everyone involved.

Professional sports teams and private corporations, and practically every other sector in society, invest in their people; law enforcement must as well. Ongoing police officer education and training are unequivocally linked to officer safety and operational success. The overall operational effectiveness of any police department is directly contingent upon the quality of training and development it provides at every level. If it is done correctly, training can increase productivity, improve morale, keep an organizational culture positive and optimistic, and even serve to protect and reduce the overall exposure to civil liability.

EXPOSURE TO CIVIL LIABILITY

The principal theme expressed throughout this book is the inherent difficulties of policing a free republic. Being a police officer in a free society is an extremely difficult responsibility, and mistakes and misconduct will happen. When they do, they are almost always resolved through timely internal investigations, public apologies, disciplinary proceedings, and promises to the community that such behavior is an aberration and will not be tolerated. But regardless of how well an agency handles such situations, there remains the problem of exposure to civil liability.

The potential exposure to civil liability on the part of the individual officer, the entire department, and the city can be manifested in many ways. Civil liability can be pursued in cases involving the use of force; direct enforcement activities such as arrests, searches, and property confiscations; perceived failure to take direct police actions; police behavior in emergency situations such as high-speed vehicle pursuits; and many other special situations resulting from some typical law enforcement action or inaction.

In some cases, the police do what they perceive to be their jobs and intervene in already bad situations. In these types of situations, citizens have typically already been injured or victimized. Policing is very reactive in nature. In many of these cases, civil lawsuits will follow that claim one of the following allegations:

- Negligent training, based on an organization's responsibility to properly train all members to perform their job assignments and tasks (*Popow* v. *City of Margate,* 1979).
- Negligent assignment, based on the assignment of employees to a job that they are unqualified or untrained to perform (*Moon* v. *Winfield,* 1974).
- Negligent entrustment, based on an organization's responsibility to prevent officers from using any equipment, such as firearms, special law enforcement vehicles, or nightsticks, that they are not qualified to use (*Hacker* v. *City of New York,* 1965).

For any of these reasons and many others, the failure to properly train members initially or the failure to sustain their qualifications annually through in-service training can serve as the basis for a wide range of civil lawsuits and civil damages under Title 42 of the United States Code, Section 1983.

For example, in the case of *City of Canton* v. *Harris* (1989), the plaintiff was arrested and taken to the police station. Upon arrival at the police station, the suspect was found lying on the floor of the police vehicle. At that time, the police asked if she needed medical attention, and she responded with the utterance of some incoherent remarks. During the subsequent arrest processing, the plaintiff again slumped to the floor. At that time, she was transported to the hospital by ambulance. Later, the plaintiff filed a United States Code, Title 42, Section 1983, suit against the police alleging that her constitutional rights to due process were violated. Evidence was provided during the trial that indicated that the tour commanders at the police station on the night of her incarceration were, in fact, authorized and expected to make a determination whether a detainee required medical attention or not. However, testimony was also provided at the trial to show that although the tour commanders were authorized and expected to make such a determination, they were not provided with any special training preparing them to make such a diagnosis. The district court decided in favor of the plaintiff on the medical claim, and the Sixth Circuit Court of Appeals affirmed the decision.

The case was appealed to the U.S. Supreme Court, which decided that "failure to train" in any area that an officer is authorized to take action in *can* be a basis of liability under Section 1983. The Court went on to further explain that the failure to train would have to be based on a "deliberate indifference" to the rights of those with whom the police come in contact (*City of Canton* v. *Harris,* 1989).

The U.S. Supreme Court then set forth what may be considered the requisites for liability based on the **deliberate indifference standard** (del Carmen and Kappeler, 1991):

- The focus must be on the adequacy of the training program in relation to the tasks the particular officer must perform.
- The fact that a particular officer may be unsatisfactorily trained will not, in and of itself, result in city liability. An officer's failure may result from factors other than a faulty training experience.
- It is not sufficient to impose liability if it can be proven that an injury or accident could have been avoided if an officer had better or more training. Officers can always have better or more training.
- The appropriate deficiency in a city's training program must be closely associated to the ultimate injury.

Clearly, at the federal level, the state level, and the local level, the legal standard in regard to the requirement to properly train police officers has been set. Aside from all the customary and business reasons for providing the necessary time and resources to ongoing training and development, the relentless and perpetual exposure to civil liability and civil damages when it comes to the day-to-day job responsibilities of a police officer provides more than enough incentive. As the bumper sticker states, "If you think education is expensive, try ignorance."

PRACTICAL CONSIDERATIONS OF IN-SERVICE TRAINING

The practical side of this issue is that providing comprehensive and timely in-service training for all civilian and sworn members of the service is an expensive, difficult, and logistically complicated task. For the most part, police officers don't like attending annual in-service training. It seems to be universally true that, from police officers' perspective, attending annual in-service presents a number of problems:

- It breaks their daily routine and upsets their personal schedules.
- It often requires them to work different tours in a different part of the city, which creates commuting problems.
- They have to listen to instructors who are sometimes less enthusiastic and less experienced in a topic than the officers themselves
- It requires them to sit in a classroom for eight hours and listen to lectures, ignoring the fact that the reason most people go into law enforcement in the first place is because they hate sitting inside all day.
- It typically consists of a series of unrelated boring lectures clearly designed to protect the department. Moreover, these blocks of instruction are inserted between late starts, long breaks, and early releases.

From a police administrator's perspective, assigning police officers to in-service training is no bargain either. It does not address the immediate priorities of responses to 911 calls, the dispatcher's many other calls for service being put on hold due to the unavailability of radio cars, crime spikes and crime patterns, and the perennial stack of community problems that need to be addressed.

Because of these traditional conflicts of both the officers and the bosses, the whole issue of career development manifested through annual in-service training becomes wedged in a downward cycle. Patrol administrators are not going to assign their scarce patrol resources to training, only to have the police officers return the next day complaining about their time being wasted. This classic dilemma of individual development for police officers simply must be reversed. Building a comprehensive in-service training model that provides a continuum of progressive and practical career development opportunities offered over the span of a twenty-year career is an excellent start. In-service training that is exciting and new, that builds on police experience from the past, and that prepares for the experiences of the future can reverse the cycle.

IN-SERVICE TRAINING MODEL

For too long, American police officers who choose to stay in patrol and perform as patrol officers have been allowed to become stagnant and bored. After a while, they perform a litany of routine calls for service and begin to perform the job on automatic pilot. Police officers who do not take promotional exams, for whatever reason, are often left to feel like they are performing one year of police work twenty times. After the first year, the excitement and the learning stop, and the routine sets in. Police officers in this situation go through a career frustrated and demoralized.

Instead, a police career should be guided by a comprehensive structure of professional development that contributes to twenty years of progressive learning. Effective in-service training can keep the officers on a professional learning curve, and it can establish horizontal professional growth. Organizationally, this can be accomplished with occasional temporary assignments to specialized units, periodic special assignments to different specialized functions, and exposure to the various functions of American policing. The only way American policing is ever going to get better is if American police officers get better. Becoming a sergeant should be only one of many channels for this to happen.

The academic discipline of policing is rich enough to sustain such a learning experience, and the complexity of patrol and the many specialized fields involved in actual police work are deep enough to sustain it. Since the typical police department is a civil service agency, the police officers are a captive audience for at least twenty years. In a field with rapidly emerging technology, changing legal issues, and constantly shifting crime patterns, why should annual in-service training ever be boring and unproductive?

To sustain excitement and interest, a department's career development model must be progressive in design and comprehensive in scope. The model must be multitiered and flexible enough to address the immediate needs of a ten- to fifteen-minute daily **roll call briefing** and the massive demand for specialized training as well as the more structured and cerebral educational blocks of instruction. Once again, the advantage is that there is no rush! It is not simply an eight-hour commitment to unrelated updates designed to meet some type of externally imposed training commitment. Career development should be viewed as a progressive twenty-year plan, built on an excellent foundation of recruit training and patrol experience.

TIERS OF PROGRESSIVE PROFESSIONAL DEVELOPMENT PLAN

1. Recruit Training
2. Field Training Program
3. Daily Roll Call Briefings
4. Annual In-Service Training
5. Annual Firearms Qualification
6. Specialized Training
7. Five-Year Refresher Class
8. Tactical Training
9. Change of Assignment Training
10. Promotional Training
11. Executive Development

Recruit Training as the Foundation

A comprehensive career development model in American policing effectively starts with the recruit training experience as a foundation. That's right, recruit training. As discussed earlier in this text, a comprehensive recruit training curriculum grounded in police science, behavioral sciences, the law, and physical training and tactics should establish an excellent foundation for a lifetime of learning. It provides the basis of knowledge to be built upon in subsequent training years, which are focused on advanced and highly specialized training experiences. Everything in a police career starts with, and builds on, patrol experience. The professional development plan should as well. Moreover, if the recruit training experience is done correctly, effective learning habits such as being on time for class, looking professional and prepared for duty, preparing, studying, reading, maintaining good physical condition, and practicing the overall personal discipline normally expected of professional police officers are all instilled in the student officer.

These same character traits should be constantly reinforced through annual in-service training. In-service training should sustain the expectations of the recruit school and demand officers demonstrate their ability to still meet the standards. To loosen up and allow veteran officers to show up for their in-service training late, in casual attire, and with a newspaper and a cup of coffee in their hands will immediately send the wrong message to the officers. If the training atmosphere is a joke, the material will also be treated like a joke.

FIELD TRAINING AND EVALUATION

As the education and training of a young police officer continue, the learning curve is especially accelerated in the field training and evaluation program. This is where all the knowledge is integrated and practical application is tested. This is where the immeasurable personality traits of physical courage and moral courage are developed and hardened. This is where an individual policing personality, representing the best from each of the FTOs, is formed that will probably be sustained for an officer's entire career. Most importantly, this is where the student officer actually stops thinking like a civilian and starts thinking like a police officer.

Daily Roll Call Briefings

To remain relevant and current, a comprehensive in-service training model must have a number of different operating levels. In-service is the most comprehensive and important. From the small agencies that employ 10 police officers or less to the New York City Police Department with its 40,000 uniformed members of the service, the bulk of the target training population is captured in the in-service component. But regardless of the size of the agency, the first level of training operation should be the **roll call briefing**.

Roll call briefing typically consists of daily updates that occur right in the local police station, barracks, or precinct for approximately ten to twenty minutes a day. Trainers should realize up front that this is normally not a very formal or especially productive commitment of time. Most police facilities are simply not designed to be, or capable of being, conducive to a learning environment. Roll call briefings typically occur in between officers picking up radio car keys, signing out police radios, looking for radar guns, and tending to an occasional screaming prisoner.

Roll call briefings can only be used for informal, short, and current information updates but remain a valuable forum for the distribution of rapidly changing information. Although they are conducted in a decentralized fashion in the local police facility by a roll call sergeant, they should still be distributed and administered as a centralized component of the police academy training program. Under the direction of the centralized police academy, the information contained in these daily briefings can be consistent both throughout the city where appropriate and locally in regard to emerging crime patterns and local precinct conditions, as needed. But centralized distribution of the training materials can ensure a department's ability to meet and document the appropriate state training standards.

In 1967, the President's Commission on Law Enforcement and the Administration of Justice recommended that peace officer standards and training commissions be established in every state. Such peace officer standards and training commissions now exist in every state but Hawaii. They effectively establish the minimum parameters and requirements for all training delivered in every local agency. The training director must ensure that all training, even local roll call–level briefings, is uniform and documented to meet or exceed these standards.

In addition to meeting state standards, the attendance at these briefings as well as the subject matter covered and the lesson plans utilized should be well documented and saved in centralized training archives. The importance of complete and thorough documentation of all police officer attendance and training records cannot be overstated. When an officer or a department is sued, at some point in the process the training director will be called to testify, and his or her testimony will only be as comprehensive and valid as the training records. Typically, trials and/or depositions involving accusations of deliberate indifference through training are conducted years after an alleged incident. For legal purposes, any training that was delivered and not properly documented simply does not exist and is useless in defending the officers or the agency involved. This vital purpose is best accomplished by the centralized control of the training function, even in the largest cities with the most personnel.

Although they are typically less formal and less structured than other professional training programs offered by police agencies, daily roll call–based briefings are essential to the fast-changing pace of American policing, especially in the medium to large law enforcement agencies where it may require a full year to cycle all the members through a structured in-service program. To them, the less formal local police facility–based briefings are effective in distributing timely but necessary information. Agency-wide information, such as legal updates, procedural updates, operations orders, large details involving the temporary reassignment of personnel, and other upcoming departmental orders and written directives, is effectively distributed through this format. Experienced officers do not require a lot of explanation with such operational documents, and they can be read during the officers' tour of duty.

Annual In-Service Training Days

The next level of training operations is the more structured annual in-service component. There are scores of structural and operational considerations to be thoroughly thought out in building an effective in-service training delivery model. Many of them are dictated by such variables as the size of the agency, the instructional methodology to be utilized, the nature of the training agenda they choose to undertake, and the organizational priority of in-service training in general.

For example, the smaller agencies can conduct their annual in-service training at one centralized location for all members of the service. They may also be able to schedule an entire week of training on five consecutive days and easily comply with any state-mandated requirements. Agencies can also utilize auditorium-style seminar-type lectures and deliver a large amount of information to a large number of officers in a small amount of time.

However, because of the sheer volume of logistical challenges, many of the larger cities often prefer to conduct their in-service training in a number of satellite or sector locations, dividing the city up geographically. Some agencies allow the officers to attend training in plainclothes, while others require them to attend in uniform in case of an unexpected mobilization during the training.

Many agencies consider two or three annual days of live fire qualification at the firearms range each year to meet the principal learning objective of firearms qualifications. Others are choosing to dedicate more time to firearms training but implementing innovative learning strategies such as **firearms simulators**, tactical awareness classes, nonlethal weapons training, or long gun qualifications, as well as other innovative training strategies involving the use of force.

None of these considerations are inherently right or wrong, better or worse than others. Instead, each agency must make its decision based on such considerations as its capabilities to administer such a program, state and/or local training mandates to be realized, and the preference of its local command staff. Every effort must be made right from the start, however, to properly align the structure and operations of the training program with the priorities and cooperation of patrol commanders.

While there are no definitive answers to the many structural issues surrounding in-service training, there clearly are some critical considerations that should be factored into the design and delivery of any professional in-service program. These factors should be discussed with patrol commanders before implementation to ensure that the effectiveness of the training and the operational efficiency of patrol operations can peacefully coexist in an agency.

Instructional Methodology

One such issue is the **instructional methodology** utilized to train police officers. Whether the structured section of the in-service training is one, two, three, or five days of instruction, perhaps the most important decision to be made is the instructional methodology to be employed. The traditional method is, of course, lecture-based delivery. Lecture-based in-service training is efficient because it can be utilized to instruct large groups of students and to deliver a considerable amount of information in a relatively short period of time. However, lecture-based methods usually do not work well with adult learners, and certainly not with police officers. Lecture-based training was once described as "a process by which facts are transmitted from the notebook of the instructor to the notebook of the student without passing through the minds of either" (Staton, 1960).

Much more effective instructional methods for teaching police officers appear to be the utilization of role plays and law enforcement simulations. In role-playing lessons, different police officers act out various parts of a typical law enforcement scenario. The lead instructor provides specific scripts for the role plays, and the role plays provide an active hands-on learning process for everyone involved. The actors learn from the experience by practicing the various verbal skills needed to effectively pull off a role play with veteran police officers. The students watching the role play are actively engaged in watching the scenario play out because they know that, at the conclusion of the session, there will be a detailed debriefing by a lead instructor. During the debriefing, everyone will be called on to critique the action of the officers involved in the scenario.

A CASE IN POINT

Day One	*Day Two*
Conducted on 4-12 tour	Conducted on day tour
In uniform	In uniform
Series of role plays	Classroom instruction
Actual street locations	Based on prior day's work
Group deb riefings	Instructor-facilitated class

The New York City Police Department has developed an excellent framework for a model of role plays that is called **in-tac training** (in-service tactical training). Most of N.Y.P.D.'s annual in-service training is accomplished through the in-tac format, and it appears to be a very effective framework for training veteran police officers. In the in-tac model, every two days a new cohort of officers shows up at eight different geographic locations throughout the city. Each location offers access to an actual street location where a scene can be sectioned off and the role plays can safely be conducted. There is also the requirement of a classroom in close proximity. In many of the locations, the trainers utilize remote streets in an industrial area of town and simply block off the locations during training. The training is designed for two consecutive days, and the officers appear in uniform, with all their gear. If at all possible, officers are encouraged to attend with their regular partner. This is helpful for two reasons: It is always advantageous for those who work together to train together, and it also keeps the officers prepared in case of a jobwide mobilization.

The entire first day of training is dedicated to a litany of comprehensive street scenario role plays. The police academy instructors are the facilitators and actors, and every scenario is carefully and uniformly scripted for safety. Scripting the role plays beforehand is necessary to ensure that the type of response anticipated from the officers will properly illustrate the lessons to be learned. Two officers working as partners are placed in a radio car around the corner and dispatched to the location. Upon their arrival on the scene, the action begins. From that point, instructors observe every aspect of the role play. Everything from officer demeanor to officer safety, use of cover and concealment, and communications skills is considered.

At the conclusion of each scenario, a group debriefing is conducted, constructively reviewing every aspect of the response. Each student is provided an opportunity to suggest what could have been done differently. An **instructional debriefing** keeps all the students actively involved in the process and provides the dimension of peer review to the evaluation.

Each scenario has a site coordinator, usually a lieutenant of police, in command to ensure safety considerations and to make sure the role plays never get out of hand. This is necessary because the scenarios can get intense, emotions can run high, and the training can take on a very real tone. With experience, police academy actors become very skilled at immediately noticing weaknesses in the police response and may choose to get the most out of those weaknesses to make a point in the subsequent instructional debriefing session.

The second day, the same officers report back to the same location, but this day is dedicated to classroom instruction. New material, videotapes from the previous day's activities, and other lessons are reviewed and discussed. This is when the police academy instructors offer the official instructional objectives and relate them to the very real lessons of the previous day's activities. Every lesson taught in the classroom environment is based on, and referenced to, a specific fact pattern of one of the street scenarios. Because much of the material is based on the previous day's activities and because the officers were personally involved in the learning process, a great deal of new and important information is shared. The information is shared in a very collaborative way, however, and not simply given as lectures to the officers.

The real value of the in-tac format lies not in the way the New York City Police Department does it but in the instructional framework. The format can be applied to any size training operation. Any new information, new material, new legal issue, or new department policy, as well as any other lesson, can be easily and effectively integrated and illustrated through this framework.

Through the in-tac framework, student officers learn by hearing, seeing, and doing—the way adult learners learn best. It allows police academy personnel to still teach the important issues of the day, but in a format better suited for adult learners. Most importantly, no matter what the instructional objectives are, every scenario is observed for the fundamental skills of effective communication and officer safety and survival.

Instructional Technology

Another possible instructional method that facilitates adult learning and makes in-service training interesting is **instructional technology**. For example, the use of firearms and driving simulators provides a format that actively involves the officers in the lessons and sustains their attention. Through the effective use of instructional technology, the student officers' reactions can be captured on computer and utilized to significantly enhance an instructional debriefing session. Marksmanship, important environmental decisions, and overall judgment can all be reviewed by senior instructors. Firearms and driving simulators are currently utilized extensively by many law enforcement agencies around the country, and the training assessments are proven to be positive and effective.

Naturally, as a comprehensive education and training program is developed for in-service veterans, a combination of many instructional methods should be incorporated. A combination of some lecture-based instruction coupled with role plays and simulators can be very constructive and productive. By doing this, the possibilities are limited only by the imagination of the instructors and the budget of the training academy. But if it is true that adults learn 10 percent of what they see, 20 percent of what they hear, and another 10 percent of what they touch, an effective method of teaching adult police officers should incorporate all three of these senses into the learning process.

It is also significant to note that the various innovative instructional methodologies enhance the role of the police academy instructor. The instructor is transformed from a mere lecturer to an active participant, a role experienced police officers are typically much better prepared to perform.

Finally, experience has shown that the more progressive instructional methodologies do have their downside. The instructors must be provided with advanced instructor training to prepare them to effectively assume the various roles needed in role plays. It is not easy to professionally facilitate role plays, and extra care must be given to ensure they do not get out of hand and compromise officer safety. Extra instructor training must be provided to teach unconventional evaluation methods. Role plays and technology-led instruction are often evaluated very differently than providing a simple multiple-choice examination at the end of the class.

Instructional technology can also be expensive in terms of time, money, training space, and personnel. Traditional classroom space will not work for role plays; an actual street scenario is required. The instructor to student ratio will also increase. More instructors and/or facilitators are needed to assume the various roles of the scenario. Some police departments have utilized restricted duty officers for this responsibility, but either way, additional instructors and resources are necessary.

Principle of Inclusion

Another critical consideration in the development of a comprehensive in-service training model is the **principle of inclusion**. Police agencies have a tendency to focus the limited educational and training resources of the agency on patrol. While patrol is, without question, a critical function and the main job of most of the personnel, every effort should be made to include all personnel in some type of in-service training component.

Many specialized police officers assigned to bureaus outside the patrol bureau are routinely excluded from training opportunities. For example, both patrol officers and detectives involved in criminal investigations should be continuously trained. Police officers assigned to specialized functions such as community affairs, fleet maintenance, staff assignments, and other remote assignments must also be cycled through training. Although such personnel may not be assigned to patrol on a daily basis, by virtue of their status as police officers, they may be called on to perform patrol at any moment. Every sworn member must stay current, certified, and prepared for the eventuality of an off-duty police action, a citywide patrol mobilization, or some other unexpected call to action.

Civilian staff, civilian managers, civilian dispatchers, and other support personnel must be included as well. Civilian personnel may be provided with access to specialized job-specific training courses, but they must also be kept current and properly trained for their job responsibilities. Ultimately, a structure of **organizational development** that trains civilian dispatchers along with the police officers they direct on a daily basis would probably make a great deal of sense. Sergeants, lieutenants, captains, and department executives should also be included in the career development process.

Finally, although it may appear to be a logistical nightmare for the larger departments, every effort should be made to build a training structure that allows various personnel to train together. People who work together should train together. Traditionally, many distinctions are made in the delivery of training services that offer administrative convenience but defy operational realities. There is no universal principle that claims that police officers and detectives cannot train together, that police officers and sergeants cannot train together, or that sworn members and civilians who support them operationally cannot train together. Think of the potential officer safety and survival benefits of civilian dispatchers, uniformed police officers, plainclothes officers, and sergeants who work in the same district spending a few days away from work together, walking through tactical training scenarios!

Although it is clearly difficult on patrol operations for that period of time, it will almost certainly lead to better operational efficiency in the field and enhanced police officer safety and survival. It seems simple: People who work together should train together. Whether a citywide task force is brought in to cover a sector for the training period or some other arrangements are made, the logistical considerations should not be allowed to nullify the many potential benefits of having officers who work together train together.

Civilian dispatchers should know the police officers in their sectors personally. They should be able to put a face and a personality with the voice they hear every day. Patrol sergeants should know the operational capabilities of the officers they supervise. Training together can establish a much-needed level of unspoken communication and understanding not normally developed during the day-to-day rigors of patrol.

Specialized Training

Another vital tier of a comprehensive career development program is the opportunity for specialized training. As an individual police officer's career develops, assignments, experiences, interests, and career goals evolve. Due to the complexity of policing, the opportunity for specialized training must exist above and beyond the standard-issue annual in-service training. Such specialized training should be comparable to electives in college. They can be classes above and beyond the annual training and firearms qualifications requirements. They should be highly specialized in design and content and should be offered to prepare law enforcement personnel for either an assignment they currently occupy or an assignment they aspire to reach.

Specialized educational opportunities may include these law enforcement–related topics:

- Computer and technology training
- Advanced tactical communications
- Foreign language classes offered in the community by community representatives
- Martial arts and advanced officer safety and survival tactics
- Advanced driving skills (such as defensive driving, driving a bus, driving specialized high-water vehicles, and driving four-wheel-drive vehicles)
- Crime scene management and forensics
- Principles of leadership
- Emerging law enforcement issues such as **COMPSTAT**, terrorism, and gangs

In addition to these internal and very traditional areas of education and training, outside opportunities should be monitored and assigned to agency personnel. Interagency training classes, both local and federal, are available and productive. Significant educational opportunities often exist at local colleges and universities and are often free to law enforcement personnel. Essentially, a professional police academy director should and must constantly scan the entire career development environment to capitalize on and promote unique and interesting opportunities for agency members.

In the end, simply requiring police officers to show up at the police academy once a year and listen to a series of unrelated lectures is obsolete, unproductive, and insufferable in law enforcement today. Police officers deserve better, and due to potential liability associated with mistakes, the expense of professional development is no longer an excuse!

FIVE-YEAR REFRESHER

The idea of a five-year refresher is somewhat of an untested and untraditional strategy in American policing. Essentially, it is built on the belief that every few years, a specialized course should be required for *all* police officers. There is nothing magical about the five-year mark; it is not based on any empirical data or some psychological milestone. The five-year mark just seems like as good a place as any to offer a refresher to experienced members of the service. The length of the class is not clearly decided either and might be four or five days long. Even the blocks of instruction are not predetermined; in fact, they can and should vary from time to time. But they would always involve some components of a physical, intellectual, and psychological refresher.

The idea of a five-year refresher for law enforcement is based on something the airline industry figured out a long time ago. When people board a plane and prepare for takeoff, they are always told that if the plane begins to suddenly lose altitude, the air masks will automatically fall. Passengers are then informed that if they are traveling with a child or a companion who needs assistance, they should put the mask on themselves first and then render aid to the child or companion. Without such a warning, most passengers on an airline would probably do the opposite. Due to the heroic instincts in most police officers, they would probably also put the air mask on a child or companion first.

Upon further reflection, the policy of the airlines makes perfect sense. It is physically impossible for a person to assist others in an emergency if he or she can't breathe—a simple premise, yet not one that seems to be practiced in American policing. Twenty-four hours a day, seven days a week, police officers are prepared to help others. Yet, a close look at most police agencies would suggest that police officers are not taking care of themselves physically, intellectually, and certainly not psychologically. Stories about police officer corruption, suicide, divorce, alcoholism, violence, burnout, and other personal problems abound. In New York City, for example, the **Mollen Commission Report** discussed widespread police corruption and wrongdoing (Mollen Commission, 1994). The report was so detailed that it prompted police psychologists to examine police behavior and to study the underlying factors such as stress and distress.

From a training prospective, the interesting aspect of many of the stories of corruption and abuse is found in the realization that, in most cases, they were not stories of a bad person who somehow

slipped through the screening procedure and became a police officer. Instead, they were typically stories of good people from good
families who became good police officers. But along the way, these
individuals were incrementally beaten down by the relentless negative cycle of police work. They were typically stories of good people who experienced physical, emotional, and psychological erosion
after being constantly exposed to negative experiences.

The police personality, if there is such a thing, is not a result
of some personality characteristic that existed prior to entry into
law enforcement. It is, instead, a result of the law enforcement culture found within each police agency that wears down the human
spirit. To exist in the face of relentless negative exposures, law
enforcement personnel systematically develop emotional **defense
mechanisms**. These defense mechanisms usually manifest themselves as a keen sense of humor, sarcasm, cynicism, a general distrust for civilians, and an overall negative "hair bag" attitude.

When this perspective sets in, and it always does, it is further
confirmed by external pressures. The political pressures normally
associated with doing police work in a society where freedom is
given such a high priority, the economic pressures associated with
police officer salaries, and the organizational decisions that sometimes leave police officers wondering whose side the bosses are on
all add up. If such a process is not interrupted by some type of
refresher training, the police personality can evolve to create an
individual who is not such a good police officer anymore, and not
such a good person either.

There clearly is a need for some type of intervention or
refresher to remind the officers of who they are and why they
entered law enforcement in the first place. A discussion about the
virtues of staying in shape and proper dieting to promote their
physical well-being is needed. An academic review of the basics of
law enforcement is required to remind the officers of the foundation
of their discipline. Finally, a psychological discussion led by a professional psychologist is appropriate to restore the compassion and
to debrief the officers on their experiences and perspectives. Over a
five-, ten-, or fifteen-year period, police officers cannot be expected
to process all they see and walk away as balanced as when they
were middle-class kids skipping through suburbia. Experienced
police officers are individuals who occasionally need to be lifted up
to make it through their twenty years of service, not locked up
when they make a mistake and behave in a manner that is perfectly consistent with their negative experiences and perspective.

Paradoxically, the same negative perspective that keeps officers alive on the street wears them down as human beings. The five-year refresher is a good start to lift officers up, and the training director must take the lead.

CONCLUSION

A comprehensive in-service education and training program is the cornerstone of healthy police officers and a healthy police organization. Since all organizations are made up of individuals, individual development must be established before any serious attempt at organizational development can be made. Police departments do not get better unless the police officers get better. While a training director may be responsible for both, the principles of sequencing must be observed.

With all the diversity, challenges, and excitement associated with policing a free republic, police officers should never be bored, and their training should never be static. Given the types of personalities normally drawn to policing, officers simply must be given the opportunity to self-actualize at work through ongoing professional development.

This cannot be accomplished, however, by bringing the officers into a classroom once a year and telling them all the things they cannot do. It can be accomplished by continuously exploring innovative instructional formats and methodologies designed to involve the officers in the learning process. After all, all police officers want is to attend in-service training and walk away eight hours later feeling like the time was well spent.

KEY TERMS

COMPSTAT
Defense Mechanisms
Deliberate Indifference
   Standard
Firearms Simulators
Instructional Debriefing
Instructional Methodology

Instructional Technology
In-tac Training
Mollen Commission Report
Organizational Development
Principle of Inclusion
Professional Development
Roll Call Briefing

QUESTIONS FOR DISCUSSION

1. Why do many police departments dedicate so much time and so many resources to recruit training and so very little time and resources to in-service training?

2. Given the facts of the *City of Canton* v. *Harris* case, as described in the text, is it reasonable to hold a tour commander responsible for making a proper medical diagnosis on all incarcerated individuals?

3. Describe the deliberate indifference standard. How far can a legal claim against the police for failure to train actually reach?

4. How important is proper training documentation to a professional training facility? What would be the best way to maintain proper and complete training records?

5. What are the various considerations about in-service training that have made it an unpleasant experience for many police officers? Can such considerations be operationally controlled?

6. What can be done to provide the incentive for patrol commanders to encourage police officers to attend an annual in-service training session?

7. At some point, is a refresher class really necessary, or should in-service training time continue to be committed to actual job-related topics?

8. What are the advantages of a centralized training component? Why not simply allow each geographic location to teach its own agenda, consistent with local issues?

9. How are recruit training and in-service training linked? Does there have to be any relationship between the two different functions?

10. How can a scenario-based training format be applied to a small law enforcement agency?

SUGGESTED READINGS

Chandler, J.T. (1990). *Modern police psychology for law enforcement and human behavior professionals.* Springfield, IL: Charles C. Thomas Press.

City of Canton v. *Harris*. (1989). 109 S.Ct. 1197.

Del Carmen, R.V., and V.E. Kappeler. (1991). Municipal and police agencies as defendants: Liability for official policy and custom. *American Journal of Police* 101(1): 1–17.

Hacker v. *City of New York*. (1965). 261 N.Y.S. 2nd 751.

Mollen Commission. (1994). *Commission to investigate allegations of police corruption and the anti-corruption procedures of the police department.* New York: Mollen Commission.

Moon v. *Winfield*. (1974). 383 F.Supp 31 (D.C., Ill. 1974).

Ostrom, Elinor. (1986). Police/law enforcement and psychology. *Behavioral Sciences and the Law* 4: 353–370.

Popow v. *City of Margate*. (1979). 476 F.Supp. 1237 (D.C., N.J. 1979).

President's Commission on Law Enforcement and Administration of Justice. (1967). *Task force report.* Washington, DC: U.S. Government Printing Office.

Staton, Thomas. (1960). *How to instruct successfully: Modern teaching methods in adult education.* New York: McGraw-Hill Book Company.

TRAINING POLICE SUPERVISORS AND MANAGERS

"Leadership and learning are indispensable to each other."
—John Fitzgerald Kennedy

INTRODUCTION

In a very vital and compelling way, the sergeants, lieutenants, captains, and civilian managerial equivalents of a police agency play an essential role in the effective and efficient day-to-day operations of an agency. Collectively, they are the real catalyst in the organization and management of the department. In fact, if American policing is ever to elevate above the status of just another civil service job and become a true profession of protecting democracy, middle management is exactly where the battle must be won.

Police supervisors and managers hold very unique job responsibilities and a very distinctive place in the organizational chain of command. They are close enough to the actual delivery of police services to deal with the officers every day. Yet, they enjoy enough authority and rank to represent a department's command structure. This rank and authority effectively require them to maintain the professional distance of a good boss yet still be visible and involved in the daily operations. The visibility also puts a department's supervisors and managers in the position of being role models for the police officers who work for them and who may aspire to be a boss one day.

Given this significance of rank in law enforcement, a professional police agency must make a considerable commitment to both the initial and ongoing preparation and development of sergeants, lieutenants, captains, and civilian managers. Present and future needs of an organization will be effectively managed in direct proportion to its commitment to management development. Without it, an agency will quickly become stagnant and inert, allowing the present and the future to manage it.

MANAGER DEVELOPMENT

To be done correctly, the preparation and development of management personnel should be comprehensive, intellectually progressive, and continual. The instructional formats must include both a **perceptual component** and a **conceptual component**. Instruction on the perceptual level should include the actual nuts-and-bolts responsibilities associated with the job; instruction on the conceptual level should include the higher-level responsibilities of management such as personnel development, a long-range vision, and the principles of organizational change and leadership.

Supervisors' classes for newly promoted sergeants and in-service sergeants should be constructed to be training-based, focusing disproportionately on the specific policies, procedures, and operational responsibilities of the rank. Once these very practical aspects of the rank are established, and the sergeants have enough technical knowledge to survive and effectively manage the police officers assigned to them, then there can be an introduction to the principles of individual management and leadership.

Lieutenants' and captains' promotional and in-service classes, on the other hand, should be disproportionately educationally based, reviewing any new or specifically significant policies and procedures of the job yet focusing heavily on the conceptual principles of organizational and transformational leadership. As a rule of thumb, the lower the rank, the more perceptual the training should be. As the rank gets higher, the **level of abstraction** of the education should be raised accordingly:

LEVEL OF ABSTRACTION IN MANAGEMENT DEVELOPMENT

Sergeants	*Lieutenants*	*Captains and Above*
80% perceptual	50% perceptual	80% conceptual
20% conceptual	50% conceptual	20% perceptual

Supervisors learn about policies and procedures; managers learn about principles of change and transformational leadership. To properly contribute to an organization's development, the education and training provided by a police academy should reflect the job responsibilities as they are now and prepare the members to envision and create the job responsibilities as they should be in the future.

Organizational Commitment to Manager Development

There are many genuine reasons for an organization to make the necessary commitment to management development. Essentially, first-line supervisors run the daily operations of a police agency, ensuring that the proper policies and procedures are followed today. Conversely, the police lieutenants and captains should be involved in leading the way toward the future by analyzing changing crime patterns and blazing new crime-fighting strategies to combat emerging crime control issues. This is more necessary today than ever before. Regardless of the size of an agency, law enforcement managers of today should be thinking about global crime, international terrorism, and other emerging issues that appear to render traditional law enforcement strategies futile and ineffective. A commitment to the professional development of the sergeants, lieutenants, and captains to perform their respective roles is critical to public safety. Facing the challenges of law enforcement today, the community cannot simply rely on the leadership of the police commissioner alone. The reality is that the supervisors and managers control the day-to-day operations of any police agency. In this regard, decisions made by a sergeant at 3 A.M. on the street in response to some terrorist threat may turn out to be just as consequential as those made at 1 P.M. in the police commissioner's boardroom.

Another major justification for such an organizational commitment to management development is the civil service nature of most American law enforcement. Because policing is typically such a closed system, new sheriffs, chiefs, and commissioners almost always are selected from within the existing ranks. Even the small-city chiefs of police, who move around from one agency to another, are almost always career law enforcement officers.

Traditionally, in law enforcement, it was assumed that the individual with the longest service record was the best one to be considered for an executive promotion. Even today, among the most respected credentials of a police executive is an extended tenure characterized by a number of years of service in the various ranks of the agency. Police commissioners are often classified in the media as those "who came up through the ranks to get the top job." Throughout the country, this practice continues today. However, to be competitive for today's top executive positions in law enforcement, a long and impressive record of public service must also be accompanied by an equally impressive transcript of educational and professional development.

The practice of selecting the future leaders of law enforcement from within has its advantages. But the practice also brings with it a decisive and necessary obligation for management development. When the U.S. military needs high-ranking leaders, it can look to the various military service academies for experienced, well-educated, and proven leadership. When corporate America looks for high-level executives, it looks to the Ivy League business schools for the finest and smartest individuals available. American policing, however, has decided to draw from a much more restricted and limited reservoir of talent. Police managers and executives are not like their counterparts in the private sector. They typically do not move around from one agency to another to expand their experiences or perspectives and advance their careers. Those who do, in the smaller to midsize agencies, are typically not fortunate enough to have had an educational assignment comparable to the U.S. Military Academy at West Point.

Instead, members of a police agency almost always stay with one police agency for at least twenty years of service, perhaps moving from patrol to a specialized unit along the way as they got promoted. Therefore, the successful education and development of first-line and middle managers become not simply a reward or a day off patrol but an organizational imperative to provide future leadership.

SERGEANTS

Education and Training

Many law enforcement executives will readily admit that the transition from police officer to sergeant was the most difficult transition to successfully make. Many other veterans will suggest that the rank of sergeant of police is the most difficult and important rank in the department. They are probably both absolutely correct.

A good sergeant no longer does the actual work but supervises those who do. In essence, a new sergeant of police has to learn to stop being a workhorse and start being a racehorse. For newly promoted sergeants who were active and involved as police officers, this can be a difficult distinction, and an even more difficult transition. Yet, this transition is exactly why it is so crucial from a training perspective for the police academy to provide a far-reaching and successful job of professional development for police supervisors.

Experience clearly demonstrates that newly promoted supervisors who are not effectively trained early on to act as supervisors will, instead, simply default and go back to doing what they are effectively trained for—being cops. Supervisors who default on their supervisory roles and responsibilities because of a lack of competence cheat their subordinates, their department, the public, and themselves. They make crucial mistakes, such as racing to a crime scene and providing assistance instead of staying back and managing the scene.

But perhaps even worse, supervisors who default on their supervisory roles and responsibilities often resort to policing their subordinates instead of supervising them. Sergeants who police their subordinates instead of supervising them run the risk of creating an overly negative, unproductive, and leaderless work environment. When that happens, necessary command and control practices break down because the sergeants are busy policing their cops, in effect treating them like street perpetrators—very subtle distinctions that can, if not realized, completely undermine officer productivity. Such interpersonal dynamics, all resulting from a lack of quality training, can actually be seen in many police agencies and are devastating to an overall organizational climate.

To prevent this phenomenon of policing subordinates instead of supervising them, newly promoted sergeants must be adequately prepared for their new role: a role that includes knowing the resources, knowing the capabilities of all subordinates, and knowing the operational, administrative, and leadership responsibilities; a role that will challenge them like never before to activate a marginally motivated patrol workforce, to identify promising young police officers and develop their careers, to plan patrol operations, to cope with the problems of other officers, to address legal concerns for the actions of others, and to actually worry about what the community might think about law enforcement.

Promotional Training

There remains a legitimate need to continue many of the traditional topics widely utilized to train newly promoted sergeants. Lectures, role plays, and discussions of the various operational, administrative, and other traditional responsibilities of the first-line supervisor are still appropriate and should be taught prior to promotion. These always have been, and continue to be, very practical and real occupational responsibilities that are immediately important to a new sergeant. These practical lessons are relatively easy to teach at the police academy.

Historically, the very same day police officers are promoted to sergeant, the stripes and gold shield they wear instantaneously provide them with the authority to tell police officers what to do. There should be no question about that in law enforcement. Indeed, one of the best advantages of working in such a highly structured rank-conscious environment is that by simply looking at the uniform of an individual who walks into a room, others can immediately tell whether they should simply nod their head in acknowledgment, salute, stand up and salute, or stand up, salute, and throw in a "Good morning, Sir." The uniform that is worn by ranking members of the service, in and of itself, immediately commands authority commensurate with the rank.

However, the reality of the situation is that becoming an effective and respected boss in law enforcement is much more complicated. As a rule, veteran police officers are just not overly impressed with authority. What makes a boss a leader in law enforcement is not the officers standing up when they walk in a room, but what the officers think when they walk out of a room.

To earn the respect and compliance of veteran police officers, a new boss has to personify the personality traits of courage, bravery, competence, and experience. These come from education and training, and they transcend, by far, the uniform one may be wearing. In fact, because police officers have so much authority themselves, many of them are immune to authority and do not respond well to authority alone.

The Leadership Challenge

The training challenge lies in the realization that rank and authority alone are not what motivate police officers to work toward a common mission for a boss—respect and leadership are. These **leadership traits** can and must be taught in the promotional schools of a police academy. Old-school police supervisors believe they can control police behavior through giving orders, imposing rank, and issuing policy directives. The new breed of leaders knows that they control behavior by setting an example and developing their subordinates. While traditional police supervisors believe that their job is to catch officers doing something wrong, contemporary leaders look to catch officers doing something right. While traditional police supervisors believe their job is to control and limit the actions of their officers, present-day leaders know their job is to empower their officers and turn them loose. Leaders know that "what gets inspected gets respected."

Taken to its logical conclusion, traditional police supervisors trained to supervise in a way that sustains the status quo serve only to lock an agency into stagnation. The status quo creates an environment where police officers are afraid to take a chance. Effective leadership, on the other hand, serves to promote personnel development and lead an agency into positive change. Creating positive change is a much more exciting prospect for a young sergeant who has studied so hard to get promoted and has earned the right to be a boss! In fact, one might argue that the seemingly persistent problems that police agencies around the country have experienced over the years, problems such as police corruption, brutality, abuse of authority, and overall cynicism, can all be traced back to one common denominator: a general lack of effective supervision and leadership.

The traditional authority of the sergeant has always been there, yet major problems persist in law enforcement. One only has to look at the national news media to find clear and compelling evidence of police misconduct and questions about police activities. For example, in 1998, a New York City police officer was convicted of sexually assaulting a Haitian immigrant with a bathroom plunger in a police facility. In 2000, the Los Angeles Police Department experienced some of the worst cases of police misconduct ever, all apparently stemming from officer corruption in a divisional gang control unit. More recently, serious allegations have been made against the New Jersey State Police for racial profiling, the Miami Police Department for a series of police shootings, the Dallas Police Department for allegedly setting up Mexican immigrants for illegal narcotics arrests, and the Philadelphia Police Department for allegations of coverups and conspiracy.

The list goes on and on, yet all of these agencies had police sergeants with the clear rank and authority to supervise the officers and control their behavior. In all of these cases, where were the sergeants? What kind of law enforcement culture did the sergeants create and/or tolerate through their supervisory practices? What level of expectations did those sergeants create for their officers? Where was the supervisory leadership in these cases? How were the sergeants trained and prepared for their supervisory roles and responsibilities?

In every case, it would seem that the authority of the sergeants was there, but not the command presence, the respect, and/or the leadership. This absence of command presence, respect, and leadership persists because, for the most part, police academies around the country are still training newly promoted sergeants in the nuts-and-bolts of policies and procedures but not educating them in the principles of leadership. Newly promoted sergeants are still being trained to police their subordinates, not to manage them.

Complexities of Teaching Leadership

Teaching newly promoted sergeants the time-tested principles of supervisory leadership will help to effectively prepare them to influence the officers working for them in a more positive way. This is a critical distinction because so much of what a police officer does is autonomous, self-directed, and unsupervised and is about the "paradox of accountability" (Crank, 1998).

Yet, it is exactly these unsupervised police–citizen interactions that constitute justice to the community. Mayors, police commissioners, and police commanders play an important role in establishing a vision for an agency. Yet it is the patrol sergeant who stands in front of the roll call every day and communicates the specifics of that vision to the actual service providers. It is the patrol sergeant who explains how the individual priorities of the day are consistent and related to the overall vision of the agency. It is the patrol sergeant who communicates, through body language, tone of voice, and **command presence**, exactly what is important and what is simply more "nonsense from the command staff." It is the patrol sergeant who establishes the level of organizational discipline and of performance expectations and creates the day-to-day culture of the squad. Street cops pick up on the subtle indicators of sergeants in a heartbeat, and the actions of the patrol sergeant can advance or sink an organizational vision just as swiftly.

Well-trained sergeants of police can inspire a young patrol force to self-actualize and work toward the mission, or they can advance and sustain a negative and cynical work environment. They can encourage officers to be productive, or they can show up at roll call and communicate to the officers, "Don't be volunteering for anything, don't wreck the radio car, and whatever you do, don't call the sergeant." This being the case, any law enforcement leader who is serious about implementing a new vision for law enforcement must do an effective job of educating and training sergeants in the traits, characteristics, and practices of leadership.

Make no mistake about it, effective and positive supervision starts at the police academy and can be directly traced to the preparation of the newly promoted managers. Yet, establishing an educational plan to develop and prepare supervisory leaders can sometimes be a complex, difficult, and nebulous endeavor because conceptualizing, operationalizing, and ultimately teaching leadership can be somewhat complicated. Over the years, many attempts to identify and examine the skills of a leader have been made. Behavioral scientists have conducted extensive studies in an attempt to identify the different leadership styles. One researcher suggests that there are three basic types of leadership: **autocratic leadership**, **democratic leadership**, and **laissez-faire leadership** (Athos and Coffey, 1968; Kuezmarski and Kuezmarski, 1995). Another study divided management approaches into five styles including authoritarian, democratic, laissez-faire, bureaucratic, and charismatic (Applewhite, 1965).

The research was based on the belief that if leadership traits could be identified and isolated, they could then be taught to aspiring students of leadership. Moreover, common wisdom taught that leaders possessed certain personality traits that provided them with a natural ability to lead others. Various studies analyzed personality traits such as intelligence, birth order, and even socioeconomic status (Bird, 1940; Bass, 1960).

Later, the literature again focused on six categories of personal factors associated with leadership (Stogdill, 1974).

1. Capacity
2. Achievement
3. Responsibility
4. Participation
5. Status
6. Situation

Years later, however, it became clear that such a narrow characterization of leadership was insufficient. In the end, all of these attempts to identify individual leadership traits led to the belief that no single characteristic could distinguish leaders from non-leaders. The inability of the research to specifically define leadership and determine its traits made it extremely difficult for educators to develop a leadership lesson plan. How can a police academy teach newly promoted sergeants a lesson on a subject that has yet to be understood or defined? Other attempts to examine leadership focused on information about the types of behaviors leaders exhibited in order to be effective. These behaviors have been categorized along two lines (Barnard, 1938; Etzioni, 1961):

1. Ability to complete organizational tasks
2. Concern for individual and interpersonal relations

Traditionally, American policing has always been able to teach efficiency and effectiveness in the completion of organizational tasks. In fact, to prepare for promotional exams, many departments require the officers to study the patrol guide and effectively memorize the volumes of policies and procedures.

But for many reasons, police academies have been somewhat less effective in educating young supervisors in the art of interpersonal skills and the personal development of sergeants. Clearly, sergeants of police are well prepared for the procedural aspects of their jobs, but not always as well prepared for the higher-level management and leadership aspects. Because of the uncertainty of leadership, police academies have historically been very good trainers but average educators. Teaching leadership remained a real challenge when the literature suggested, "Effective leadership behavior tends most often to be associated with the high perform-ance on both dimensions" (Halpin, 1966).

At this point, it seems that an effective educational and train-ing plan must focus on both, the very specific traits of supervision and the more general conceptual traits of leadership. Apparently, just teaching supervision with no leadership component will sim-ply produce managers who are only partially prepared for their role. Simply teaching leadership traits with no management skills will likely produce supervisors with no credibility with the officers and an inability to perform the day-to-day job responsibilities expected of them. Neither is acceptable.

Today, leadership traits can be taught to newly promoted ser-geants in conjunction with effective management skills. New police sergeants must learn: "Managers are people who do things right, and leaders are people who do the right thing" (Bennis and Nanus, 1985); "Managers are transactors and leaders are transformers" (Burns, 1978); and "Management controls, arranges, does things right; leadership unleashes energy, states the vision so people do the right thing" (Bennis and Nanus, 1985).

Most importantly, new police supervisors must be prepared in a way that makes it clear that effective supervisors are both—good managers and good leaders. This realization about the way newly promoted sergeants of police should be educated and trained can lit-erally transform and elevate American police to an ideal that repre-sents who they should be: protectors of the American Republic.

Role Responsibilities

Closely related to the issue of leadership is the need to train indi-viduals for the key roles and responsibilities of the police supervi-sor. At the end of the day, the roles and responsibilities of a good police supervisor are to ensure that whatever tasks needed to be accomplished to further the mission were, in fact, accomplished. Police sergeants are concerned with the day-to-day operations of patrol and investigative commands. From a supervisory perspec-tive, the roles and responsibilities of a sergeant are different. To the most experienced police officers, this difference can seem over-whelming. It is one thing to have experience and know the job of policing, and it is quite another to see the job from a supervisor's perspective.

Accordingly, the essential skills of a first-line supervisor must be taught at the police academy. Probably more than any other person, the immediate supervisor has a direct impact on the productivity, morale, integrity, day-to-day work environment, and overall effectiveness of the patrol officer.

Good supervisors can develop and advance a career through mentoring, honest and constructive performance evaluations, and fair job assignments. They can have a profound impact on the quality of the day-to-day work of an officer as well as the officer's future development. A good training program must stress the role of the supervisor as a trainer, as the one who represents the link between the vision of the commissioner and the actual actions and operations of the patrol officer.

To make this happen, a new sergeant must be taught how to manage crime data and patrol assignments, identify problems and make decisions, handle personnel problems and conflict, and manage equal employment opportunity concerns, performance evaluations, and other considerations.

Resources

Since a professional law enforcement organization is going to hold sergeants accountable for activity, or the lack thereof, sergeants must be effectively trained in the various resources available to them to bring about their personnel's needed compliance. For example, if a police officer is performing well, a supervisor should never miss an opportunity to immediately acknowledge that positive behavior. Conversely, if a police officer has a problem or is not performing well, it is the responsibility of a good supervisor to diagnose exactly why the behavior in question is occurring.

If a supervisor determines that an officer wants to do a good job but does not know how, that supervisor should refer the officer to retraining or specialized training. If, however, a supervisor believes that an officer knows how to do what is expected but simply chooses not to, other disciplinary options are more appropriate. In this case, supervisors should be trained to refer the problem officer to Internal Affairs, the Chaplains Unit, the Drug Screening Unit, the Counseling Unit, the Alcohol Referral Unit, the Early Intervention Unit, or some other appropriate support service. In any case, the sergeants must be trained to make such a diagnosis and not tolerate poor performance. Ignoring a poorly performing police officer and allowing him or her to remain in a unit will serve only to undermine the mission and destroy the morale of the productive police officers. Essentially, this is precisely what separates a sergeant who is respected by the good officers from a sergeant who is not.

It is often said that one can judge the quality of a patrol sergeant by his or her enemies. If the lazy police officers don't like a sergeant, that is usually because that sergeant has the required moral courage to do the job. Being a demanding sergeant is often difficult to do, but it is exactly what encourages subordinates to be productive at work.

Operational Responsibilities

Sergeants must also be well trained in the operational responsibilities of the rank. Since all sergeants come from the rank of patrol officer, they should have the advantage of a firm understanding of the types of routine operational responsibilities required in police work. However, as a sergeant, the actual responsibility is increased because a supervisor is responsible not only for himself or herself but for the actions of subordinates at a scene. Sergeants must be trained to manage patrol operations by learning how to run a roll call, how to communicate the commanding officer's wishes, how to manage calls for service and general dispatcher operations, how to communicate to the officers such things as current crime patterns and trends, and how to inform the officers to be aware of them. Operational decisions relative to manpower deployment, special patrol details, fixed post assignments, patrol allocations, tactical and plainclothes operations scheduled in the area, assignment of radio cars, and scheduling of days off, vacation days, and emergency excuses are all critical components of a sergeant's operational concerns.

Sergeants should also be trained in the various operational resources available to them and the officers under their command. For example, they should be taught the capabilities and contact numbers of the Bomb Squad Unit, Crime Scene Units, Public Information Officer, and Emergency Service and Hostage Negotiation Units. These specialized units and people can save lives and may be needed quickly at a crime scene. Being aware of their capabilities and availability can make a supervisor appear to be decisive and in command.

Administrative Responsibilities

One of the key differences officers notice once they become a supervisor is the administrative responsibilities and **tactical supervision** that now come with the rank. An effective training program must include preparation for matters such as acting as the desk officer, preparing roll calls, carrying out uniformed inspections, counseling subordinates, completing officer performance evaluations, knowing equal employment opportunity concerns, handling disciplinary matters, using quality control for written reports, and dealing with citizen concerns and other administrative issues.

In-Service Training

In addition to an effective promotional training course for sergeants, it is equally important to provide for the ongoing professional development of sergeants. Naturally, they will still be required to appear at the firearms range twice a year to maintain their firearms proficiency. Above and beyond that, sergeants should also attend a few days of additional situational-based role-play training. Sergeants' training days should be structured with the instructional methods

---

PROMOTIONAL CURRICULUM FOR SERGEANTS

Role of the Sergeant
Principles of Supervision
Sergeant as Trainer
Mentoring and Coaching
Role of Discipline

Administrative Responsibilities
Desk Officer Duties
Preparing Roll Calls
Uniform Inspections
Performance Evaluations
Managing Diversity
Quality Control

Operational Responsibilities
Resources of a Sergeant
Conducting Roll Calls
Managing Patrol Operations
Supervising Critical Incidents
Managing Use of Force
Tactical Supervision
Supervisory Ethics

Supervisory Leadership
Creating a Culture
Inspiring Police Officers
Aligning Your People

Total = Approximately 100 Hours of Instruction

---

of role plays and scenario-based training. The actual lessons illustrated through the role plays should be based on the principles of tactical supervision and effective decision making. As a general rule, sergeants of police are individuals of advanced maturity and action and simply do not respond well to a typical classroom lecture format. It is clear that when one is training police personnel, the instructional methodology is just as important as the message.

Additional supervisory training opportunities can be formatted as a collection of seminars that act as electives for the sergeants, or it can be a required format to include a few days annually. Individual agencies should make a determination that is most consistent with local resources and priorities. In either case, the seminars should test the sergeants' leadership skills and promote an environment of learning and decision making. Relevant and emerging topics of concern to the sergeants should be offered to keep them up-to-date on the ever-changing environment they are asked to supervise.

LIEUTENANTS

Education and Training

Although the transition from sergeant to lieutenant is somewhat easier than the transition from police officer to sergeant, the necessity for effective preparation and training is by no means less consequential. In the typically hierarchical and bureaucratic organizational structure of American policing, lieutenants continue to play an important role. Whether an agency is doing community policing, traditional policing, or strategy-driven policing, the rank of lieutenant always seems to emerge as a key level of responsibility. It may be in patrol as a tour commander, in investigative assignments as a squad commander, or in administrative assignments as a personnel officer, a budget officer, or a desk officer. In any case, the lieutenant must also be effectively trained in the roles and responsibilities of the rank.

Although many of the issues and topics required in a lieutenant's promotional course are similar to those of other ranks, the level of discussion and the level of responsibility are clearly different and one notch higher.

The Leadership Challenge

The importance of effectively preparing lieutenants for the leadership challenge is every bit as critical as it is for sergeants, but it is just designed more conceptually and delivered from a higher operational altitude. As stated earlier, sergeants should be prepared to assume supervisory roles as well as individual leadership responsibilities. Lieutenants, on the other hand, should be educated and trained at a higher, more progressive level of leadership, **organizational leadership**.

As sergeants assume their responsibilities over a squad, lieutenants move up in their organizational responsibilities to a tour, watch, section, or division. Lieutenants manage the supervisors and assume more of a high-profile, front-and-center leadership role in the command. But success at such a high-profile rank in law enforcement requires a special type of respect, a respect that has to be earned. Some believe that the hallmark of a good leader at the lieutenant rank "is motivation, and that strong leaders are good communicators, outgoing, persistent yet patient, sensitive, trustworthy, appreciative of others, optimistic, people oriented, realistic, organized and prepared" (Farr, 1998). Others who have studied leadership at the management level add such characteristics as honesty, courage, dependability, creativity, confidence, personal energy, loyalty, tact, and humility (Fulton, 1998b). Either way, the promotional training of lieutenants must properly prepare them for a very complex role.

Shared Leadership

Newly promoted lieutenants should be prepared to understand that their leadership role is one of **shared leadership**. They should be equipped to forget the assumption that leadership is an individual strength and begin to understand the concept that "shared leadership can also be exercised by a team of individuals" (Slater and Doig, 1988). At the shared level, leadership ability assumes much more of an organizational role, and such a definition of leadership is appropriate and necessary at the lieutenant level of operations.

Organizational leadership for lieutenants requires the teaching of some new and different skills and perspectives. Self-development, management for the overall good of the service, public speaking and effective interpersonal communication skills, sharing of the department's vision, development of the careers of subordinates, and other skills move to the forefront.

As lieutenants prepare to assume a key role in organizational leadership, they should be encouraged to embark on a journey of self-development because, at that level, leadership development is a process of self-development. Proficiency in leadership comes from self-development. Lieutenants should be advised that from now on if they want things to get better, they have to get better, and if they want things to change, they have to change. Only through such self-development can one find the ability and confidence to lead others (Kouzes and Posner, 1990).

At the lieutenant level, one must begin to understand a significantly broader vision of law enforcement and must effectively integrate what is going on at the precinct, division, department, and citywide level. Lieutenants must understand the political realities of their job, community concerns, and global patterns and the relationship of these issues to what police officers do every day. Lieutenants must be prepared to solve complex problems that would have been resolved already by sergeants if they were easy. They must understand, believe in, and communicate the department's vision and direction. Finally, they must recognize their own limitations and strive to get better as they lead a segment of their organization forward.

These are the leadership challenges facing lieutenants, and a professional police department must prepare newly promoted members through education and training to meet these challenges.

Role Responsibilities

In their role as middle managers, lieutenants should be briefed on their various day-to-day responsibilities. As second in command to a captain, most of the actual daily operations will fall on them. In general, the lieutenants' responsibilities can be classified as operational responsibilities, administrative responsibilities, and organizational leadership responsibilities. These distinctions have proved to provide an effective structure to classify the training blocks of the curriculum. When the successful application of all these skills comes together, it will collectively create a workplace that is productive, empowering, and focused on the core functions of policing.

Operational Responsibilities

The operational responsibilities that a lieutenant must be prepared for through training are varied and flexible. They are also somewhat governed by practical and structural considerations such as the size of an agency and the nature of an assignment within that agency. For the most part, the types of operational responsibilities in which lieutenants should be trained include establishing the priorities for the assignments of both police officers in patrol commands and detectives in investigative commands.

Personnel assignments typically have to be made based on a review of timely and relevant crime analysis data, patrol officer safety and survival, and other important operational, environmental, and even political considerations. Once the resources are allocated, typical lieutenant operational responsibilities often include media relations on major crime scenes, especially on the night tour when other higher-ranking members are usually not on duty. Managing critical incidents that often change rapidly and that require the immediate redeployment of personnel and other valuable departmental resources, managing special operations involving different police officers in various types of assignments, managing community relations, and managing equipment such as radios and cars all require effective organizational leadership from a lieutenant of police. These types of organizational responsibilities are crucial to the effective operations of a police department, and they are clearly *not* skills that can just be learned on the job.

Administrative Responsibilities

At the rank of lieutenant (the next line of management below the commanding officer), administrative responsibilities are considerable and crucial. It is the responsibility of the police academy to understand these administrative responsibilities, understand their linkages to departmental priorities, and effectively teach that information to a level of high competency.

Such administrative responsibilities include the following:

- Managing community relations
- Communicating the vision, priorities, and strategies of the commanding officer
- Communicating to maintain a balance in the area of labor relations

- Managing station-level Internal Affairs investigations and integrity issues
- Reviewing performance evaluations
- Acting as desk officer
- Managing patrol operations and/or criminal investigations
- Inspecting command logs and physical property

At the rank of lieutenant, members of the service must be prepared to act more like a manager and less like a street cop. As many police managers learn the hard way, it is possible to promote yourself out of doing what you enjoy the most. Lieutenants often feel as if they have been promoted out of police work and into administration . . . because they have. Promotional training can and must play a crucial role in facilitating this management transformation.

In-Service Training

As managers, the ongoing professional development of lieutenants remains an essential organizational priority. Just as with all law enforcement personnel, the instructional methodology remains

---

PROMOTIONAL CURRICULUM FOR LIEUTENANTS

Role of the Lieutenant
Principles of Administration
Duties of Executive Officer
Professional Communications
Time Management Skills

Administrative Responsibilities
Command Liaison Officer
Managing Diversity/E.E.O.
Integrity Control/Inspections
Labor Relations
Managing Patrol Operations
Managing Criminal Investigations
Performance Evaluations

Operational Responsibilities
Managing Crime Analysis
Resource Management
Media Relations
Community Relations
Special Operations

Organizational Leadership
External Environment
Shared Leadership
Coaching Subordinates
Team Building in Policing
Establishing Direction
Group Problem Solving

Total = Approximately 70 Hours of Instruction

crucial. Lieutenants of police should be exposed to a number of executive development–type seminars, each assiduously designed to facilitate the professional exchange of information.

These seminars can be developed to illustrate the evolving strategies of management and organizational leadership. Veteran lieutenants should receive at least two or three days annually of educational seminars designed to progressively build on their foundation of communication skills, management skills, leadership skills, political survival skills, media relations skills, crime data interpretation skills, and general decision-making competencies.

Lieutenants play an integral role in the functioning of any police agency. Their education and training are a genuine moral and legal responsibility of the agency and must be offered on an ongoing basis to keep them prepared to face the ever-changing issues associated with their leadership roles.

LEADERSHIP TRAINING FOR ORGANIZATIONAL STABILITY

In any successful police agency, operational continuity is an essential concern. That is why every police chief has an assistant police chief, and that is why successful departments usually promote a new chief from within the ranks. Only departments that want a change bring in a new chief from outside their agency.

In public administration, a continuity of operations enjoyed through **organizational stability** or a concern for the long-term welfare of an agency that transcends an individual's tenure is complicated. Mayors come and go, police commissioners come and go, and training directors come and go. Political administrations change every couple of years from Democrats being in control to Republicans being in control, and vice versa. The tenure of many police commissioners or sheriffs is often relatively short, and long-term professional development agendas vanish in the confusion.

In a political democracy, a police executive is subjected to conflicting political pressures from diverse influences and special-interest groups throughout the community. Essentially, the politics of American law enforcement threatens the very organizational stability necessary to successfully fight crime for at least four reasons:

1. Most of the more successful crime control strategies and tactics require time, resources, and experience to implement. Street crime rarely begins to drop right away. Crime control efforts should be sustained over a long period of time.

2. There is traditionally an organizational low and/or a loss of momentum and morale when there is a change in executive leadership. Often, members of an agency will ease up on enforcement activities and wait for new priorities to emerge.
3. A change in police leadership is typically followed by the retirement and loss of many other top-level chiefs and deputy commissioners who were closely aligned with the departing police executive.
4. Perhaps most importantly, sergeants, lieutenants, and captains are typically at the point in their careers where they are just below the radar screen to be adversely affected by an executive transition. Yet, they typically have developed the necessary practical experience to implement the more successful crime control strategies and can continue to do so if they are allowed to.

Therefore, a true leader who understands the essential responsibility of establishing organizational stability and operational success that transcend individual tenure will recognize that the professional development of middle managers is a primary mandate. Investing in the law enforcement leaders of the future is, indeed, the best way to establish organizational stability.

A CASE IN POINT

A fine example of this type of leadership is William J. Bratton, the former police commissioner of New York City. During his tenure, Police Commissioner Bratton was such a visionary and advocate for the professional development of his people that the New York City Police Department has sustained his vision, his operational priorities, and his success in crime fighting long after his retirement. This is the case, at least in part, because the "diamonds in the rough" that Commissioner Bratton identified and invested in during his tenure are the leaders of the New York City Police Department today. As a result, crime continues to drop almost ten years later. Without such an investment, there could not have been any organizational continuity.

When there is a significant change in leadership in American policing, individual executives who come and go with the leadership do not sustain positive change. Sergeants, lieutenants, and captains who were educated, developed, experienced, and respected along the way normally do.

There is no substitute for the loyalty that proper leadership can engender. It is the responsibility of the police academy, through the direction of the command staff, to make such professional development happen. This type of executive leadership in American policing must take place, and it can only be accomplished by investing in the professional development of future leaders.

CONCLUSION

The sergeants and lieutenants of a police agency play a crucial role in the delivery of police services today and the future of a police agency tomorrow. They are where the "rubber meets the road" in American policing. They are the only individuals who can actually carry out the vision and mission of a police executive.

They are, by virtue of their place in the command structure, the most visible form of management for the everyday working police officer. To the average police officers, a sergeant or lieutenant is as high in the chain of command as they ever need to go to accomplish their mission. Indeed, in American policing, it is typically not a good thing for a police officer to be required to report to someone of any higher rank.

Therefore, it is the duty of a law enforcement agency to properly invest in its middle managers. It is the responsibility of the police academy to provide the design and structure for a continuum of progressive educational and training opportunities specifically designed for their personal development. The responsibilities of sergeants and lieutenants are far too important to default to on-the-job learning.

The civil and/or criminal stakes and liabilities are much too real to leave a department potentially exposed to the ever-expanding "failure to train," "failure to supervise," or "failure to protect" lawsuits taking place in the twenty-first century. Given the complexities, it is the operational, managerial, legal, and indeed moral obligation of an agency to provide professional development.

It is not at all an exaggeration to say that police officers in the American Republic are heroes and are essential to freedom. But even heroes must be supported, managed, developed, and led. As the theme of this text suggests, police officers can be agents of justice and freedom. Nothing is more important to the American Republic than a good police officer, and nothing can be more devastating than a bad one. If bosses are not educated and trained to manage this enormous responsibility properly, serious problems will remain. However, when police officers are provided with the effective management and leadership they need and deserve, this is a realistic and reachable ideal.

Investing in the professional development of the supervision, management, and leadership of a law enforcement agency is a significant commitment. It is a long-term approach to an often-immediate public policy question as well as an expensive proposition. However, effective supervision, management, and leadership development will work, and it will stop police misconduct cases and end the erosion of public confidence in law enforcement!

Clearly, it is not an easy solution or the quick fix that is normally preferred by elected officials. Instead, it is a progressive, intelligent educational process designed to produce greatness. As we have always known, education, not additional layers of civilian oversight, is the antidote to ignorance. Dedicate the resources and make the organizational commitment to the personal development of the sergeants and lieutenants, and the American Republic will prosper.

KEY TERMS

Autocratic Leadership

Command Presence

Conceptual Component

Democratic Leadership

Laissez-Faire Leadership

Leadership Traits

Level of Abstraction

Organizational Leadership

Organizational Stability

Perceptual Component

Shared Leadership

Tactical Supervision

QUESTIONS FOR DISCUSSION

1. What is the role of a sergeant of police in law enforcement?
2. From a department's perspective, is it best to provide leadership training before or after an individual is promoted? Why?

3. What is the expense involved in providing education as well as training to sergeants and lieutenants? Why is it worth the expense?

4. Who has the most influence over the day-to-day activities of a police officer?

5. How are the future leaders of law enforcement selected? What education and training are required to be a captain of police?

6. Is it better to select a police executive from within the ranks of an agency or to select an outsider? What are the advantages and disadvantages of each option?

7. What will most newly promoted police supervisors do if they have not received the necessary training for their new supervisory role?

8. What motivates police officers to be productive . . . rank or leadership?

9. What is organizational leadership, and how can a police academy teach organizational leadership?

10. What are the complexities associated with teaching leadership? Can they be overcome in a promotional class for law enforcement managers?

SUGGESTED READINGS

Applewhite, Philip B. (1965). *Organizational behavior*. Englewood Cliffs, NJ: Prentice-Hall.

Athos, Anthony G., and Robert E. Coffey. (1968). *Behavior in organizations: A multi-dimensional view*. Englewood Cliffs, NJ: Prentice-Hall.

Barnard, C.I. (1938). *The function of the executive*. Cambridge, MA: Harvard University Press.

Bass, B.M. (1960). *Leadership, psychology, and organizational behavior*. New York: Harper & Brothers.

Bennis, Warren. (1990). Managing the dream: Leadership in the 21st century. *Training: The Magazine of Human Resource Development* 27: 44–46.

Bennis, Warren, and Burt Nanus. (1985). *Leaders: The strategies for taking charge*. New York: Harper & Row.

Bird, C. (1940). *Social psychology*. New York: D. Appleton-Century Company.

Burns, J.M. (1978). *Leadership.* New York: Harper & Row.

Crank, John. (1998). *Understanding police culture.* Cincinnati, OH: Anderson Press.

Etzioni, A. (1961). *A comparative analysis of complex organizations.* New York: Free Press.

Farr, James N. (1998). Where you lead, will they follow? *Norwest Business Advantage Magazine,* Fall/Winter.

Fulton, Roger. (1998a). Leaders do what managers don't. *Law Enforcement Technology* 25 (8): August.

Fulton, Roger. (1998b). 10 leadership traits you should possess. *Law Enforcement Technology* 25 (9).

Halpin, A. W. (1966). *Theory and research in administration.* New York: Macmillan.

Kouzes, James M., and Barry Z. Posner. (1990). *The leadership challenge.* San Francisco: Jossey-Bass Publishers.

Kuezmarski, Susan, and Thomas D. Kuezmarski. (1995). *Values based leadership: Rebuilding employee commitment.* Englewood Cliffs, NJ: Prentice-Hall.

Los Angeles Police Department. (2000). Board of inquiry report into the Rampart Area corruption incident. LAPD online, http://lapdonline.org/whats_new/boi/boi_report.htm.

Slater, R.O., and J.W. Doig. (1988). Leadership in education: Issues of entrepreneurship. *Education and Urban Society* 20: 294–301.

Stogdill, R.M. (1974). *Handbook of leadership: A survey of theory and research.* New York: Free Press.

chapter **12**

A Model for Executive Development in Law Enforcement

"I think good people deserve good leadership."
—Debi Coleman,
Vice President and Chief Financial Officer
of Apple Computer

INTRODUCTION

Executive development in American policing is an extraordinary challenge, extraordinary in that police executives come in many different ranks and/or classifications. Generally speaking, they may be called captain of police, deputy inspector, full inspector, deputy chief, assistant chief, deputy director, director, deputy commissioner, chief of police, or sheriff as well as other executive titles. Beyond their job classifications or titles, they are all very different individuals, accomplished men and women who are diverse in their professional experiences, academic preparations, intellectual capacities, and career aspirations. Although general statements are frequently heard about police executives, as a group they are very divergent and resistant to classification.

Most police executives are sworn members of the service who have been promoted up through the ranks to the executive staff. This typically happens from within a law enforcement agency through a combination of the successful completion of traditional civil service examinations and career appointments. However, even though most sworn executives are selected from within a law enforcement agency, they may still have very different and varied professional backgrounds and experiences.

Some law enforcement executives are knowledgeable in conducting criminal investigations, managing criminal investigations, and understanding forensic operations. Upon promotion to chief, such individuals typically need additional professional development in administrative operations and/or uniformed patrol operations. Other law enforcement executives may have spent an entire career in uniformed patrol yet never actually conducted or managed a criminal investigation. Still others may have been fortunate and diversified enough to have gained experience in both uniformed patrol and investigative operations but need additional professional development in administrative issues such as budget management, management of capital construction projects, political survival skills, time management, dealings with special-interest groups, organizational discipline, or even public speaking skills.

At the highest levels of policing, some law enforcement executives are great street cops but are not very articulate or polished as professionals. Others are very polished and experienced administrators but have not been around uniformed police officers for a very long time. Through the unique promotional practices of American law enforcement, all of these scenarios are possible. This is true in the medium and large law enforcement agencies, where specialization of function is utilized extensively. And it is true in very small agencies, where the opportunity to gain a great deal of highly specialized experience is simply not available. Essentially, it is true everywhere in policing.

There are also civilian executive ranks where the same diversity is apparent. Civilian executives may be called assistant directors, deputy directors, directors, assistant wardens, and deputy commissioners. Aside from their job classifications and/or ranks, they may or may not have any actual police experience. Civilian executives typically have developed a certain professional expertise that is valuable to a police agency. They are utilized in professional command areas such as chief of staff, education and training, building maintenance, fleet maintenance, planning and research, and communications.

Finally, some police executives come to be sheriffs, police chiefs, or police commissioners from outside a particular law enforcement agency, but with significant law enforcement experience in another law enforcement agency, another city, or even another discipline such as law, politics, or education. Regardless of their individual professional backgrounds, most senior police executives are political appointees, so a new sheriff, police chief, or police commissioner may be selected from virtually any number of possible professional experiences and/or disciplines.

Because of all the various career paths one may pursue to become a law enforcement executive in America, educational levels are also countless and quite different. Educational standards in the executive ranks run the full range from high school equivalencies to some college, university degrees, law degrees, and doctorates.

The point is that effective professional development remains important to an organization, even at the executive level. It is irresponsible to assume that merely because an individual is promoted from captain to deputy inspector, he or she will automatically have all the necessary advanced skills of public administration. The inherent complexities of public administration, coupled with the diverse backgrounds of those who practice it, often create mystery and uncertainty in the executive development arena.

EXECUTIVE DEVELOPMENT FORMAT

Creating an instructional design for executive development requires imagination and courage: imagination, because there simply is no standardized class structure, format, or instructional methodology that can address all the variables of such a dissimilar population; courage, because executive development is a high-profile endeavor, and no training director wants to invite his or her colleagues to a seminar that turns out to be wasteful or uninteresting. At the lower ranks, the education and training systems tend to be standardized across the board, with minor variations allowing for assignment or rank. At the executive level, a professional development agenda simply must be custom-designed around the strengths and weaknesses of the individual.

When an individual is appointed to the rank of captain of police or an equivalent civilian position, there should be a personalized session scheduled with the executive staff of the police academy. During that session, the new executive should be guided through a very confidential **self-assessment inventory** of exercises and instruments. An honest self-assessment inventory can be very beneficial in completing a comprehensive review of an individual's professional strengths and weaknesses, personality type, and most appropriate leadership styles. A personalized professional development plan for the future can then be carefully and thoughtfully constructed for each individual executive. At that point, a professional development package can be specifically tailored to the mutual benefit of the individual executive and, of course, the service.

An effective executive development agenda for law enforcement personnel must be personalized, multitiered, and comprehensive in scope.

EXECUTIVE DEVELOPMENT OPPORTUNITIES

In the arena of executive development, the training director becomes more of a facilitator and less of a direct service provider. The search for educational opportunities must be very expansive and proactive. To meet such a challenge, the police academy must facilitate educational seminars from inside the agency. But it must also scan the external environment for professional development opportunities. The police academy should be building relationships with professional training consultants and local colleges and universities.

Police academies should be constantly aware of available private seminars and conferences, executive educational opportunities in corporate America, state-sponsored educational seminars, and other external development opportunities. At the executive development level, more than ever, individuals should have a **global perspective**, and that comes from being much more global in their interactions. If it is true that "Where you stand depends on where you sit," the purpose of executive development is to put the executive in as many different seats as possible.

A comprehensive executive development plan should take full advantage of the many outstanding programs for executive development that exist around the country. Most major corporations are more than happy to invite local police executives to their executive development seminars and develop professional ties with local and national law enforcement officers.

But perhaps most importantly, training directors must not let executives fall into the traditional traps that always seem to put an end to professional development. Police executives claim that they are too important, too experienced, or too busy for ongoing executive development. Yet, it is precisely the busy executives who need the opportunity for professional development the most. It is difficult, but important, for them to occasionally step back from their day-to-day command responsibilities and pressures of management to reflect. It is refreshing to the spirit and the mind to be exposed to as many positive outside influences as possible. In the **kaleidoscope of management**, reality and priorities constantly evolve and change. To be responsive and relevant, executive development must keep pace and change along with it.

TRANSFORMATIONAL LEADERSHIP

An interesting phenomenon seems to happen to law enforcement executives. Due to the inherent complexities of managing a law enforcement agency, immediately upon promotion very few executives are completely prepared for all the various aspects of police administration. Instead, law enforcement executives, at least the successful ones, almost all seem to grow into the job as time goes on. No matter how well prepared individuals may be, no matter how diversified and broad their professional experiences, the most successful police executives seem to literally grow into the role. Along the way, they incrementally define the job responsibilities directly along the lines of their strengths and preferences, thereby accentuating their competencies and allowing themselves time to develop in their areas of weakness.

In fact, it may be argued that it is precisely this ability to quickly and honestly identify the various dimensions of a job, and then to assess and identify individual strengths and weaknesses as they relate to the job dimensions, that marks a truly successful police executive. Therefore, it is exactly this type of ability, **transformational leadership**, that should be the core focus of development for professional law enforcement executives. Truly successful police executives must be able to transform themselves before they can ever transform an entire agency. Private victory must precede public victory (Covey, 1989). The philosophical cornerstone of an executive development program, then, should be facilitating transformational leadership.

Other, more specific seminars teaching the peripheral skills necessary to supplement transformational leadership will always be necessary and appropriate. These would include executive-level educational opportunities on such matters as effective communication and public speaking skills; political and special-interest group survival; legal issues; management of patrol operations, criminal investigations, and change; **infrastructure**; **COMPSTAT** preparation and survival skills; international terrorism; management of the intelligence function; **critical incident management**; ethics and integrity; executive stress; and budget preparation, just to name a few.

EXECUTIVE DEVELOPMENT SEMINARS

Transformational Leadership	Managing Critical Incidents
Effective Public Speaking	Executive Stress
Legal Issues in Public Administration	External Environment
Managing Patrol Operations	Political Survival Skills
Managing Criminal Investigations	Managing Public Budgets
Managing Change	Conceptual Thinking
Issues in Ethics and Integrity	Human Resources
Issues in Infrastructure	Executive Discussions
Executive Firearms Cycle	Managing Diversity
Executive Health and Nutrition	Leadership in Private Sector

Transformational leadership, defined not as a set of specific behaviors taught to sergeants and lieutenants but rather as "a process by which leaders and followers raise one another to higher levels of morality and motivation," emerges as the foundation for executives (Burns, 1978). Developing the conceptual ability to evaluate the present and envision the future is critical. Developing and articulating a road map to enable an agency to face the future—**forecasting** all the probable political, social, financial, technological, and operational roadblocks to be overcome—is what is expected from the successful law enforcement executive.

Some of the most compelling success stories in American policing are all examples of transformational leadership, and this is no coincidence. In the early 1980s, Chief of Police Lee P. Brown transformed the Houston Police Department through the application of transformational leadership principles. Chief Brown assumed command of a police department with a small-city mentality, and he very quickly and effectively turned it into one of the finest big-city police departments in the country. This was accomplished, at least in part, through a sincere commitment to effective executive development in transformational leadership. Chief Brown proficiently developed his executive staff, and they constructed and relentlessly communicated a vision of community policing.

The Houston Police Department's transformation began to take hold and soon became apparent in the crime data and police officer morale. Good things began to happen, and interest in what was happening grew around the world. Everyone wanted to know the secrets of the Houston model.

In the wake of that success, many of Houston's senior executives went on to assume leadership roles in other police agencies around the country, a true mark of success. During that time, the marketplace value of the executives from the Houston Police Department was not based on their overly specific knowledge of policing strategies and tactics. Crime control knowledge is not rare; it can easily be found. Instead, the proven ability of the Houston executives to transform themselves and an entire police department was what was rare. Their proven abilities in transformational leadership made them valuable to every other city in the country looking for a new chief of police.

Another example can be found in the early 1990s when Chief William J. Bratton assumed command of the New York City Transit Police Department and very quickly transformed it from a second-class specialty police department into one of the most effective law enforcement agencies in the country. Under Commissioner Bratton's leadership, crime in the New York City subways plummeted, the quality of life on and around the transit system improved significantly, police officer morale drastically increased, and the slogan for the New York City Transit Police became "Second to none." Bratton's unique ability to bring about a transformation in such a deeply entrenched bureaucracy illustrates the first hallmark of transformational leadership, the ability to "go beyond the individual needs and focus on a common purpose, addressing intrinsic rewards and higher psychological needs such as self-actualization, and developing commitment with and in followers" (Bennis and Nanus, 1985; Bennis, 1990; Sergiovanni, 1990; Leithwood, 1992).

This leadership ability was so immediately apparent in the New York City subways that, upon his election, Mayor-Elect Rudolph W. Giuliani appointed William Bratton as the police commissioner of New York City. Mayor Giuliani commissioned Commissioner Bratton to transform the N.Y.P.D., a mammoth organization of some 42,000 uniformed and 15,000 civilian members. Once again, Commissioner Bratton quickly took on the role, and his ability to transform an agency paid immediate dividends. Police Commissioner Bratton immediately revealed an aggressive agenda, including an investment in education and training to prepare the members of the New York City Police Department to accomplish his crime reduction strategies. He empowered the police academy, and he used lectures, personal appearances at promotional classes, constant videotaped messages, and every conceivable resource to constantly develop the officers and communicate his vision. This investment in training contributed in a positive way and supported the ongoing organizational transformation of the New York City Police Department.

Just as in Houston, many senior executives of the New York City Police Department were recruited for chief of police positions in other cities. Just as in Houston, the ability of an executive to transform an agency and turn it in the right direction was recognized as extremely valuable.

CONCLUSION

It has been proven time and time again that transformational leadership is clearly what high-level executives need. This is true in policing, professional sports, business, and anywhere the stakes are high and the need for results is real. The leadership ability to transform an organization, energize a workforce, and get results can get police managers noticed and promoted. Conversely, the inability to inspire a workforce can end a career, even at the highest levels.

Therefore, reading, teaching, discussing, and practicing transformational leadership must be a cornerstone of any agency's executive development program. In the final analysis, nothing else will matter.

KEY TERMS

Critical Incident Management
COMPSTAT
Forecasting
Global Perspective

Infrastructure
Kaleidoscope of Management
Self-Assessment Inventory
Transformational Leadership

QUESTIONS FOR DISCUSSION

1. What are the various career paths one can follow to become a chief of police?
2. What educational background does one need to become a sheriff or a chief of police in a large city?
3. What are the various benefits of a top law enforcement executive taking time out of his or her schedule to attend a professional seminar?
4. Identify and discuss some examples of transformational leadership in professional sports and American business.
5. In the kaleidoscope of public administration, what types of changes can occur that would significantly impact law enforcement?

SUGGESTED READINGS

Bennis, Warren. (1990). Managing the dream: Leadership in the 21st century. *Training: The Magazine of Human Resource Development* 27: 44–46.

Bennis, Warren and Burt Nanus. (1985). *Leaders: The strategies for taking charge*. New York: Harper & Row.

Bratton, William, and Peter Knobler. (1998). *Turnaround: How America's top cop reversed the crime epidemic*. New York: Random House.

Burns, James M. (1978). *Leadership*. New York: Harper & Row.

Covey, Steven R. (1989). *The seven habits of highly effective people: Powerful lessons in personal change*. New York: Simon & Schuster.

Leithwood, K.A. (1992). The move toward transformational leadership. *Educational Leadership* 49 (5): 8–12.

Sergiovanni, T.J. (1990). Adding value to leadership gets extraordinary results. *Educational Leadership* 47 (8): 23–27.

chapter **13**

BUILDING A LAW ENFORCEMENT ORGANIZATION TO SUSTAIN THE AMERICAN REPUBLIC

"The imagination is a great thing . . . you can't predict the future,
but you can create it."

—Albert Einstein

INTRODUCTION

The passage to becoming a civilized society that personifies the virtues of sustained peace, freedom, justice, equality, and mutual respect is an extraordinarily complex journey. Historically, it always has been, and it promises to always be in the future. It is a journey that is never really accomplished. The American Republic, as a philosophically ideal state, is really a process, not a destination. To make real progress in such a process requires constant vigilance, public debate, social compromise, and collective efforts.

The occurrences of global organized crime, international terrorism, high-level white-collar crime, local street crime, violations against the innocent, and other real or perceived injustices threaten the very complex and momentary balance of a free society. Crime and social problems did not go away in the preceding centuries, and they are not likely to disappear in the twenty-first century.

The leaders of American law enforcement cannot predict the future with any certainty. But, as Albert Einstein said, with a good imagination and the necessary education and training, perhaps they can create it.

PERSPECTIVES ON SUSTAINING JUSTICE

The many public and private institutions established to provide criminal justice, civil justice, and social justice must all work together to sustain a continuously emerging concept of justice. But, by any definition, the cornerstone institution in any such effort will be American law enforcement.

The challenge lies in the realization that any effort to provide justice will be directly related to the clarity with which it is defined. Over the years, various perspectives of justice have emerged. Naturally, these perspectives include a **philosophical justice**, in which Rawls proposes the idea of a "social contract" in which "the principles of justice for the basic structure of society are the principles that free and rational persons . . . would accept in an initial situation of equality as defining the fundamental terms of their association" (Rawls, 1971).

Other philosophical perspectives of justice proliferate throughout history (Plato, 1986; Aristotle, 1953; Kant, 1959; Hart, 1961; Mill, 1961; Locke, 1967; Hume, 1975; and Rawls, 1975). Interestingly, there is also a well-defined perspective examining the concept of **economic justice** as it relates to wealth, the fair distribution of wealth, economic theory, and the overall economic system (Clark, 1902; Smith, 1937; Aristotle, 1941; Marx, 1967; Lowry, 1969; Bronfenbrenner, 1971; Clark and Gintis, 1978; Harris, 1978; Dworkin, 1980; and Worland, 1983).

A perspective of **political justice** also exists that examines the notion of justice within the context of the political framework that exists to sustain it (Friedman, 1962; Hobbes, 1968; Alchian and Allen, 1969; Gewirth, 1973; Smart, 1978; Galston, 1980; Schweickart, 1980; Wood, 1980; Dworkin, 1981; Elshtain, 1981; and DiQuattro, 1983).

A perspective of **sociological justice** is available that considers the concept of justice as a relative one, relative to the social structure of those who live under it (Durkheim, 1933; Bendix and Lipset, 1953; Dahrendorf, 1959; Blau, 1964; Rossi, Waite, Bose, and Berk, 1974; Hamilton and Rytina, 1980; Coleman, 1982; Walzer, 1983; and Axelrod, 1984).

Even a perspective of **anthropological justice** can be found that essentially looks at the notion of justice from an anthropological paradigm and the way indigenous people have defined the notion of balance in their societies (Barton, 1919; Lowie, 1925; Mair, 1972; Black, 1976; Evans-Prichard, 1976; Craig, 1979; Lerner, 1980; and Berreman, 1981).

These are but a few of the many examples of the numerous perspectives that can be applied to the study of justice, and they demonstrate the complexity of understanding the concept. They are all interesting and worthy of study. But given the complexity of defining justice, let alone actually delivering it on a day-by-day basis, how can a society possibly sustain justice?

Perhaps in the end, justice can be claimed when citizens of a free and democratic society receive what they are due, and it is automatically acknowledged that they are due not only fundamental fairness but also treatment consistent with their natural rights as human beings. In a very real way, providing citizens what they are due has historically been the responsibility of local law enforcement. When average citizens are denied what they are due, they will typically call 911 to complain. Local police officers are then dispatched to the scene, and it becomes the responsibility of the police to make things right again. That may be accomplished through an arrest, a referral, a conversation, or simply a police report along with a concern for the aggrieved. In any case, no other social institution in a free society provides such a direct linkage between fundamental fairness and the average citizen in the community. Routine interactions between the police and the community play a deciding role in the manifestation of justice.

In law enforcement today, the challenges of providing and sustaining justice remain immense and complex. An institution charged with the mission of actually policing a free republic must be philosophically, intellectually, ethically, and operationally prepared to reduce crime and disorder on the streets. That much is abundantly clear. But the real responsibilities of law enforcement can be so much more than just that. Arresting a bad guy is only one way of delivering justice in America. But that is where the confusion sometimes begins.

For a true definition of justice to emerge, law enforcement officers cannot simply be trained to fight crime by administering force. That is too easy, and the mandate is significantly more complex and important than that. Instead, law enforcement must be prepared to perpetuate justice, freedom, and the fundamental premise of human dignity by practicing voluntary compliance and mutual respect whenever possible. Voluntary compliance to law enforcement and mutual respect, in the final analysis, can only be accomplished by excellent education and training for the police officers, along with an unconditional requirement of civility from everyone.

Clearly, a law enforcement agency built to sustain justice in society must have the operational and administrative capacities to manage a rapidly changing crime picture in a society obsessed with individual rights and fundamental freedoms. It must have an Internal Affairs Unit strong enough and autonomous enough to ensure professionalism, internal integrity, and constant awareness of the limits of authority. The law enforcement agency must have the fiscal and political resources necessary to support the accomplishment of the mandate. Most importantly, it must have the confidence and support of the citizens it is sworn to protect.

To sustain the delicate balance justice requires, law enforcement must be in a position to perform its duties with a sense of fairness and equality for *all* human beings, regardless of their social station in life. Law enforcement officers must be accountable to the public for their enforcement authority in a very open and responsive manner. There must always be an open and accessible avenue for public redress as a means of holding those in authority accountable for unlawful and/or unreasonable treatment.

PREEMINENCE OF EDUCATION AND TRAINING

For the most part, these are all relatively routine considerations long since figured out by professional police administrators and elected officials. What still remains to be developed, however, is an integrated, sustained commitment to the philosophical, intellectual, and spiritual education and training of the human resources involved in law enforcement. The human resources of American policing continue to need the education and training to carry out the contradictory mandate of policing a free society. They need to be provided with significant education, knowledge, physical skills, physical and moral courage, and proven strategies and tactics to prevail. Such an imperative responsibility remains a critical function in any law enforcement agency, regardless of its size, and it must be assigned top priority.

ORGANIZATIONAL STRUCTURE OF LAW ENFORCEMENT

In addition to the professional development of the individual, law enforcement agencies must also provide the officers with an organizational structure that empowers them to utilize professional discretion and to self-actualize. Given the nature of American policing, the best way to improve policing is to improve the individual service provider. Improving the individual service provider will only work if the organizational structure supports self-actualization.

The ancient teachings of the Taoist masters of the early Han dynasty once said, "You must never put a monkey in a cage, because if you do, the monkey becomes no better than a pig" (Cleary, 1992). Perhaps what that meant is that a monkey has a relatively high level of ability to think, but if the monkey is put in a cage, all of its ability to think is thereby taken away and the monkey becomes no better than the pig, which has very little conceptual ability.

This ancient Taoist principle applies to law enforcement today. Many agencies maintain very traditional and bureaucratic police organizational structures, and the rigid command and control practices they perpetuate essentially put good, smart police officers in a metaphorical cage, not bound by bars but by an abundance of restrictive policies, standard operating procedures, overbearing supervisors obsessed with doing things right instead of doing the right thing, and an overall lack of optimism and trust. If these types of traditional organizational structures and practices are continued, the very same virtues of justice, freedom, and mutual respect that the police are expected to implement in the community become nonexistent in their department.

In philosophy, it is taught that if the answer to a question sounds counterintuitive or even preposterous, check your premise. Perhaps over the years, the limited investment that has been made in the education and training of the American police would suggest an incorrect premise.

As the new millennium begins, American policing finds itself in a somewhat peculiar situation. The community policing movement is being implemented and taught in many communities and in police academies, colleges, and universities around the nation. Community policing is an operational philosophy that is based on an active working partnership between the police and the community in addressing crime problems (Kelling et al., 1988).

Community policing calls for a broader role for policing through the community's empowerment and shared problem-solving responsibility with the police to improve the overall quality of life for the community. Not a bad premise for policing a free society! Yet, social problems in the community, often involving allegations of police abuse, violence in the streets and schools, crime, disorder, urban decay, and a perceived absence of justice, persist.

In other communities, traditional policing advocates are going back in time and calling for a law and order approach or zero-tolerance enforcement. The law and order approach to law enforcement involves activities such as more arrests, increased numbers of summonses, and the strict enforcement of quality-of-life infractions. Traditional police executives also call for zero-tolerance enforcement, as if there could ever be such a thing in a free society. Yet, even then, it appears that part of the solution is still missing.

A CASE IN POINT

The New York City Police Department closed out the year 2001 with violent crime down 12.3 percent, making it one of the safest large cities in America. A comparison of the crime data between the years 1993 and 2001 shows a remarkable 66.7 percent reduction in murder, a 40 percent reduction in rape, a 67 percent reduction in both robbery and burglary, and a 73 percent reduction in auto theft (N.Y.P.D., 2001)—an astonishing crime-fighting story by any standard.

Yet, public allegations of police abuse of authority and police brutality as well as a significant community distrust of the police persist. Cries can still be heard on the streets of New York, "No justice—no peace!"

How can this be? How can a department make so much progress in reducing violence and street crime and yet still be struggling to provide a genuine sense of peace and justice in the community? How can a police department accomplish so much in terms of crime reduction and still leave the members of the community feeling a lack of any sense of individual fairness and/or justice and respect? Perhaps the fundamental premise of the law enforcement mandate in a free society should be reconsidered. A proper underlying premise, or philosophy, is important to all things, even police work—especially police work.

THE AMERICAN REPUBLIC

If a true republic can ever actually exist, the United States of America is it. The United States of America is the perennial role model of freedom, justice, and human dignity. In fact, the principles of justice, freedom, and human dignity are so ingrained in the American people that they are even ingrained in their military. As the men and women of the U.S. Armed Forces engaged in the war on terrorism in Afghanistan by dropping smart bombs with one hand, they helped innocent civilians with food drops and medical supplies with the other. The United States of America even fights its wars with compassion and respect for human dignity, which makes it a living personification of justice with mercy—the philosophy of the American democracy that drives its freedoms. The American military, sent to Afghanistan to fight a war, acted more like agents of social justice than the Afghanistan government ever did.

It is exactly this type of precise and decisive action (superimposed on a solid foundation of education and training), which the U.S. military demonstrated in the war on terrorism, that must be established in American policing. There were no U.S. military morale problems in Afghanistan. The types of missions and the expected behaviors of the U.S. military were unmistakably linked to the fundamental American virtues of justice and freedom. The American soldiers were educated and trained to understand that. There can be no morale problems when there is a deep understanding of the philosophical principles that are at stake undergirding a mandate.

When the American police are educated to understand that this same link exists between the fundamental American virtues and their mandate, they too will be empowered and enriched.

When the organizational commitment to their education and training is established, they too can become domestic agents of justice and freedom, just like the U.S. military has been abroad. Then, and only then, will the full potential and the true ideals of the American Republic naturally emerge.

AMERICAN JUSTICE

True justice will come to a society only to the extent that criminal justice, social justice, and restorative justice are practiced and advanced. First and foremost, in a free society, the physical manifestations of justice are practiced and advanced by the police. In America, law enforcement provides what is perhaps the most fundamental civil right of them all, the right to live in peace and free of the will of others who may be bigger and stronger. When justice and freedom are prevalent, a society can and will flourish. However, where there is no justice, there will never be a sustained peace, and no free and democratic society can be sustained.

If the fundamental principles of justice, freedom, mutual respect, and individual autonomy are ever to be realized in a multicultural and multiethnic nation, the basic philosophical premise of policing must be unequivocally understood and communicated to police officers through a comprehensive system of education and training. The overriding goals of policing a free society *are not* to reduce street crime at any cost, to maintain law and order by physically forcing compliance, or to blindly enforce the will of the majority through the application of force. Instead, the overriding goal *is* to sustain and advance the virtues of freedom, justice, and mutual respect in society, and to do so in a manner consistent with the citizens' natural rights as human beings.

Clearly, this is partially accomplished by reducing crime, protecting the innocent from the guilty, and not allowing might to equal right. But such accomplishments are only "lipstick on a pig" if they are accomplished without the police leaving behind a sense of justice and fundamental fairness in the wake of citizen encounters. In a free society, voluntary compliance is the best compliance.

No one understands better than street cops that justice and freedom are clearly individual and relative concepts. Police officers know that justice is often defined on the street as "who gets their way." And experience tells police officers that some street encounters simply cannot be structured to produce a win-win scenario.

Sometimes someone has to lose, and sometimes someone has to go to jail. And truly, sometimes voluntary compliance is simply not an option with perpetrators who need to be forced to comply. But proper training can prepare officers to utilize the virtues of professionalism and fundamental fairness in the vast majority of actions they take, even most enforcement actions.

It may be that protecting the republic by advancing justice and freedom is not an operational, tactical, procedural, or even political challenge, but a philosophical challenge, a philosophical challenge that can only be appropriately addressed by a significant investment in the education and training of the police officers involved in the mission. Police officers must understand that justice, freedom, individual autonomy, and mutual respect in a republic are not principles simply guaranteed to every citizen by virtue of the Constitution or the Bill of Rights. They are, instead, principles owed to every human being, citizen or not, by virtue of being a human being. As Immanuel Kant once said, "A good will is good not because of what it performs or effects, not by its aptness for the attainment of some proposed end, but simply by virtue of the volition, that is, it is good in itself. . . . Then, like a jewel, it would still shine by its own light, as a thing which has its own value in itself."

Law enforcement operating under an assumption that *all* people possess a right to human dignity by virtue of their birth into the human race could eliminate many problems. Individual characteristics such as race, gender, sexual orientation, and/or legal status become moot, and justice is much less relative.

In so many ways, the future of the American Republic is intrinsically linked to the ability of law enforcement to protect it. One cannot exist without the other. But as Albert Einstein said, the future belongs to those who have the imagination to create it. In policing, this requires an imagination vivid enough to envision a significant reallocation of resources to the development of its personnel, resources that, for the most part, already exist.

Law enforcement executives deal with choices and rapidly changing priorities every day. It is, by any account, an extraordinarily difficult and thankless job. But those who choose to assume such responsibilities should do so with a complete understanding of what is at stake. They must do so with an understanding of the problems of the past and the philosophical framework to move an agency forward into the future. As they plan for the future, police executives already have direct command and control over the two most critical management prerogatives: budget and personnel. Police executives know that controlling the budget and personnel is essential to controlling a department. However, a broader definition of the personnel function is necessary. Currently, police executives define control over personnel to mean controlling the hiring, assignment, promotion, and the disciplinary functions. To break the status quo and move forward will require a more significant commitment to the development of personnel.

CONCLUSION

Currently, the American police, for the most part, are simply not educated and trained extensively enough to assume the role of agents of social justice. Instead, police recruits are adequately trained up front in the law enforcement role as recruits, and cities simply make up the difference by paying for it on the back end. Unfortunately, on the back end, the social costs are significant. Justice can be denied and freedoms can perish. But society also pays for law enforcement mistakes in the way of successful lawsuits for civil rights violations. Across the nation, billions of dollars, which could be better directed to significantly enhance education and training on the front end, are instead utilized to pay for liability insurance, litigation expenses, out-of-court settlements for police misconduct, and punitive damage awards.

In fact, a survey conducted by the National Institute of Municipal Law Officers found that the 215 municipalities surveyed had more than $4.3 billion in pending liability lawsuits. Moreover, it was estimated that these figures, applied to the existing 39,000 local governments, could represent as much as $780 billion in pending liability litigation against local governments (Bates, Cutler, and Clink, 1981).

One study of the New York City Police Department (1992) found that between 1987 and 1991, New York City alone paid out $44 million in claims to settle police misconduct cases. Over that five-year period, the average settlement or judgment on police misconduct cases more than doubled from $23,000 to $52,000. Also during the same period, "The comptroller's office saw a jump from 977 to 1,498 in the number of claims alleging misuse of force."

In the end, police officers are clearly the best agents of criminal, social, and restorative justice in the American Republic. Police officers are in the best position, on a day-to-day basis, to provide and advance justice at all levels of society. However, to effectively deliver on such an awesome responsibility, they simply must receive the very best education and training. Police officers must be prepared to be agents of justice, not simply law enforcement officers. This does not come easy, and it does not come cheap. It requires a significant commitment of resources at the city, state, and federal levels.

Throughout history, the struggle to provide justice, freedom, and human dignity and the struggle to establish a democratic form of government with the ability to provide such virtues have unfolded together. Along the way, the journey has demonstrated one undeniable truth: The more advanced a free republic strives to be, the better educated and trained its police must be.

In the dialogues of Plato's *Republic*, a group of citizens forced Socrates to stay and explain his words and actions to them. Today, a group of citizens often force police officers to stay and explain their words and actions to them, usually in the form of a grand jury. In Plato's *Republic*, important democratic ideals emerge during the dialogues of Socrates. Today, important democratic ideals emerge through the individual actions of police officers in the way they resolve social conflict.

Finally, just as democratic Athens put the philosopher Socrates on trial and ultimately killed him for impiety, democratic America sometimes kills police officers too, for what they represent. Justice, freedom, and human dignity are the most important virtues of all if the social order is to be sustained. Socrates knew this and ultimately gave his life for it. Soldiers, police officers, and other public safety workers of the American Republic also know this, and they sometimes give their lives for it.

Throughout history, all of the great leaders knew this, and today, the American people know it. On September 11, 2001, shortly after the worst terrorist attack in American history, three New York City firefighters bravely faced grave danger in the ruins of the World Trade Center and defiantly raised the American flag. Those New York City firefighters knew how resilient the spirit of American freedom and democracy was, and they proved it that day by their actions. But these virtues must be studied and operationalized in the police academies, colleges, and universities around the country to actually be manifested in society. Political will, civil liability, administrative policies and procedures, and negative discipline alone will not effectively change police behavior, but education and training will.

Hopefully, the value of this text lies not in the criticisms, but in the conceptual framework it provides to do exactly that!

KEY TERMS

Anthropological Justice

Economic Justice

Philosophical Justice

Political Justice

Sociological Justice

QUESTIONS FOR DISCUSSION

1. Explain and discuss the distinctions between criminal justice, civil justice, social justice, and restorative justice.
2. What social institutions are responsible for justice in society?
3. On an individual level, how would you define justice? Whom would you call if you felt that you were denied justice?
4. Specifically, what type of training should the police receive to help them to provide justice to the community?
5. How can American law enforcement create the future of freedom?
6. What did the ancient teachings of the Taoist masters contribute to the discussion about the structure of a law enforcement agency?
7. Why is it not enough for a police agency to successfully reduce crime? What else is necessary?
8. Should the American military show compassion for civilians during time of war?
9. How is the virtue of justice typically defined on the street?
10. Should the police aspire to be agents of social change in a free society?

SUGGESTED READINGS

Alchian, A., and W. Allen. (1969). *Exchange and production: Theory in use*. Belmont, CA: Wadsworth Publishing.

Aristotle. (1941). Politics. In R. McKeon (ed.), *The basic works of Aristotle*. New York: Random House.

Aristotle. (1953). *Nichomachean ethics,* translated by J.A.K. Thompson. London: George, Allen & Unwin.

Axelrod, R. (1984). *The evolution of cooperation.* New York: Basic Books.

Barton, R. (1919). *Ifugao law,* Volume 15. Berkeley, CA: University of California Publications in Archeology and Ethnology.

Bates, R.D., R.F. Cutler, and M.J. Clink. (1981). Prepared statement on behalf of the National Institute of Municipal Law Officers. Presented before the Subcommittee on the Constitution, Senate Committee on the Judiciary, May 1981. Washington, D.C.

Bendix, R., and S. Lipset. (1953). *Class, status, and power.* New York: Free Press.

Berreman, G. (1981). Social inequality: A cross-cultural analysis. In G. Berreman (ed.), *Social inequality: Comparative and developmental approaches.* New York: Academic Press.

Black, D. (1976). *The behavior of law.* New York: Academic Press.

Blau, P.M. (1964). *Exchange and power in social life.* New York: Wiley.

Bronfenbrenner, M. (1971). *Income distribution theory.* Chicago: Aldine–Atherton.

Clark, B., and H. Gintis. (1978). Rawlsian justice and economic systems. *Philosophy and Public Affairs* 7: 302–325.

Clark, J.B. (1902). *The distribution of wealth.* New York: Macmillan.

Cleary, Thomas. (1992). *The book of leadership & strategy: Lessons from the Chinese masters.* Boston, MA: Shambhala Lion Publications.

Coleman, J.S. (1982). *The asymmetrical society.* Syracuse, NY: Syracuse University Press.

Craig, D. (1979). Traditional and legal reform in an Iranian Village. In K.F. Koch (ed.), *Access to justice.* Milan, Italy: Giuffre Editore.

Dahrendorf, R. (1959). *Class and class conflict in industrial society.* Palo Alto, CA: Stanford University Press.

DiQuattro, A. (1983). Rawls and left criticism. *Political Theory* 11: 53–78.

Durkheim, E. (1933) (Originally published in 1893). *The division of labor in society.* New York: Free Press.

Dworkin, R.M. (1980). Is wealth a virtue? *Journal of Legal Studies* 9: 191–227.

Dworkin, R.M. (1981). What is equality? *Philosophy and Public Affairs* 10: 283–345.

Elshtain, J.B. (1981). *Public man, private women*. Princeton, NJ: Princeton University Press.

Evans-Prichard, E.E. (1976) (originally published in 1937). *Witchcraft, oracles, and magic among the Azande*. Oxford, England: Clarendon Press.

Friedman, M. (1962). *Capitalism and freedom*. Chicago: University of Chicago Press.

Galston, W. (1980). *Justice and the human good*. Chicago: University of Chicago Press.

Gewirth, A. (1973). The justification of egalitarian justice. In R. Flathman (ed.), *Concepts in social and political philosophy*. New York: Macmillan.

Hamilton, V.L., and S. Rytina. (1980). Social consensus on norms of justice. *American Journal of Sociology* 85: 1117–1144.

Harris, D.J. (1978). *Capital accumulation and income distribution*. Stanford, CA: Stanford University Press.

Hart, H.L.A. (1961). *The concept of law*. Oxford, England: Clarendon Press.

Hobbes, Thomas. (1968) (originally published in 1651). *Leviathan*, edited by C.B. McPherson. New York: Penguin Press.

Hume, David. (1975) (originally published in 1775). An enquiry concerning the principle of morals. In L.A. Selby-Bigge (ed.), *Enquires concerning human understanding and concerning the principles of morals*. Oxford, England: Clarendon Press.

Kant, Immanuel. (1959) (originally published in 1785). *Foundations of the metaphysics of morals,* translated by L.W. Beck. New York: Bobbs-Merrill.

Kant, Immanuel. (1986). *Fundamental principles of the metaphysics of morals,* translated by T.K. Abbott. Buffalo, NY: Prometheus Books.

Kelling, G., et al. (1988). *Perspectives on policing: Police accountability and community policing*. Washington, DC: U.S. Department of Justice.

Lerner, M.J. (1980). *The belief in a just world*. New York: Plenum Press.

Locke, John. (1967) (originally published in 1698). *Two treatises of government,* 2nd edition, edited by P. Laslett. Cambridge, England: Cambridge University Press.

Lowie, R.H. (1925). *Primitive society*. New York: Boni & Liveright.

Lowry, S.T. (1969). Aristotle's mathematical analysis of exchange. *History of Political Economy* 1: 44–66.

Mair, L. (1972). *An introduction to social anthropology,* 2nd edition. New York: Oxford University Press.

Marx, Karl. (1967) (original English edition published in 1887). *Capital.* New York: International Publishers.

Mill, John S. (1961) (originally published in 1861). *Utilitarianism.* Garden City, NY: Doubleday.

New York City Police Department fails to monitor police misconduct suits. (1992). *Chief Leader,* March, pp. 20–22.

Plato. (1986). *The Republic,* translated by Benjamin Jowett. Buffalo, NY: Prometheus Books.

Rawls, John. (1971). *A theory of justice.* Cambridge, MA: Harvard University Press.

Rawls, John. (1975). Fairness to goodness. *Philosophical Review* 84: 536–554.

Rossi, P., E. Waite, C. Bose, and R. Berk. (1974). The seriousness of crimes. *American Sociological Review* 39: 224–237.

Schweickart, D. (1980). *Capitalism or worker control?* New York: Praeger.

Smart, J.C. (1978). Distributive justice and utilitarianism. In J. Arthur and W. Shaw (eds.), *Justice and economic distribution.* Englewood Cliffs, NJ: Prentice-Hall.

Smith, Adam. (1937) (originally published in 1776). *The wealth of nations,* Modern Library Edition. New York: Random House.

Walzer, M. (1983). *Spheres of justice.* New York: Basic Books.

Werner, Jaeger. (1957). *Aristotle: Fundamentals of the history of his development,* translated by Richard Robinson. Oxford, England: Oxford University Press.

Wood, A. (1980). The Marxian critique of justice. In M. Cohen, T. Nagel, and T. Scanlon (eds.), *Marx, justice, and history.* Princeton, NJ: Princeton University Press.

Worland, S.T. (1983). Economic justice and the founding father. In R. Skurski (ed.), *New directions in economic justice.* Notre Dame, IN: Notre Dame University Press.

INDEX